Iowa History Reference Guide

COMPILED BY

WILLIAM J. PETERSEN

THE STATE HISTORICAL SOCIETY OF IOWA
IOWA CITY 1952

PRINTED IN THE UNITED STATES OF AMERICA
BY THE ATHENS PRESS, IOWA CITY, IOWA

EXPLANATION

THIS Reference Guide is designed to facilitate the study of Iowa history. Ever since the State Historical Society was founded in 1857 a deep appreciation of the work of the pioneers has prevailed. This interest in historical foundations has been cultivated by the Society which, especially under the leadership of Dr. Benjamin F. Shambaugh, has been most active in the dissemination of trustworthy information. Research and publication have kept pace with the growing attention to the history of this Commonwealth so that the available materials are now very extensive. In 1933 Iowans observed the 100th anniversary of the beginnings of permanent settlement in the Black Hawk Purchase. The establishment of the Territory of Iowa in 1838 and the admission of Iowa into the Union in 1846 have been duly observed by citizens of the Hawkeye State, whose knowledge of our heritage has been greatly enlarged by these centennial observances. The decade of the 1950's will be marked by scores of important centennials, among which one might mention the election of James W. Grimes, the settlement of the Amanas, the return of the Tama Indians, the birth of the Republican Party, the opening of the State University of Iowa, the adoption of the Constitution of 1857, and the colorful episodes that preceded the outbreak of the Civil War in 1861. It is hoped that this compilation of historical writings will stimulate further investigation and understanding of the record of past achievements.

The purpose of this *Iowa History Reference Guide* is to provide useful lists of references on many topics. Like *One Hundred Topics in Iowa History* issued in 1914, *Two Hundred Topics in Iowa History* issued in 1932, and *A Reference Guide to Iowa History* issued in 1942, this guide will be especially helpful to teachers, to persons interested in local history and active in county historical societies, to students who wish to read systematically, and to clubs which prepare programs in Iowa history. The object has been to cite materials which are available and accessible to general readers, rather than to present an exhaustive bibliography for research scholars.

In general the main divisions of the Reference Guide are arranged in logical sequence beginning with the natural setting of Iowa history and proceeding through the periods of exploration and settlement to the principal fields of activity and to the people who have made history in this Commonwealth. The order of the topics in each division follows a similar plan, but the specific references under each topic are listed alphabetically. To find a specific topic or reference, consult the detailed table of contents in the front or the index at the end of the book.

A large number of the references are to historical magazines and periodicals—four of which have been published by the State Historical Society of Iowa, namely: the *Annals of Iowa;* the *Iowa Historical Record;* the *Iowa Journal of History and Politics;* and the *Palimpsest.* The *Annals of Iowa,* first series, cited here as *Annals (1),* includes twelve volumes and covers the years 1863 to 1874. This series is now out of print, and only a few libraries in the State have complete sets. A second series of the *Annals of Iowa,* cited here as *Annals (2),* containing three volumes, was published from 1882 to 1884. In 1885 the State Historical Society of Iowa began the publication of the *Iowa Historical Record,* cited here as *Historical Record.* It was continued until 1902 and contains eighteen volumes. The *Annals of Iowa,* third series, cited herein as *Annals (3),* is now published at Des Moines by the State Department of History and Archives.

At present the State Historical Society of Iowa publishes two historical magazines: the *Iowa Journal of History* (referred to in the citations as the *Iowa Journal*), a quarterly which was begun in 1903; and the *Palimpsest,* a monthly periodical which was first issued in 1920.

Books published by the State Historical Society are marked SHSI, followed by the date of publication. In the case of books not published by the Society, the name of the publisher and the place and date of publication are given. Only a few references to rare and out-of-print books have been included.

The compiler is indebted to his staff members for assistance in verifying and proof-reading, especially to Christine Adrian, Mrs. Adelaide Seemuth, Dr. Frederick Kuhns, and Dr. Mildred Throne. The index was compiled by Robert A. Rutland.

WILLIAM J. PETERSEN

OFFICE OF THE EDITOR
THE STATE HISTORICAL SOCIETY OF IOWA
IOWA CITY, IOWA

CONTENTS

Physical Foundations

Natural Phenomena

Wild Life

The Indians of Iowa

Discovery and Exploration

Soldiers on the Frontier

Early Settlements and the Pioneers

The Land and Its Owners

Immigration

Travel

Territorial Government

State Government

Administration of Justice

Suffrage, Parties, and Elections

Iowa and National Affairs

Local Government

Cities and Towns

Iowa and the Civil War

Iowa and Foreign Wars

Education in Iowa

Religion in Iowa

Cultural Activities

Amusements and Recreation

Health in Iowa

Social and Economic Problems

Printing and Publishing

Transportation and Communication

Business and Industry

Agriculture

Iowa History

Biographies of Iowans

IOWA HISTORY REFERENCE GUIDE

(For an explanation of abbreviations used in the following references and for other information see pages 3 and 4.)

Physical Foundations

GEOGRAPHY OF IOWA

Aitchison, Alison E., *Iowa State Geography*. Ginn, New York. 1921.

Brigham, Albert P., and Charles T. McFarlane, *Our Home State and Continent* — Iowa section by George F. Kay and Marjorie Kay McLaughlin. American Book Co., New York. 1934.

Gallaher, Ruth A., *Notes on an Old Geography*, Palimpsest, 27: 126-128, April, 1946.

Lees, James H., *Dodge-Lackey Geography of Iowa*. Rand McNally, Chicago. 1931.

Petersen, William J., *The Geography of Iowa Territory*, Palimpsest, 19: 264-274, July, 1938.

Petersen, William J., *The Geography of Wisconsin Territory*, Palimpsest. 19: 12-21, Jan., 1938.

Petersen, William J., *Iowa: The Rivers of Her Valleys*. SHSI. 1941.

Petersen, William J., *The Story of Iowa*. Lewis Historical Publishing Company, New York. 1952. 4 vols. 1: 12-27. The first two volumes are devoted exclusively to history and were written by Dr. Petersen. The last two volumes are biographical, the material being collected, written, and edited by the Lewis Historical Publishing Company.

See also the Iowa sections of the various geographies in use in Iowa schools.

GEOLOGY OF IOWA

Aitchison, Alison E., *Iowa State Geography*, 5-24. Ginn, New York. 1921.

Black, Jean Phyllis, *A Geological Report*, Palimpsest, 25: 332-339, Nov., 1944.

Briggs, John E., *A Geological Palimpsest*, Palimpsest, 1: 133-142, Nov., 1920.

Briggs, John E., *Iowa in the Beginning*, Palimpsest, 5: 353-356, Oct., 1924

Briggs, John E., *Iowa Old and New*, 1-22. University Publishing Co., Lincoln, Nebr. 1939.

Calvin, Samuel, *Pleistocene Iowa*, Annals (3), 3: 1-22, April, 1897.

Hendrickson, Walter B., *David Dale Owen, and the First Geological Survey of Iowa*, Annals (3), 24: 3-13, July, 1942.

Hendrickson, Walter B., *Iowa's First Survey—David Dale Owen, Pioneer Geologist of Middle West*, Annals (3), 26: 136-137, Oct., 1944.

Iowa Academy of Science, *Proceedings,* 35 vols., 1887-1928, State of Iowa, Des Moines.

Iowa Geological Survey, *Annual Report,* 37 vols., 1892 to date. State of Iowa, Des Moines.

Irish, Charles W., *Movements of the Glaciers of the Ice Period in Iowa and Its Vicinity,* Historical Record, 1: 63-67, 115-123, 162-185, April, July, Oct., 1885.

Kay, George F., *Pleistocene History and Early Man in America,* Bull. of the Geol. Soc. of Amer., 50: 453-464, March, 1939.

Kay, George F., and James H. Lees, *Sketches of the Geology of Iowa.* Iowa Geological Survey, Des Moines. 1926.

Keyes, Charles Rollin, *Aboriginal Use of Mineral Coal and its Discovery in the West,* Annals (3), 10: 431-434, July, 1912.

Keyes, Charles Rollin, *Evolution of the General Rock Scheme in Iowa,* Annals (3), 12: 98-100, July, 1915.

Keyes, Charles Rollin, *The Geological Surveys of Iowa,* Annals (3), 3: 111-123, July, 1897.

Lees, James H., Annals (3), 20: 309-311, April, 1936.

Leverett, Frank, *Old Channels of the Mississippi in Southeastern Iowa,* Annals (3), 5: 38-51, April, 1901.

Petersen, William J., *The Story of Iowa,* 1: 1-11. Lewis Historical Co., New York. 1952.

Savage, T. E., *The Iowa Corals,* Annals (3), 6: 534-545, Oct., 1904.

Wilson, Ben H., *The Geode Beds of Iowa,* Palimpsest, 29: 145-154, May, 1948.

GEOLOGY OF IOWA COUNTIES

These valuable reports may be found scattered through the annual Reports of the Iowa Geological Survey. They contain a wealth of material on the geology, physiography, stratigraphy, and economic products of the counties. Maps and pictures are included.

Adair, 27; Adams, 37; Allamakee, 4; Appanoose, 5;

Benton, 15; Black Hawk, 16; Boone, 5; Bremer, 16; Buchanan, 8; Buena Vista, 12; Butler, 20;

Carroll, 9; Cass, 27; Cedar, 11; Cerro Gordo, 7; Cherokee, 12; Chickasaw, 13; Clay, 11; Clayton, 16; Clarke, 17; Clinton, 15; Crawford, 32;

Dallas, 8; Davis, 20; Decatur, 8; Delaware, 8; Des Moines, 3; Dickinson, 10; Dubuque, 10;

Emmet, 15;

Fayette, 15; Franklin, 16; Fremont, 13;

Grundy, 20; Guthrie, 7;

Hamilton, 20; Hancock, 13; Hardin, 10; Harrison, 20; Henry, 12; Howard, 13; Humboldt, 9;

Ida, 16; Iowa, 20;

Jackson, 16; Jasper, 15; Jefferson, 12; Johnson, 7; Jones, 5;

Keokuk, 4; Kossuth, 13;

Lee, 3; Linn, 4; Louisa, 11; Lucas, 32; Lyon, 10;

Madison, 7; Mahaska, 4; Marion, 11; Marshall, 7; Mills, 13; Mitchell, 13; Monroe, 13; Monona, 20; Montgomery, 4; Muscatine, 9;

O'Brien, 11: Osceola, 10;

Page, 11; Palo Alto, 15; Plymouth, 8; Pocahontas, 15; Polk, 7; Pottawattamie, 11; Poweshiek, 20;

Ringgold, 27;

Sac, 16; Scott, 9; Sioux, 10; Story, 9;

Tama, 13; Taylor, 27;

Van Buren, 4;

Wapello, 12; Warren, 5; Washington, 5; Wayne, 20; Webster, 12; Winnebago, 13; Winneshiek, 16; Woodbury, 5; Worth, 10; Wright, 20.

SOIL SURVEYS OF IOWA COUNTIES

Soil Survey Reports, Nos. 1-82, issued by the Iowa Agricultural Experiment Station, Ames, Iowa, 1917-1942. The following counties have been surveyed and the number of the report of each is indicated.

Adair, 27; Appanoose, 53;

Benton, 46; Black Hawk, 14; Boone, 34; Bremer, 1; Buchanan, 67; Buena Vista, 16; Butler, 70;

Calhoun, 72; Carroll, 60; Cedar, 28; Cherokee, 59; Chickasaw, 63; Clarke, 51; Clay, 12; Clayton, 65; Clinton, 8; Crawford, 73;

Dallas, 39; Decatur, 80; Delaware, 56; Des Moines, 45; Dickinson, 37; Dubuque, 35;

Emmet, 36;

Fayette, 30; Floyd, 48; Franklin, 79; Fremont, 58;

Greene, 44; Grundy, 47; Guthrie, 75;

Hamilton, 20; Hancock, 76; Hardin, 38; Harrison, 55; Henry, 15; Howard, 61;

Ida, 82;

Jasper, 42; Jefferson, 50; Johnson, 32; Jones, 57;

Kossuth, 64;

Lee, 5; Linn, 17; Louisa, 21; Lyon, 66;

Madison, 26; Mahaska, 29; Marion, 81; Marshall, 25; Mills, 33; Mitchell, 11; Monroe, 78; Montgomery, 13; Muscatine, 3;

O'Brien, 43;

Page, 41; Palo Alto, 22; Plymouth, 54; Pocahontas, 69; Polk, 24; Pottawattamie, 2; Poweshiek, 74;

Ringgold, 10;

Sac, 71; Scott, 9; Sioux 6;

Union, 68;

Van Buren, 7;

Wapello, 18; Warren, 62; Washington, 77; Wayne, 19; Webster, 4; Winnebago, 23; Winneshiek, 52; Woodbury, 40; Worth, 49; Wright, 31.

RIVERS OF IOWA

Chief of Army Engineers, *Report on the Big and Little Sioux Rivers* (1931). House Document No. 189, 72nd Congress, 1st Session.

Chief of Army Engineers, *Report on the Des Moines River* (1930). House Document No. 682, 71st Congress, 3rd Session.

Chief of Army Engineers, *Report on the Grand River* (1932). House Document No. 236, 72nd Congress, 1st Session.

Chief of Army Engineers, *Report on the Iowa River* (1929). House Document No. 134, 71st Congress, 2nd Session.

Chief of Army Engineers, *Report on the Skunk River* (1931). House Document No. 170, 72nd Congress, 1st Session.

Chief of Army Engineers, *Report on the Turkey River* (1933). House Document No. 98, 73rd Congress, 1st Session.

Iowa State Planning Board, *Stream Flow Records of Iowa, 1873-1932.* State of Iowa, Des Moines. 1935.

Lea, Albert M., *Notes on Wisconsin Territory, with a Map,* 22-33. Reprinted as *The Book That Gave to Iowa its Name.* SHSI. 1935.

Nicollet, Joseph N., *Rivers of Iowa,* Palimpsest, 8: 284-294, Aug., 1927.

Petersen, William J., *Iowa: The Rivers of Her Valleys,* SHSI. 1941.

Petersen, William J., *The Mississippi River Through Many Eyes,* Iowa Journal, 46: 339-377, Oct., 1948.

Petersen, William J., *On River and Highway,* Palimpsest, 19: 73-88, March, 1938.

Petersen, William J., *The Story of Iowa,* 1: 39-75. Lewis Historical Co., New York. 1952.

Natural Phenomena

THE WEATHER

Haefner, John H., *What About the Weather,* Palimpsest, 20: 226-237, July, 1939.

Iowa Weather and Crop Service, *Annual Report.* Since 1878. State of Iowa, Des Moines.

Iowa Weather and Crop Service, *Monthly Review.* Since 1890. U. S. Department of Agriculture, Washington, D. C.

The *Iowa Year Book of Agriculture* also contains the annual report of the Weather Division.

Millsap, Kenneth F., *The Weather,* Palimpsest, 32: 345-350, Sept., 1951.

Petersen, William J., *Sunburn, Dust, and Insects,* Palimpsest, 16: 233-237, Aug., 1935.

Petersen, William J., *The Weather,* Palimpsest, 17: 249-254, Aug., 1936; 18: 245-251, Aug., 1937.

Petersen, William J., *The Story of Iowa,* 1:28-38. Lewis Historical Co., New York. 1952.

Tjernagel, N., *Variable Iowa Weather,* Annals (3), 31: 205-214, Jan., 1952.

WINTER

Aldrich, Charles, *A Winter Night on the Open Prairie*, Historical Record, 12: 450-458, April, 1896.

Bailey, Belle, *To Market with Hogs*, Palimpsest, 12: 57-63, Feb., 1931.

Briggs, John E., *The Milton Lott Tragedy*, Palimpsest, 23: 113-120, April, 1942.

Donovan, Josephine B., *The Winter of Eighty-One*, Palimpsest, 4: 113-120, April, 1923.

Houser, Hazel E., *Caught in a Blizzard*, Palimpsest, 14: 149-159, April, 1933.

Niles' National Register, *One Who Dissented*, Palimpsest, 9: 311-313, Aug., 1928.

Petersen, William J., *Variable Winters*, Palimpsest, 26: 87-96, March, 1945.

Petersen, William J., *When Blizzards Blow*, Palimpsest, 26: 72-86, March, 1945.

Petersen, William J., *Sleighing Time*, Palimpsest, 26: 33-46, Feb., 1945.

Richardson, David N., *Winter Peril*, Palimpsest, 26: 65-71, March, 1945.

Williams, Ira A., *Lost in an Iowa Blizzard*, Palimpsest, 2: 1-15, Jan., 1921.

STORMS AND FLOODS

Briggs, John E., *The Flood of 1851*, Palimpsest, 15: 207-215, June, 1934.

Clayton, B. F., *A Cyclone Sketched by an Eye-Witness* (Macedonia), Midland Monthly, 2: 49-50, July, 1894.

Geary, Thomas C., *Flood Time at Cascade*, Palimpsest, 17: 235-246, July, 1936.

Gist, W. W., *A Story of Devastation* (Emmetsburg to Cresco), Midland Monthly, 2: 377-384, Nov., 1894.

Grahame, Pauline P., *The Rockdale Flood*, Palimpsest, 10: 233-242, July, 1929.

The Great Tornado (Camanche), Harper's Weekly, June 23, 1860.

Herrick, S. H., *The Grinnell Cyclone of June 17, 1882*, Annals (3), 3: 81-96, July, 1897.

Hussey, Tacitus, *The Flood of 1851*, Annals (3), 5: 401-424, July, 1902.

Levering, N., *High Water in Western Iowa*, Palimpsest, 8: 169-176, May, 1927.

Petersen, William J., *Iowa: The Rivers of Her Valleys*, SHSI. 1941.

Richards, W. Avery, *The Cyclone* (Pomeroy), Historical Record, 13: 120-123, July, 1897.

Sherman, Jay J., *The Pomeroy Cyclone*, Palimpsest, 7: 172-183, June, 1926.

Swisher, Jacob A., *Floods in Iowa*, Iowa Journal, 45: 347-379, Oct., 1947.

Swisher, Jacob A., *Kate Shelley*, Palimpsest, 6: 45-55, Feb., 1925.

Wagner, Dorothy, *The Camanche Tornado*, Palimpsest, 14: 137-148, April, 1933.

Wilson, Ben Hur, *High Water in Canaan*, Palimpsest, 25: 78-81, March, 1944.

Astronomical Incidents

Irish, C. W., *Some Remarkable Meteors and Meteoric Falls*, Historical Record,
2: 221-232, Jan., 1886.

Williams, Ora, *On the Trail of the Corona*, Annals (3), 29: Part 1, 81-
107, Oct., 1947.

Wilson, Ben H., *The Amana Meteor*, Palimpsest, 8: 379-390, Nov., 1927.

Wilson, Ben H., *The Eclipse of 1869*, Palimpsest, 6: 56-72, Feb., 1925.

Wilson, Ben H., *The Estherville Meteor*, Palimpsest, 9: 317-333, Sept., 1928.

Wilson, Ben H., *The Forest City Meteor*, Palimpsest, 10: 145-155, April,
1929.

Wilson, Ben H., *The Great Comet of 1882*, Palimpsest, 21: 286-296, Sept.,
1940.

Wilson, Ben H., *The Leonid Shower of 1867*, Palimpsest, 18: 48-59, Feb.,
1937.

Wilson, Ben H., *The Mapleton Meteorite*, Palimpsest, 25: 129-140, May,
1944.

Wilson, Ben H., *The Marion Meteor*, Palimpsest, 18: 33-47, Feb., 1937.

Wilson, Ben H., *The Morehouse Comet*, Palimpsest, 23: 351-358, Nov., 1942.

Earthquakes

Heck, Nicholas H., *Earthquakes*. Princeton University Press, Princeton. 1936.

Petersen, William J., *Earthquakes in Iowa*, Palimpsest, 14: 160-174, April,
1933.

Wild Life

Wild Game in Early Iowa

Bennett, H. Arnold, *Fish and Game Legislation in Iowa*, Iowa Journal, 24:
335-444, July, 1926.

Bennett, H. Arnold, *The Great Snake Hunt*, Palimpsest, 9: 334-337, Sept.,
1928.

Bennett, H. Arnold, *The Mystery of the Iowa Buffalo*, Iowa Journal, 32:
60-73, Jan., 1934.

Bennett, H. Arnold, *Wild Life in Early Iowa*, Iowa Journal, 25: 450-471,
July, 1927.

Harlan, James R., *The Game Book of George E. Poyneer*, Annals (3), 23:
189-211, Jan., 1942.

Hornaday, William T., *John F. Lacey*, Annals (3), 11: 582-584, Jan., 1915.

Lacey, John F., *"Our Vanishing Wild Life" by Dr. William Temple Hornaday*, Annals (3), 11: 336-341, April, 1914.

Macbride, Thomas H., *In Cabins and Sod-Houses*, SHSI. 1928.

Macbride, Thomas H., *The Landscapes of Early Iowa*, Historical Record,
11: 341-349, Oct., 1895.

Murray, Charles A., *Big Game Hunting in Iowa*, Palimpsest, 2: 144-157,
May, 1921.

Musgrove, Jack W., *Market Hunting in Northern Iowa,* Annals (3), 26: 173-197, Jan., 1945.

Musgrove, Jack W., and Mary R., *Waterfowl in Iowa.* State Conservation Commission, Des Moines. 1943.

Osborn, Herbert, *The Recently Extinct and Vanishing Animals of Iowa,* Annals (3), 6: 561-570, Jan., 1905.

Pammel, Louis H., *Buffalo in Iowa,* Annals (3), 17: 403-434, Oct., 1930.

Pammel, Louis H., *Dr. Edwin James,* Annals (3), 8: 161-185, 277-295, Oct., 1907, Jan., 1908.

Petersen, William J., *Buffalo Hunting with Keokuk,* Palimpsest, 16: 33-49, Feb., 1935.

Petersen, William J., *Wolves in Iowa,* Iowa Journal, 38: 50-93, Jan., 1940.

Swisher, Jacob A., *Deer in Iowa,* Palimpsest, 21: 398-409, Dec., 1940.

Wilson, Ellis E., *Buffalo Wallows and Trails in Black Hawk County,* Annals (3), 18: 181-188, Jan., 1932.

Thompson, F. O., *Hunting in Northwestern Iowa,* Iowa Journal, 35: 73-90, Jan., 1937.

See also the files of the Iowa Conservation Commission's *Iowa Conservationist,* 1942-1952.

BIRDS IN IOWA

Aitken, Walter W., *Birds That Have Vanished,* Palimpsest, 12: 137-143, April, 1931.

Harlan, James R., *The Game Book of George E. Poyneer,* Annals (3), 23: 189-211, Jan., 1942.

Iowa Conservationist, 1942 to date.

MacMartin, Faye Brice, *Iowa Birds Then and Now,* Palimpsest, 26: 202-214, July, 1945.

Mott, David C., *John J. Audubon and His Visit to Iowa,* Annals (3), 16: 403-419, Oct., 1928.

Musgrove, Jack W., *Goose Flight of Western Iowa,* Annals (3), 29: Part 1, 145-152, Oct., 1947.

Musgrove, Jack W., Mary R. Musgrove, and Kenneth E. Colton, *Birds of Iowa Pioneer Days,* Annals (3), 22: 543-555, Jan., 1941.

Musgrove, Jack W., and Mary R., *Waterfowl in Iowa.* State Conservation Commission, Des Moines. 1943.

Nauman, E. D., *Birds of Early Iowa,* Palimpsest, 5: 133-138, April, 1924.

Nauman, E. D., *Roasted Eggs,* Palimpsest, 13: 198-201, May, 1932.

Nauman, E. D., *Vanished Hosts,* Palimpsest, 16: 169-173, June, 1935.

Savage, David L., *Birds of the Midland Region,* Midland Monthly, 7: 490-495, June, 1897; 8: 122-128, 461-465, 523-528, Aug., Nov., Dec., 1897.

Tyler, Inez Sheldon, *The Goldfinch,* Annals (3), 29: Part I, 107, Oct., 1947.

The Indians of Iowa

PREHISTORIC MAN IN IOWA

Calvin, Samuel, *Prehistoric Iowa*, Iowa Historical Lectures, 1892, 5-29. SHSI.

Christensen, Thomas P., *The Mound Builders*, Annals (3), 31: 300-308, April, 1952.

Gilder, Robert F., *Prehistoric Village Sites of Harrison County, Iowa*, Annals (3), 10: 401-407, July, 1912.

Harlan, Edgar R., *Indian Mounds of Southeastern Iowa*, Annals (3), 19: 387-394, July, 1934.

Keyes, Charles Reuben, *Antiquities of the Upper Iowa*, Palimpsest, 15: 321-354, Oct., 1934.

Keyes, Charles Reuben, *Minott's Rock Shelter*, Palimpsest, 24: 1-40, Jan., 1943.

Keyes, Charles Reuben, *Prehistoric Indians of Iowa*, Palimpsest, 32: 285-344, Aug., 1951.

Keyes, Charles Reuben, *Prehistoric Man in Iowa*, Palimpsest, 8: 185-229, June, 1927.

Keyes, Charles Reuben, *Prehistoric Red Men*, Palimpsest, 9: 33-37, Feb., 1928.

Keyes, Charles Reuben, *Progress of the Archeological Survey of Iowa*, Iowa Journal, 23: 339-352, July, 1925.

Keyes, Charles Reuben, *Report of the Work of the Iowa Archeological Survey*, Iowa Journal, 38: 94-96, Jan., 1940; 39: 88-91, Jan., 1941.

Keyes, Charles Reuben, *Some Materials for the Study of Iowa Archeology*, Iowa Journal, 18: 357-370, July, 1920.

Keyes, Charles Reuben, *A Unique Survey* (Lewis-Hill), Palimpsest, 11: 214-226, May, 1930.

Mott, Mildred, *Maps Showing Indian Tribes in the Iowa Area*, Iowa Journal, 36: 305-314, July, 1938.

Mott, Mildred, *The Relation of Historic Indian Tribes to Archaeological Manifestations in Iowa*, Iowa Journal, 36: 227-304, July, 1938.

Petersen, William J., *The Story of Iowa*, 1: 76-101. Lewis Historical Co., New York. 1952.

Robinson, Charles H., *Primitive Man of Iowa, and How He Lived*, Annals (3), 3: 161-178, Oct., 1897.

Shetrone, Henry C., *The Mound-Builders*, 291-340. Appleton, New York. 1930.

Ward, Duren J. H., *Anthropological Instruction in Iowa*, Iowa Journal, 1: 312-328, July, 1903.

Ward, Duren J. H., *Historico-Anthropological Possibilities in Iowa*, Iowa Journal, 1: 47-76, Jan., 1903.

Ward, Duren J. H., *The Problem of the Mounds*, Iowa Journal, 3: 20-40, Jan., 1905.

Ward, Duren J. H., *Some Iowa Mounds—An Anthropological Survey*, Iowa Journal, 2: 34-68, Jan., 1904.

Ward, Duren J. H., *First Yearly Meeting of the Iowa Anthropological Association*, Iowa Journal, 2: 342-368, July, 1904; *Second Yearly Meeting*, Iowa Journal, 3: 422-458, July, 1905.

Much valuable material may also be found in the *Proceedings of the Davenport Academy of Sciences*.

THE RED MEN OF IOWA

Briggs, John E., *Implacable Foes*, Palimpsest, 8: 306-314, Sept., 1927.

Briggs, John E., *Indian Affairs*, Palimpsest, 21: 261-277, Sept., 1940.

Briggs, John E., *Indian Affairs in 1845*, Palimpsest, 26: 225-238, Aug., 1945.

Briggs, John E., *Iowa Old and New*, 115-149. University Publishing Co., Lincoln, Nebr. 1939.

Briggs, John E., *Wisaka*, Palimpsest, 7: 97-112, April, 1926.

Clark, Charles A., *Indians of Iowa*, Annals (3), 6: 81-106, July, 1903.

Clark, Dan E., *The Indians of Iowa in 1842*, Iowa Journal, 13: 250-263, April, 1915.

Cole, Cyrenus, *A History of the People of Iowa*, 49-120, 173-177, 218-222, 294-301. Torch Press, Cedar Rapids. 1921.

Cole, Cyrenus, *Iowa Through the Years*, 53-98, 124-128, 153-158, 250-255. SHSI. 1940.

Frontier Fear of the Indians, Annals (3), 29: 315-322, April, 1948.

Fulton, A. R., *The Red Men of Iowa*. Mills & Co., Des Moines. 1882.

Garretson, O. A., *Indian Jim*, Palimpsest, 7: 11-14, Jan., 1926.

Harlan, Edgar R., *Adoption Among the Indians of Iowa*, Annals (3), 17: 59-66, July, 1929.

Harlan, Edgar R., *Some Methods of Collecting Indian Lore*, Annals (3), 18: 403-412, Oct., 1932.

Indians of Iowa, Palimpsest, 9: 33-88, Feb., 1928.

Jones, William, *Notes on the Fox Indians*, Iowa Journal, 10, 70-112, Jan., 1912.

Keyes, Charles Reuben, *Minott's Rock Shelter*, Palimpsest, 24: 1-40, Jan., 1943.

Lucas, Robert, *Indian Affairs of Iowa in 1840*, Annals (3), 15: 255-280, April, 1926.

Lyon, Bessie L., *Hungry Indians*, Palimpsest, 9: 357-370, Oct., 1928.

Mahan, Bruce E., and Ruth A. Gallaher, *Stories of Iowa for Boys and Girls*, 79-168. Macmillan, New York. 1929.

Mullin, Frank A., *Father De Smet and the Pottawattamie Indian Mission*, Iowa Journal, 23: 192-216, April, 1925.

New York Spirit of the Times, *A Theatre Scene—Indian Gallantry*, Annals (3), 27: 70-72, July, 1945.

Niles' National Register, *Indians at Boston*, Palimpsest, 9: 338-346, Sept., 1928.

Parish, John C., *Liquor and the Indians*, Palimpsest, 3: 201-213, July, 1922.

Petersen, William J., *The Story of Iowa*, 1: 102-172. Lewis Historical Co., New York. 1952.

Pickard, J. L., *Indian Tribes in Iowa Before 1846*, Annals (3), 2: 174-185, July-Oct., 1895.

Pickard, J. L., *Iowa Indians*, Iowa Historical Lectures, 1892, 30-52. SHSI.

Pruitt, O. J., *An Indian Play Pot*, Annals (3), 31: 200-204, Jan., 1952.

Pruitt, O. J., *Indian Burials of Pottawattamie County*, Annals (3), 25: 246-255, April, 1944.

Pruitt, O. J., *Tales of the Cherokees in Iowa*, Annals (3), 30: 359-367, July, 1950.

Richman, Irving B., *Indians of Iowa*, Palimpsest, 5: 357-362, Oct., 1924.

Richman, Irving B., *Ioway to Iowa*, 45-69, 123-146. SHSI. 1931.

Rule, Edith, and William J. Petersen, *True Tales of Iowa*, 99-150. Yelland and Hanes, Mason City. 1932.

Skinner, Alanson, *An Ioway Village*, Palimpsest, 6: 164-173, May, 1925.

Smith, Ada Gray, *Indians at Gray's Ford*, Palimpsest, 15: 216-222, June, 1934.

Street, Ida M., *A Chapter of Indian History*, Annals (3), 3: 601-623, Jan., 1899.

Street, Joseph M., *Backgrounds of Indian Traditions*, Annals (3), 15: 613-620, April, 1927.

Van der Zee, Jacob, *Episodes in the Early History of the Western Iowa Country*, Iowa Journal, 11: 323-363, July, 1913.

Vestal, Stanley, *Preservation of Indian Pictures*, Annals (3), 26: 299, April, 1945.

THE IOWAY INDIANS

Aumann, Francis R., *The Ioway*, Palimpsest, 9: 38-41, Feb., 1928.

Aumann, Francis R., *Mahaska*, Palimpsest, 8: 361-369, Nov., 1927.

Fulton, A. R., *The Red Men of Iowa*, 107-125. Mills & Co., Des Moines. 1882.

Gallaher, Ruth A., *Rantchewaime*, Palimpsest, 7: 165-171, June, 1926.

Miner, William H., *The Iowa*. Torch Press, Cedar Rapids. 1911.

Mott, Mildred, *Maps Showing Indian Tribes in the Iowa Area*, Iowa Journal, 36: 305-314, July, 1938.

Mott, Mildred, *The Relation of Historic Indian Tribes to Archaeological Manifestations in Iowa*, Iowa Journal, 36: 227-304, July, 1938.

Petersen, William J., *The Ioways Bid Farewell*, Palimpsest, 19: 397-400, Oct., 1938.

Richman, Irving B., *Ioway to Iowa*, 58-69. SHSI. 1931.

Skinner, Alanson, *An Ioway Village*, Palimpsest, 6: 164-173, May, 1925.

THE SAUK AND FOX INDIANS

Aumann, Francis R., *Poweshiek*, Palimpsest, 8: 297-305, Sept., 1927.

Aumann, Francis R., *Wapello*, Palimpsest, 9: 1-7, Jan., 1928.

Beach, John, *Sac and Fox Indian Council of 1842*, Annals (3), 12: 331-345, July, 1920.

Briggs, John E., *Implacable Foes*, Palimpsest, 8: 306-314, Sept., 1927.

Briggs, John E., *No Sale,* Palimpsest, 22: 193-212, July, 1941.

Briggs, John E., *The Indian Cession of 1842,* Palimpsest, 23: 287-297, Sept., 1942.

Briggs, John E., *The Sacs and Foxes,* Palimpsest, 9: 45-48, Feb., 1928.

Briggs, John E., *Wisaka,* Palimpsest, 7: 97-112, April, 1926.

Fulton, A. R., *The Red Men of Iowa,* 126-145, 186-280. Mills & Co., Des Moines. 1882.

Garretson, O. A., *Indian Jim,* Palimpsest, 7: 11-14, Jan., 1926.

Grimes, James W., *Sac and Fox Indian Council of 1841,* Annals (3), 12: 321-331, July, 1920.

Jones, William, *Notes on the Fox Indians,* Iowa Journal, 10: 70-112, Jan., 1912.

Mahan, Bruce E., *Making the Treaty of 1842,* Palimpsest, 10: 174-180, May, 1929.

Mitchell, J. Leland T., *Crying in the Bottoms,* Palimpsest, 26: 239-246, Aug., 1945.

Petersen, William J., *The Second Purchase,* Palimpsest, 18: 88-97, March, 1937.

Poweshiek, Jonas, *Indians Again on the Warpath,* Annals (3), 26: 291-299, April, 1945.

Rounseville, Wm., *The Indian Outlaw,* Annals (3), 25: 275-281, April, 1944.

Williams, Ora, *Chief Poweshiek at Des Moines,* Annals (3), 25: 58-60, July, 1943.

THE TAMA INDIANS

Bicknell, A. D., *The Tama County Indians,* Annals (3), 4: 196-208, Oct., 1899.

Evans, Samuel B., *A Patch of Barbarism,* Midland Monthly, 4: 515-524, Dec., 1895.

Gallaher, Ruth A., *Indian Agents in Iowa,* Iowa Journal, 14: 559-596, Oct., 1916.

Gallaher, Ruth A., *The Tama Indians,* Palimpsest, 7: 44-53, Feb., 1926.

Gallaher, Ruth A., *The Tama Indians,* Palimpsest, 31: 249-259, July, 1950.

Harlan, Edgar R., *Mesquakie Indians and the Wheeler-Howard Bill,* Annals (3), 20: 381-384, July, 1936.

Harlan, Edgar R., *An Original Study of Mesquakie (Fox) Life,* Annals (3), 19: 115-125, Oct., 1933, 221-234, Jan., 1934, 352-362, July, 1934; 20: 123-139, Oct., 1935, 510-526, Jan., 1937.

Owen, Mary A., *Folk-Lore of the Musquakie Indians of North America.* David Nutt, for the Folk-Lore Society, London. 1904.

Poweshiek, Jonas M., *An Autobiography,* Annals (3), 20: 435-443, Oct., 1936.

Preston, Ruth I., *Tama Indians and the Scare of 1864,* Historical Record, 14: 249-256, April, 1898.

Rebok, Horace M., *The Last of the Mus-qua-kies,* Historical Record, 17: 305-335, July, 1901.

Rebok, Horace M., *The Last of the Mus-qua-kies and the Indian Congress.* 1898. 1900.

Spencer III, Dick, *Powwow Time*, Palimpsest, 31: 260-280, July, 1950.

Ward, Duren J. H., *Meskwakia and the Meskwaki People of To-day*, Iowa Journal, 4: 179-219, April, 1906.

THE POTTAWATTAMIE INDIANS

Babbitt, Charles H., *The Old Pottawattamie Mill*, Palimpsest, 6: 319-334, Sept., 1925.

Dean, Seth, *Wabaunsee, The Indian Chief*, Annals (3), 16: 1-24, July, 1927.

Fulton, A. R., *The Red Men of Iowa*, 163-172. Mills & Co., Des Moines. 1882.

Hayden, Lucretia June, *Johnny Green's High Ambition*, Annals (3), 25: 239-245, April, 1944.

Mahan, Bruce E., *The Winnebago and Pottawattamie*, Palimpsest, 9: 53-55, Feb., 1928.

Mullin, Frank A., *Father De Smet and the Pottawattamie Indian Mission*, Iowa Journal, 23: 192-216, April, 1925.

Swisher, J. A., *Chief Waubonsie*, Palimpsest, 29: 353-361, Dec., 1948.

Wick, Barthinius L., *Shabbona and the Part He Played in the Pioneer History of the Mississippi Valley*, Annals (3), 17: 168-172, Jan., 1930.

THE WINNEBAGO INDIANS

Beall, Walter H., *The Tegarden Massacre*, Palimpsest, 24: 82-91, March, 1943.

Fulton, A. R., *The Red Men of Iowa*, 146-162. Mills & Co., Des Moines. 1882.

Mahan, Bruce E., *Moving the Winnebago*, Palimpsest, 3: 33-52, Feb., 1922.

Mahan, Bruce E., *Old Fort Crawford and the Frontier*, 100-119, 140-161, 201-240. SHSI. 1926.

Mahan, Bruce E., *The School on Yellow River*, Palimpsest, 5: 446-452, Dec., 1924.

Mahan, Bruce E., *Winnebago and Pottawattamie*, Palimpsest, 9: 53-55, Feb., 1928.

Pruitt, O. J., *Mud Turtle's Last Hunt*, Annals (3), 29: 553-556, Jan., 1949.

THE SIOUX INDIANS

Briggs, John E., *Implacable Foes*, Palimpsest, 8: 306-314, Sept., 1927.

Call, Ambrose A., *Indians Repelled in Kossuth*, Annals (3), 31: 81-90, Oct., 1951.

Fulton, A. R., *The Red Men of Iowa*, 173-185, 281-333. Mills & Co., Des Moines. 1882.

Lyon, Bessie L., *Hungry Indians*, Palimpsest, 9: 357-370, Oct., 1928.

Peterson, Harold D., *Wahkonsa*, Palimpsest, 23: 121-135, April, 1942.

Swisher, Jacob A., *The Sioux*, Palimpsest, 9: 49-52, Feb., 1928.

Swisher, Jacob A., *War Eagle*, Palimpsest, 30: 33-41, Feb., 1949.
Wylie, Helen, *Omaha, Oto, and Missouri*, Palimpsest, 9: 42-44, Feb., 1928.

THE SPIRIT LAKE MASSACRE

Carpenter, Cyrus C., *Major William Williams*, Annals (3), 2: 146-160, July-Oct., 1895.
Carpenter, Cyrus C., *The Spirit Lake Expedition*, Annals (3), 3: 481-553, Oct., 1898.
Carpenter, Cyrus C., *The Spirit Lake Massacre*, Midland Monthly, 4: 17-31, July, 1895.
Clark, Dan E., *Frontier Defense in Iowa, 1850-1865*, Iowa Journal, 16: 315-386, July, 1918.
Clark, Dan E., *The Spirit Lake Massacre*, Iowa and War, No. 11, May, 1918. SHSI.
Herriott, Frank I., *The Aftermath of the Spirit Lake Massacre, March 8-15, 1857*, Annals (3), 18: 434-470, Oct., 1932, 483-517, Jan., 1933, 597-631, April, 1933.
Herriott, Frank I., *Dr. Isaac H. Harriott*, Annals (3), 18: 243-294, April, 1932.
Herriott, Frank I., *The Origins of the Indian Massacre Between the Okobojis, March 8, 1857*, Annals (3), 18: 323-382, July, 1932.
Howe, Orlando C., *The Discovery of the Spirit Lake Massacre*, Annals (3), 11: 408-430, July, 1914.
Ingham, Harvey, *Ink-Pa-Du-Tah's Revenge*, Midland Monthly, 4: 269-272, Sept., 1895.
Ingham, William H., *The Iowa Northern Border Brigade of 1862-3*, Annals (3), 5: 481-523, Oct., 1902.
Lyon, Bessie L., *Hungry Indians*, Palimpsest, 9: 357-370, Oct., 1928.
Richards, Charles B., *Organization and Service of the Frontier Guards*, Annals (3), 11: 1-15, April, 1913.
Richman, Irving B., *John Brown Among the Quakers, and Other Sketches*, 203-235. Historical Department, Des Moines. 1904.
Sharp, Abbie G., *History of the Spirit Lake Massacre and Captivity of Miss Abbie Gardner* (Several Editions).
The Spirit Lake and Okoboji Monument, Annals (3), 2: 69-73, April, 1895.
Taylor, Landon, *Indian Alarm*, Palimpsest, 25: 12-15, Jan., 1944.
Teakle, Thomas, *The Spirit Lake Massacre*. SHSI. 1918.

FAMOUS INDIANS OF IOWA

Aumann, Francis R., *Indian Oratory*, Palimpsest, 9: 149-154, April, 1928.
Aumann, Francis R., *Mahaska*, Palimpsest, 8: 361-369, Nov., 1927.
Aumann, Francis R., *Poweshiek*, Palimpsest, 8: 297-305, Sept., 1927.
Aumann, Francis R., *Wapello*, Palimpsest, 9: 1-7, Jan., 1928.
Barnhart, Cornelia Mallet, *Osceola and Oskaloosa*, Palimpsest, 28: 300-309, Oct., 1947.

Cole, Cyrenus, *A History of the People of Iowa*, 81-113. Torch Press, Cedar Rapids. 1921.

Cole, Cyrenus, *Iowa Through the Years*, 53-98, SHSI. 1940.

Dean, Seth, *Wabaunsee, The Indian Chief*, Annals (3), 16: 1-24, July, 1927.

English, Emory H., *A Mesquakie Chief's Burial*, Annals (3), 30: 545-550, Jan., 1951.

Fulton, A. R., *The Red Men of Iowa*, 208-299. Mills & Co., Des Moines. 1882.

Gallaher, Ruth A., *Rantchewaime*, Palimpsest, 7: 165-171, June, 1926.

Hayden, Lucretia June, *Johnny Green's High Ambition*, Annals (3), 25: 239-245, April, 1944.

Petersen, William J., *The Story of Iowa*, 1: 102-153. Lewis Historical Co., New York. 1952.

Swisher, J. A., *Chief Waubonsie*, Palimpsest, 29: 353-361, Dec., 1948.

Swisher, J. A., *War Eagle*, Palimpsest, 30: 33-41, Feb., 1949.

Wick, Barthinius L., *Shabbona and the Part He Played in the Pioneer History of the Mississippi Valley*, Annals (3), 17: 168-172, Jan., 1930.

Williams, Ora, *Chief Poweshiek at Des Moines*, Annals (3), 25: 58-60, July, 1943.

Williams, Ora, *The Keokuk Pictures*, Annals (3), 25: 60, July, 1943.

See also Black Hawk and the Black Hawk War and Keokuk.

BLACK HAWK AND THE BLACK HAWK WAR

Aldrich, Charles, *Jefferson Davis and Black Hawk*, Midland Monthly, 5: 406-411, May, 1896.

Armstrong, Perry A., *The Sauks and the Black Hawk War*. H. W. Rokker, Springfield, Ill. 1887.

Cole, Cyrenus, *A History of the People of Iowa*, 81-113. Torch Press, Cedar Rapids. 1921.

Cole, Cyrenus, *I Am a Man: The Indian Black Hawk*. SHSI. 1938.

Drake, Benjamin, *The Life and Adventures of Black Hawk*. E. Morgan & Co., Cincinnati. 1839. This volume went through several editions.

Engle, Paul, *Futile Defiance*, Palimpsest, 13: 55-73, Feb., 1932.

Fulton, A. R., *The Red Men of Iowa*, 186-230. Mills & Co., Des Moines. 1882.

Patterson, J. B., *Life of Ma-Ka-Tai-Me-She-Kia-Kiak or Black Hawk*. Russell, Odiorne & Metcalf, Boston. 1834.

Peck, Mrs. W. F., *Black Hawk*, Annals (3), 2: 450-464, July, 1896.

Petersen, William J., *The Terms of Peace*, Palimpsest, 13: 74-89, Feb., 1932.

Petersen, William J., *The Story of Iowa*, 1: 117-135. Lewis Historical Co., New York. 1952.

Quaife, Milo M., *Life of Black Hawk*. R. R. Donnelley, Chicago. 1916. This is a reprint of the autobiography issued by J. B. Patterson.

Richman, Irving B., *John Brown Among the Quakers, and Other Sketches*, 79-119. Historical Department, Des Moines. 1904.

Shambaugh, Benj. F. (editor), *Life of Ma-Ka-Tai-Me-She-Kia-Kiak or Black Hawk* (Reprint of the Patterson volume). SHSI. 1932.

Smith, Grace Noll, *To Black Hawk—A Poem*, Annals (3), 29: 46, July, 1947.

Stevens, Frank E., *The Black Hawk War Including a Review of Black Hawk's Life*. Frank E. Stevens, Chicago. 1903.

Swisher, Jacob A., *Chief of the Sauks*, Palimpsest, 13: 41-54, Feb., 1932.

Van der Zee, Jacob, *The Black Hawk War and the Treaty of 1832*, Iowa Journal, 13: 416-428, July, 1915.

Van der Zee, Jacob, *The Black Hawk War*, Iowa and War, No. 9, March, 1918. SHSI.

Wakefield, John A., *History of the Black Hawk War* (Edited by Frank E. Stevens). The Caxton Club, Chicago. 1908.

KEOKUK

Aumann, Francis R., *Indian Oratory*, Palimpsest, 9: 149-154, April, 1928.

Aumann, Francis R., *The Watchful Fox*, Palimpsest, 9: 121-132, April, 1928.

Briggs, John E., *The Council on the Iowa*, Palimpsest, 9: 133-148, April, 1928.

Cole, Cyrenus, *A History of the People of Iowa*, 81-113. Torch Press, Cedar Rapids. 1921.

Cole, Cyrenus, *Iowa Through the Years*, 63-98. SHSI. 1940.

Fulton, A. R., *The Red Men of Iowa*, 231-247. Mills & Co., Des Moines. 1882.

Petersen, William J., *Buffalo Hunting with Keokuk*, Palimpsest, 16: 33-49, Feb., 1935.

Petersen, William J., *The Story of Iowa*, 1: 117-134. Lewis Historical Co., New York. 1952.

Richman, Irving B., *John Brown Among the Quakers, and Other Sketches*, 79-119. Historical Department, Des Moines. 1904.

Williams, Ora, *The Keokuk Pictures*, Annals (3), 25: 60, July, 1943.

INDIAN TREATIES

Abernethy, Alonzo, *Early Iowa Indian Treaties and Boundaries*, Annals (3), 11: 241-259, 358-380, Jan., April, 1914.

Abernethy, Alonzo, *Iowa Under Territorial Governments and the Removal of the Indians*, Annals (3), 7: 431-445, July, 1906.

Acquisition of Iowa Lands from the Indians, The, Annals (3), 7: 283-290, Jan., 1906.

Beach, John, *Sac and Fox Indian Council of 1842*, Annals (3), 12: 331-345, July, 1920.

Briggs, John E., *The Indian Cession of 1842*, Palimpsest, 23: 287-297, Sept., 1942.

Briggs, John E., *No Sale*, Palimpsest, 22: 193-212, July, 1941.

Council with the Sac and Fox Indians in 1840, Iowa Journal, 15: 429-436, July, 1917.

Edwards, James G., *Indian Affairs*, Palimpsest, 10: 161-173, May, 1929.

Grahame, Pauline P., *The Promised Land*, Palimpsest, 10: 187-198, May, 1929.

Grimes, James W., *Sac and Fox Indian Council of 1841*, Annals (3), 12: 321-331, July, 1920.

Kappler, Charles J., *Indian Affairs, Laws and Treaties*, Vol. II (Treaties). Government Printing Office, Washington. 1903.

Mahan, Bruce E., *Making the Treaty of 1842*, Palimpsest, 10: 174-180, May, 1929.

Niles' National Register, *Westward*, Palimpsest, 10: 181-186, May, 1929.

Parish, John C., *John Chambers*, 162-189. SHSI. 1909.

Petersen, William J., *The Ioways Bid Farewell*, Palimpsest, 19: 397-400, Oct., 1938.

Petersen, William J., *The Second Purchase*, Palimpsest, 18: 88-97, March, 1937.

Petersen, William J., *The Terms of Peace*, Palimpsest, 13: 74-89, Feb., 1932.

Proceedings of a Council with the Chippewa Indians, Iowa Journal, 9: 408-437, July, 1911.

The Sac and Fox Indians and the Treaty of 1842, Iowa Journal, 10: 261-265, April, 1912.

Stiles, Cassius C., *The White Breast Boundary Line*, Annals (3), 10: 1-33, April, 1911.

Van der Zee, Jacob, *The Black Hawk War and the Treaty of 1832*, Iowa Journal, 13: 416-428, July, 1915.

THE HALF-BREED TRACT

Dr. Galland's Account of the Half-Breed Tract, Annals (3), 10: 450-466, July, 1912.

Harlan, Edgar R., *A Map of the Half Breed Tract*, Annals (3), 14: 422-423, Oct., 1924.

Mason, Charles, *Decree in Partition of the Half Breed Tract in Lee County, Iowa, 1840*, Annals (3), 14: 424-460, Oct., 1924.

Petersen, William J., *Some Beginnings in Iowa*, Iowa Journal, 28: 3-54, Jan., 1930.

Swisher, Jacob A., *The Half-breed Tract*, Palimpsest, 14: 69-76, Feb., 1933.

Taylor, Hawkins, *Judge Mason and the Half-Breed Tract*, Historical Record, 2: 350-355, Oct., 1886.

Van der Zee, Jacob, *The Half-breed Tract*, Iowa Journal, 13: 151-164, April, 1915.

Van der Zee, Jacob, *The Oldest Land Titles in the State of Iowa*, Iowa Journal, 13: 238-249, April, 1915.

Wick, Barthinius L., *The Struggle for the Half-Breed Tract*, Annals (3), 7: 16-29, April, 1905.

THE NEUTRAL GROUND

Barrows, Willard, *In the Neutral Ground*, Palimpsest, 3: 106-124, April, 1922.

Hildreth, A. B. F., *A Winnebago Encampment*, Palimpsest, 16: 299-302, Sept., 1935.

Mahan, Bruce E., *The Great Council of 1825*, Palimpsest, 6: 305-318, Sept., 1925.

Mahan, Bruce E., *Moving the Winnebago*, Palimpsest, 3: 33-52, Feb., 1922.

Mahan, Bruce E., *Old Fort Crawford and the Frontier*, 89-99, 140-161, 201-240. SHSI. 1926.

Mahan, Bruce E., *The School on Yellow River*, Palimpsest, 5: 446-452, Dec., 1924.

Van der Zee, Jacob, *The Neutral Ground*, Iowa Journal, 13: 311-348, July, 1915.

INDIAN AGENTS

Beach, John, *Sac and Fox Indian Council of 1842*, Annals (3), 12: 331-345, July, 1920.

Fulton, A. R., *The Red Men of Iowa*, 340-355. Mills & Co., Des Moines. 1882.

Gallaher, Ruth A., *The Indian Agent in the United States*, Iowa Journal, 14: 3-55, 173-238, Jan., April, 1916.

Gallaher, Ruth A., *Indian Agents in Iowa*, Iowa Journal, 14: 348-394, 559-596, July, Oct., 1916.

Leggett, Richard C., *An Historic Indian Agency*, Annals (3), 25: 257-274, April, 1944.

Petersen, William J., *The Story of Iowa*, 1: 153-160. Lewis Historical Co., New York. 1952.

Scanlan, P. J., *Nichols Boilvin, Indian Agent*, Annals (3), 25: 281, April, 1944.

Street, Ida M., *A Chapter of Indian History*, Annals (3), 3: 601-623, Jan., 1899.

Street, Ida M., *Joseph M. Street's Last Fight With the Fur Traders*, Annals (3), 17: 105-148, Oct., 1929.

Street, Ida M., *A Second Chapter of Indian History*, Annals (3), 6: 364-375, April, 1904.

Street, Ida M., *The Simon Cameron Indian Commission of 1838*, Annals (3), 7: 115-139, 172-195, July, Oct., 1905.

Street, Joseph M., *Backgrounds of Indian Traditions*, Annals (3), 15: 613-620, April, 1927.

Street, Joseph M., *Indian Affairs of the Iowa Region, 1827-1830*, Annals (3), 16: 25-42, July, 1927.

Street, Joseph M., *Letters of Joseph M. Street to Dr. Alexander Posey*, Annals (3), 12: 533-539, Jan., 1921.

Street, William B., *General Joseph M. Street*, Annals (3), 2: 81-105, July-Oct., 1895.

Discovery and Exploration

THE FRENCH IN IOWA

Briggs, John E., *When Iowa was Young* (De Noyelles Expedition), Palimpsest, 6: 117-127, April, 1925.

Cole, Cyrenus, *A History of the People of Iowa*, 19-37. Torch Press, Cedar Rapids. 1921.

Parish, John C., *The Man With the Iron Hand* (Tonty). Houghton Mifflin, Boston. 1913.

Parish, John C., *Michel Aco—Squaw-Man*, Palimpsest, 2: 161-177, June, 1921.

Petersen, William J., *Historical Setting of the Mound Region in Northeastern Iowa*, Iowa Journal, 31: 47-86, Jan., 1933.

Petersen, William J., *Perrot's Mines*, Palimpsest, 12: 405-413, Nov., 1931.

Petersen, William J., *The Story of Iowa*, 1: 173-200. Lewis Historical Co., New York. 1952.

Salter, William, *Nicolas Perrot*, Annals (3), 4: 610-613, Jan., 1901.

Shambaugh, Benj. F., *Iowa History from 1699 to 1821*, Historical Record, 16: 29-46, Jan., 1900.

Thwaites, Reuben G., *France in America*. Harper, New York. 1905.

Van der Zee, Jacob, *Captivity of a Party of Frenchmen Among Indians in the Iowa Country, 1728-1729*, Iowa Journal, 14: 96-118, Jan., 1916.

Van der Zee, Jacob, *French Discovery and Exploration of the Eastern Iowa Country Before 1763*, Iowa Journal, 12: 323-354, July, 1914.

See also Joliet and Marquette in Iowa.

JOLIET AND MARQUETTE IN IOWA

Briggs, John E., *Louis Joliet*, Palimpsest, 4: 240-248, July, 1923.

Mahan, Bruce E., *The Discovery of Iowa*, Palimpsest, 4: 215-228, July, 1923.

Middaugh, Ruth B., *Father Marquette*, Palimpsest, 4: 229-239, July, 1923.

Petersen, William J., *The Story of Iowa*, 1: 182-192. Lewis Historical Co., New York. 1952.

Steck, Francis B., *The Jolliet-Marquette Expedition, 1673*. Catholic University of America, Washington. 1927.

Thwaites, Reuben G., *Father Marquette*. Dodd, Mead, New York. 1904.

Van der Zee, Jacob, *French Discovery and Exploration of the Eastern Iowa Country Before 1763*, Iowa Journal, 12: 323-354, July, 1914.

Weld, Laenas G., *Joliet and Marquette in Iowa*, Iowa Journal, 1: 3-16, Jan., 1903.

Weld, Laenas G., *On the Way to Iowa*, 21-31. SHSI. 1910.

Weld, Laenas G., *Pointing the Way*, Palimpsest, 4: 205-214, July, 1923.

THE IOWA COUNTRY UNDER SPAIN

Bourne, Edward G., *Spain in America*. Harper, New York. 1906.

Cole, Cyrenus, *Iowa Through the Years*, 36-44. SHSI. 1940.

Garretson, O. A., *Iowa and the Spanish Pioneers*, Iowa Journal, 30: 395-403, July, 1932.

Nasatir, Abraham P., *Anglo-Spanish Frontier on the Upper Mississippi 1786-1796*, Iowa Journal, 29: 155-232, April, 1931.

Nasatir, Abraham P., *Anglo-Spanish Rivalry in the Iowa Country 1797-1798*, Iowa Journal, 28: 337-389, July, 1930.

Petersen, William J., *Jean Marie Cardinal*, Palimpsest, 12: 414-420, Nov., 1931.

Petersen, William J., *The Story of Iowa*, 1: 200-214. Lewis Historical Co., New York. 1952.

Quigley, Iola B., *The Giard Tract*, Palimpsest, 12: 1-6, Jan., 1931.

Scanlan, P. L., and Marian Scanlan, *Basil Giard and His Land Claim in Iowa*, Iowa Journal, 30: 219-247, April, 1932.

Tesson Claim in Lee County and the Earliest Orchard in Iowa, The, Annals (3), 17: 547-553, Jan., 1931.

Van der Zee, Jacob, *Early History of Lead Mining in the Iowa Country*, Iowa Journal, 13: 3-52, Jan., 1915.

Van der Zee, Jacob, *Fur Trade Operations in the Eastern Iowa Country under the Spanish Régime*, Iowa Journal, 12: 355-372, July, 1914.

Whitaker, A. P., *The Spanish American Frontier*. Houghton Mifflin, Boston. 1927.

Wilson, Ben H., *Tesson's Apple Orchard*, Palimpsest, 4: 121-131, April, 1923.

JULIEN DUBUQUE AND THE MINES OF SPAIN

Clark, Dan E., *Adventures of First White Settlers in the Mississippi Valley*, Journal of American History, 3: 505-510, Oct.-Dec., 1909.

Gue, Benjamin F., *History of Iowa*, 1: 109-116. 4 vols. Century History Co., New York. 1903.

Ham, M. M., *The First White Man in Iowa*, Annals (3), 2: 329-344, April, 1896.

Ham, M. M., *Who Was Peosta?*, Annals (3), 2: 470-472, July, 1896.

Herrmann, Richard, *Julien Dubuque, His Life and Adventures*. Times-Journal Co., Dubuque. 1922.

Hoffmann, M. M., *Antique Dubuque 1673-1833*. Telegraph-Herald Press, Dubuque. 1930.

Keyes, Charles Rollin, *Spanish Mines: An Episode in Primitive American Lead-Mining*, Annals (3), 10: 539-546, Oct., 1912.

Langworthy, Lucius H., *Dubuque: Its History, Mines, Indian Legends, Etc.*, Dubuque Literary Institute, Dubuque. 1855. Reprinted in Iowa Journal, 8: 366-422, July, 1910.

Pelzer, Louis, *The Spanish Land Grants of Upper Louisiana*, Iowa Journal, 11: 3-37, Jan., 1913.

Petersen, William J., *The Mines of Spain*, Palimpsest, 12: 405-440, Nov., 1931.

Petersen, William J., *The Story of Iowa*, 1: 204-212. Lewis Historical Co., New York. 1952.

Shiras, Oliver P., *The Mines of Spain*, Annals (3), 5: 321-334, April, 1902.
W (unknown). *A Visit to Dubuque's Grave*, Palimpsest, 3: 125-128, April, 1922.

THE FUR TRADE IN THE IOWA COUNTRY

Briggs, John E., *Two Connecticut Yankees* (Carver and Pond), Palimpsest, 7: 15-29, Jan., 1926.
Chittenden, Hiram M., *The American Fur Trade of the Far West*. 3 vols. Francis P. Harper, New York. 1902.
Hussey, Tacitus, *The Old-Time Trapper*, Annals (3), 9: 301-310, Jan., 1910.
Murray, Charles A., *Big Game Hunting in Iowa*, Palimpsest, 2: 144-157, May, 1921.
Parish, John C., *Liquor and the Indians*, Palimpsest, 3: 201-213, July, 1922.
Petersen, William J., *The Story of Iowa*, 1: 245-252. Lewis Historical Co., New York. 1952.
Petersen, William J., *Wolves in Iowa*, Iowa Journal, 38: 50-93, Jan., 1940.
Robeson, George F., *The Fur Trade*, Palimpsest, 6: 1-41, Jan., 1925.
Swisher, Jacob A., *Deer in Iowa*, Palimpsest, 21: 398-409, Dec., 1940.
Van der Zee, Jacob, *Fur Trade Operations in the Eastern Iowa Country from 1800 to 1833*, Iowa Journal, 12: 479-567, Oct., 1914.
Van der Zee, Jacob, *Fur Trade Operations in the Eastern Iowa Country under the Spanish Régime*, Iowa Journal, 12: 355-372, July, 1914.

THE LEWIS AND CLARK EXPEDITION

Brooks, Mary E., *Sergeant Floyd's Grave*, Midland Monthly, 4: 419-424, Nov., 1895.
Caldwell, E. W., *The Floyd Monument*, Historical Record, 17: 362-370, Oct., 1901.
Catlin, George, *The Grave of Sergeant Floyd*, Palimpsest, 7: 337-341, Nov., 1926.
Coues, Elliott, *History of the Expedition under the Command of Lewis and Clark*. 4 vols. Francis P. Harper, New York. 1893.
Dye, Eva Emery, *The Conquest: The True Story of Lewis and Clark* (historical novel). McClurg, Chicago. 1902.
Garver, F. H., *Tents for Lewis and Clark*, Palimpsest, 25: 90-96, March, 1944.
Hosmer, James K., *History of the Expedition of Lewis and Clark*. 2 vols. McClurg, Chicago. 1902.
Kasson, John A., *The Expansion of the Republic West of the Mississippi*, Annals (3), 5: 177-198, Oct., 1901.
Mahan, Bruce E., *Explorations of Iowa*, Palimpsest, 5: 363-369, Oct., 1924.
Mott, David C., *The Lewis and Clark Expedition in its Relation to Iowa History and Geography*, Annals (3), 13: 99-125, 163-192, Oct., 1921, Jan., 1922.
Petersen, William J., *The Story of Iowa*, 1: 220-229. Lewis Historical Co., New York. 1952.

Quaife, M. M., *The Journals of Captain Meriwether Lewis and Sergeant John Ordway.* State Historical Society of Wisconsin, Madison. 1916.

Riegel, Robert E., *America Moves West,* 97-113. Henry Holt, New York. 1930.

Salter, William, *The Western Border of Iowa in 1804 and 1806,* Historical Record, 10: 71-78, April, 1894.

Thwaites, Reuben G., *Original Journals of the Lewis and Clark Expedition.* 8 vols., including atlas. Dodd, Mead, New York. 1904.

Wakefield, George W., *Sergeant Charles Floyd,* Annals (3), 2: 305-314, Jan., 1896.

Wheeler, O. D., *The Trail of Lewis and Clark, 1804-1904.* 2 vols., G. P. Putnam's Sons, New York. 1904.

ZEBULON M. PIKE'S EXPEDITION UP THE MISSISSIPPI

Coues, Elliott, *The Expeditions of Zebulon Montgomery Pike.* 3 vols. Francis P. Harper, New York. 1895.

Mahan, Bruce E., *Pike's Hill,* Palimpsest, 2: 282-289, Sept., 1921.

Martin, Ethyl E., *The Expedition of Zebulon Montgomery Pike to the Sources of the Mississippi,* Iowa Journal, 9: 335-358, July, 1911.

Meigs, Cornelia, *As the Crow Flies.* Macmillan, New York. 1927.

Petersen, William J., *The Story of Iowa,* 1: 229-236. Lewis Historical Co., New York. 1952.

Salter, William, *The Eastern Border of Iowa in 1805-6,* Historical Record, 10: 107-121, July, 1894.

ALBERT MILLER LEA AND HIS PLACE IN IOWA HISTORY

Gallaher, Ruth A., *Albert Miller Lea,* Palimpsest, 16: 65-80, March, 1935.

Gallaher, Ruth A., *Albert Miller Lea,* Iowa Journal, 33: 195-241, July, 1935.

Lea, Albert M., *Albert Miller Lea,* Historical Record, 8: 200-207, Jan., 1892.

Lea, Albert M., *Early Explorations in Iowa,* Historical Record, 6: 535-553, Oct., 1890.

Lea, Albert M., *The Expedition of 1835,* Palimpsest, 16: 105-134, April, 1935.

Lea, Albert M., *Iowa and Missouri Boundary,* Historical Record, 2: 193-207, Jan., 1886.

Lea, Albert M., *Notes on the Wisconsin Territory.* H. S. Tanner, Philadelphia. 1836. Reprinted as *The Book that Gave to Iowa its Name.* SHSI. 1935. Also reprinted in Annals (3), 11: 115-167, July-Oct., 1913.

Powell, Clifford, *The Contributions of Albert Miller Lea to the Literature of Iowa History,* Iowa Journal, 9: 3-32, Jan., 1911.

Report Made by Lieutenant Albert Miller Lea on the Des Moines River, Iowa Journal, 33: 242-246, July, 1935.

Report Made by Albert Miller Lea on the Iowa-Missouri Boundary, Iowa Journal, 33: 246-259, July, 1935.

Soldiers on the Frontier

EARLY FORTS IN IOWA

Beers, Henry P., *The Western Military Frontier 1815-1846*. Published by the author, Philadelphia. 1935.

Bloomer, D. C., *The Old Blockhouse in Council Bluffs*, Annals (3), 2: 549-552, Oct., 1896.

Briggs, John E., *Iowa Old and New*, 85-114. University Publishing Co., Lincoln, Nebr. 1939.

Briggs, John E., *The Second Fort Des Moines*, Palimpsest, 24: 161-172, May, 1943.

Clark, Dan E., *Border Defense in Iowa During the Civil War*, Iowa and War, No. 10, April, 1918. SHSI.

Flagler, D. W., *A History of the Rock Island Arsenal*. Government Printing Office, Washington. 1877.

Fort Atkinson, Iowa, Annals (3), 4: 448-453, July, 1900.

Fort Des Moines, No. 2, Annals (3), 4: 161-178, Oct., 1899.

Fort Dodge, Iowa, Annals (3), 4: 534-538, Oct., 1900.

Fort Sanford, Iowa, Annals (3), 4: 289-293, Jan., 1900.

Gallaher, Ruth A., *Fort Des Moines in Iowa History*, Iowa and War, No. 22, April, 1919. SHSI.

Gallaher, Ruth A., *The Military-Indian Frontier 1830-1835*, Iowa Journal, 15: 393-428, July, 1917.

Grahl, Charles H., *Fort Des Moines' 100th Anniversary*, Annals (3), 25: 38-42, July, 1943.

Hansen, Marcus L., *Old Fort Snelling*, Iowa and War, No. 1, July, 1917. SHSI.

Hansen, Marcus L., *Old Fort Snelling: 1819-1858*. SHSI. 1918.

Mahan, Bruce E., *Old Fort Atkinson*, Palimpsest, 2: 333-350, Nov., 1921.

Mahan, Bruce E., *Old Fort Crawford and the Frontier*. SHSI. 1926.

McLaughlin, W. M., *Old Fort Des Moines*, Annals (3), 25: 31-37, July, 1943.

Peck, Mrs. Maria, *Fort Armstrong*, Annals (3), 1: 602-613, Jan., 1895.

Petersen, William J., *The Story of Iowa*, 1: 252-260. Lewis Historical Co., New York. 1952.

Seeburger, Vernon R., *Fort Des Moines and Des Moines*, Annals (3), 25: 20-31, July, 1943.

Three Forts Des Moines—100th Anniversary of Establishment of Military Post at Des Moines, Annals (3), 25: 3-7, July, 1943.

Van der Zee, Jacob, *Forts in the Iowa Country*, Iowa Journal, 12: 163-204, April, 1914.

Wesley, Edgar B., *Guarding the Frontier: A Study of Frontier Defense from 1815-1825*. University of Minnesota Press, Minneapolis. 1935.

Williams, Ora, *Des Moines' First Hundred Years*, Annals (3), 25: 7-20, July, 1943.

OLD FORT MADISON—THE FIRST AMERICAN FORT IN IOWA

Cole, Cyrenus, A History of the People of Iowa, 62-74. Torch Press, Cedar Rapids. 1921.

Fort Madison, Annals (3), 3: 97-110, July, 1897.

Petersen, William J., The Story of Iowa, 1: 237-245. Lewis Historical Co., New York. 1952.

Van der Zee, Jacob, Forts in the Iowa Country, Iowa Journal, 12: 163-204, April, 1914.

Van der Zee, Jacob, Fur Trade Operations in the Eastern Iowa Country from 1800 to 1833, Iowa Journal, 12: 479-567, Oct., 1914.

Van der Zee, Jacob, Old Fort Madison, Iowa and War, No. 7, Jan., 1918.

Van der Zee, Jacob, Old Fort Madison: Some Source Materials, Iowa Journal, 11: 517-545, Oct., 1913.

MILITARY EXPEDITIONS IN THE IOWA COUNTRY

Briggs, John E., When Iowa Was Young, Palimpsest, 6: 117-127, April, 1925.

Briggs, John E., With Captain Allen in 1844, Palimpsest, 25: 193-209, July, 1944.

Captain Allen's Explorations, Annals (3), 30: 222, Jan., 1950.

Gallaher, Ruth A., The Military-Indian Frontier 1830-1835, Iowa Journal, 15: 393-428, July, 1917.

Kearny, Stephen W., An Expedition Across Iowa in 1820, Annals (3), 10: 343-371, Jan.-April, 1912.

Lea, Albert M., Early Explorations in Iowa, Historical Record, 6: 535-553, Oct., 1890.

Lea, Albert M., The Expedition of 1835, Palimpsest, 16: 105-134, April, 1935.

Lucas, Senator J. G., March of the Dragoons, Annals (3), 27: 85-96, Oct., 1945.

Pelzer, Louis, A Journal of Marches by the First United States Dragoons 1834-1835, Iowa Journal, 7: 331-378, July, 1909.

Pelzer, Louis, Marches of the Dragoons in the Mississippi Valley, 49-63. SHSI. 1917.

Petersen, William J., Across the Prairies of Iowa, Palimpsest, 12: 326-334, Aug., 1931.

Petersen, William J., Jean Marie Cardinal, Palimpsest, 12: 414-420, Nov., 1931.

Petersen, William J., Trailmaking on the Frontier, Palimpsest, 12: 298-314, Aug., 1931.

Petersen, William J., Up the Missouri with Atkinson, Palimpsest, 12: 315-325, Aug., 1931.

Petersen, William J., The Story of Iowa, 1: 261-272. Lewis Historical Co., New York. 1952.

Van der Zee, Jacob, Captain James Allen's Dragoon Expedition from Fort Des Moines, Territory of Iowa, in 1844, Iowa Journal, 11: 68-108, Jan., 1913.

Van der Zee, Jacob, *Edwin V. Sumner's Dragoon Expedition in the Territory of Iowa in the Summer of 1845*, Iowa Journal, 11: 258-267, April, 1913.

Early Settlements and the Pioneers

SETTLEMENTS ALONG THE MISSISSIPPI

Allen, James D., *Iowa's "Little Switzerland,"* Annals (3), 30: 378-384, July, 1950.

Duffield, George C., *Coming into Iowa in 1837*, Annals (3), 6: 1-8, April, 1903.

Goodwin, Cardinal, *The American Occupation of Iowa 1833 to 1860*, Iowa Journal, 17: 83-102, Jan., 1919.

Goodwin, Cardinal, *The Movement of American Settlers into Wisconsin and Minnesota*, Iowa Journal, 17: 406-428, July, 1919.

Haefner, Marie, *Rivalry Among the River Towns*, Palimpsest, 18: 160-174, May, 1937.

Kelly, Henry C., *Northern Iowa—1858*, Palimpsest, 30: 42-60, Feb., 1949.

Knapp, Henry E., *General John H. Knapp, The First Permanent Settler of Fort Madison, Iowa*, Annals (3), 10: 161-165, Oct., 1911.

Langworthy, Lucius H., *Dubuque: Its History, Mines, Indian Legends, Etc.*, Iowa Journal, 8: 366-422, July, 1910.

Meyer, Marie E., *River Towns*, Palimpsest, 7: 381-389, Dec., 1926.

Mullin, Frank A., *Gleanings of an Editor*, Palimpsest, 6: 250-261, July, 1925.

Oldest Midwest Settlement, Annals (3), 29: 615, April, 1949.

Parish, John C., *Iowa in the Days of Lucas*, Palimpsest, 3: 244-249, Aug., 1922.

Pelzer, Louis, *Early Burlington*, Palimpsest, 15: 225-254, July, 1934.

Pelzer, Louis, *Squatter Settlements*, Palimpsest, 14: 77-84, Feb., 1933.

Petersen, William J., *Beginnings of Davenport*, Palimpsest, 20: 241-280, Aug., 1939.

Petersen, William J., *Beginnings of Dubuque*, Palimpsest, 21: 345-392, Nov., 1940.

Petersen, William J., *Beginnings of Muscatine*, Palimpsest, 20: 345-384, Nov., 1939.

Petersen, William J., *Some Beginnings in Iowa*, Iowa Journal, 28: 3-54, Jan., 1930.

Richman, Irving B., *Ioway to Iowa*, 105-134. SHSI. 1931.

Salter, William, *Iowa: The First Free State in the Louisiana Purchase*, 124-231. McClurg, Chicago. 1905.

The Settlers Came 1833, Palimpsest, 14: 41-100, Feb., 1933.

Material may be found also in the various county histories. See also Towns of Iowa, Burlington, Davenport, Dubuque, Fort Madison, Keokuk, Muscatine.

Settlements in the Interior of Iowa

Bohach, Leona J., *Settlement of St. Ansgar—Miniature Melting Pot*, Iowa Journal, 46: 296-315, July, 1948.

Brown, H. Clark, *Bradford—A Prairie Village*, Palimpsest, 2: 65-71, March, 1921.

Daniels, John J., *The Earliest Settlers of Linn County*, Annals (3), 6: 581-589, Jan., 1905.

Ericson, Charles J. A., *Memories of a Swedish Immigrant of 1852*, Annals (3), 8: 1-12, April, 1907.

Lucas, C. L., *Recollections of Early Times in Iowa*, Annals (3), 6: 376-384, April, 1904.

Lyon, Bessie L., *Prospecting for a New Home*, Palimpsest, 6: 225-232, July, 1925.

Mann, T. E., *Union Grove*, Palimpsest, 26: 28-32, Jan., 1945.

Marsh, James, *First Iowans Settled by Streams*, Annals (3), 31: 229-230, Jan., 1952.

Parker, George F., *A Typical Iowa Pioneer Community* (Carlisle), Iowa Journal, 20: 348-363, July, 1922.

Parker, L. F., and Samuel J. Buck, *Old Settlers of Grinnell*, Historical Record, 14: 266-283, April, 1898.

Pelzer, Louis, *Iowa City: A Miniature Frontier of the Forties*, Iowa Journal, 29: 3-26, Jan., 1931.

Petersen, William J., *Come to the Turkey Valley*, Palimpsest, 24: 352-364, Nov., 1943.

Raleigh, O. H., *Northern Iowa One Hundred Years Ago*, Annals (3), 27: 200-206, Oct., 1945.

Shambaugh, Benj. F., *Iowa City: A Contribution to the Early History of Iowa*. SHSI. 1893.

Shambaugh, Benj. F., *The Old Stone Capitol Remembers*. SHSI. 1939.

Stiles, Cassius C., *The Kentucky Settlement in Madison County, Iowa*, Annals (3), 20: 3-10, July, 1935.

Swisher, Jacob A., *Hopeville*, Palimpsest, 26: 303-315, Oct., 1945.

Material may be found also in the various county histories. See also Towns of Iowa, Cedar Falls, Cedar Rapids, Des Moines, Fort Dodge, Iowa City, Marshalltown, Mason City, Waterloo.

White Men Along the Missouri

Allen, Arthur F., *Northwestern Iowa: Its History and Traditions 1804-1926*. 3 vols. S. J. Clarke, Chicago. 1927.

Bloomer, D. C., *Notes on the Early History of Pottawattamie County*, Annals (1), 9: 523-533, 666-683, April, Oct., 1871.

Briggs, John E., *The Grasshopper Plagues in Iowa*, Iowa Journal, 13: 349-391, July, 1915.

Garver, Frank H., *The Settlement of Woodbury County*, Iowa Journal, 9: 359-384, July, 1911.

Ingalsbe, J. L., *Northwestern Iowa in 1855*, Iowa Journal, 18: 271-300, April, 1920.

Keck, Inez, A. J. Whisman, Pioneer (Washta), Palimpsest, 6: 337-345, Oct., 1925.

Pruitt, O. J., On the Road to Bethlehem, Annals (3), 30: 617-624, April, 1951.

Sly, Blanche C., Magnolia, Palimpsest, 2: 290-297, Sept., 1921.

Titus, Lydia A., From New York to Iowa (Bedford), Palimpsest, 2: 311-321, Oct., 1921.

Tweito, Thomas E., A Destined Land, Palimpsest, 29: 155-160, May, 1948.

Van der Zee, Jacob, Episodes in the Early History of the Western Iowa Country, Iowa Journal, 11: 323-363, July, 1913.

Material may be found also in histories of the various western border counties. See also Towns of Iowa, Council Bluffs, and Sioux City.

PIONEER LIFE IN IOWA

Aldrich, Charles, Things Remembered, Historical Record, 11: 312-323, July, 1895.

Athearn, Robert G., Across the Plains in 1863: The Diary of Peter Winne, Iowa Journal, 49: 221-240, July, 1951.

Aurner, Clarence R., Story of an Iowa Woman, Palimpsest, 28: 161-171, June, 1947.

Baily, Matie L., Christmas of a Pioneer Family, Annals (3), 31: 152-153, Oct., 1951.

Baily, Matie L. Turner, Prairie Homesteading, Palimpsest, 23: 229-238, July, 1942.

Beall, Walter H., Dutton's Cave, Palimpsest, 25: 156-160, May, 1944.

Benedict, Abbie M., My Early Days in Iowa, Annals (3), 17: 323-356, July, 1930.

Bereman, T. A., A Right Smart Hostilry, Palimpsest, 23: 239-240, July, 1942.

Berry, William J., The Influence of Natural Environment in North-Central Iowa, Iowa Journal, 25: 277-298, April, 1927.

Bishop, J. C., Letters of Jerome Carskaddan, 1853-1854, Iowa Journal, 48: 247-266, July, 1950.

Briggs, John E., Earning a Living, Palimpsest, 8: 14-17, Jan., 1927.

Briggs, John E., Earning a Living, Palimpsest, 32: 14-17, Jan., 1951.

Briggs, John E., Iowa Old and New, 150-212. University Publishing Co., Lincoln, Nebr. 1939.

Burrows, J. M. D., A Pioneer Journey, Palimpsest, 4: 301-306, Sept., 1923.

Clarke, George W., Pages From Bygone Days in and about Drakeville, Iowa, Annals (3), 14: 323-356, July, 1924.

Clarke, George W., Power of the Natural Man, Annals (3), 29: 544-552, Jan., 1949.

Closz, Harriet Bonebright, Reminiscences of Newcastle, Iowa, 1848. Historical Department, Des Moines. 1921.

Colegrove, Kenneth W., The Attitude of Congress Toward the Pioneers of the West from 1789 to 1820, Iowa Journal, 8: 3-129, Jan., 1910; 9: 196-302, April, 1911.

Collins, Hubert E., *The Story of Mahlon Day Collins*, Iowa Journal, 28: 55-131, Jan., 1930.

Cowman, Evangeline S., *For Value Received*, Palimpsest, 7: 277-282, Sept., 1926.

Cruikshank, Charles W., *The Making of a Pioneer*, Iowa Journal, 45: 290-310, July, 1947.

Davenport Courier, 1855, *Pioneering Handicap*, Annals (3), 26: 89, Oct., 1944.

Dubell, Susan I., *Rural Pioneering*, Palimpsest, 22: 225-239, Aug., 1941.

Dutton, Claude W., *Experiences of Francis Parker*, Annals (3), 29: Part 1, 108-131, Oct., 1947.

Fay, Barbara Brice, *An Iowa Blue Stocking*, Palimpsest, 28: 334-342, Nov., 1947.

Felton, Oliver J., *Pioneer Life in Jones County*, Iowa Journal, 29: 233-281, April, 1931.

Galer, Roger S., *Recollections of Busy Years*, Iowa Journal, 42: 3-72, Jan., 1944.

Gallaher, Ruth A., *From Connecticut to Iowa*, Palimpsest, 22: 65-78, March, 1941.

Gallaher, Ruth A., *Pioneer Life in Iowa*, Midland Schools, Jan., 1932.

Gallaher, Ruth A., *Pioneers in Person*, Palimpsest, 14: 85-97, Feb., 1933.

Garretson, O. A., *The Lewelling Family—Pioneers*, Iowa Journal, 27: 548-563, Oct., 1929.

Grahame, Pauline P., *On the Highway*, Palimpsest, 8: 24-27, Jan., 1927.

Gue, Benjamin F., *Early Iowa Reminiscences*, Historical Record, 16: 106-125, July, 1900.

Haines, Joanna Harris, *Seventy Years in Iowa*, Annals (3), 27: 97-118, Oct., 1945.

Hedge, Thomas, *Installation of the Temple Tablet, June 17, 1913*, Annals (3), 11: 168-179, July-Oct., 1913.

Henderson, A. M., *My Years in Story County*, Annals (3), 30: 604-616, April, 1951.

Herrick, John P., *Oley Nelson—An Unforgettable Character*, Annals (3), 25: 117-121, Oct., 1943.

Hill, James L., *Formative Influences in Early Iowa*, Annals (3), 10: 202-228, Oct., 1911.

Hoffmann, Phil, *The Lost Creek Disaster*, Palimpsest, 26: 21-27, Jan., 1945.

Hoffmann, Phil, *The Powder House Explosion*, Palimpsest, 26: 247-256, Aug., 1945.

Horack, Frank E., *An Account Book of Jesse Berry*, Historical Record, 13: 110-119, July, 1897.

Ingham, William H., *Hardships of Pioneers in Northwestern Iowa*, Annals (3), 5: 135-142, July, 1901.

Iowa Was Prosperous in 1869, Annals (3), 27: 316-317, April, 1946.

Irish, John P., *A Reminiscence*, Palimpsest, 2: 123-124, April, 1921.

Jarchow, Merrill E., *Life on a Jones County Farm, 1873-1912*, Iowa Journal, 49: 311-338, Oct., 1951.

Jarchow, Merrill E., *Social Life of an Iowa Farm Family, 1873-1912*, Iowa Journal, 50: 123-154, April, 1952.

Jennings, Rosa Schreurs, *Second-Generation Americans,* Annals (3), 29: 589-598, April, 1949.

Jordan, Philip D., *Quiet Please!,* Palimpsest, 26: 1-11, Jan., 1945.

Kaloupek, Walter E., *The Career of a Pioneer,* Palimpsest, 18: 317-334, Oct., 1937.

Kirkpatrick, C. D., *Buying a Farm in 1866,* Palimpsest, 6: 346-350, Oct., 1925.

Kuhns, Frederick I., *Diary of S. S. Howell, 1868,* Iowa Journal, 49: 143-167, April, 1951.

Lyon, Bessie L., *Grandmother's Story,* Palimpsest, 5: 1-8, Jan., 1924.

Lyon, Bessie L., *Gunda's Coffee Pot,* Palimpsest, 13: 416-425, Oct., 1932.

Lyon, Bessie L., *Hungry Indians,* Palimpsest, 9: 357-370, Oct., 1928.

Lyon, Bessie L., *Prospecting for a New Home,* Palimpsest, 6: 225-232, July, 1925.

McNamara, Agnes, *The First Four Years,* Palimpsest, 21: 91-98, March, 1940.

Mahan, Bruce E., and Ruth A. Gallaher, *Stories of Iowa for Boys and Girls,* 171-230. Macmillan, New York. 1929.

Mann, T. E., *Union Grove,* Palimpsest, 26: 28-32, Jan., 1945.

Men That History Forgot, Annals (3), 30: 223-224, Jan., 1950.

Mitchell, Thomas, *Mitchell's Early Settlement,* Annals (3), 31: 72-73, July, 1951.

Montzheimer, O. H., *Old Dutch Fred,* Palimpsest, 23: 16-23, Jan., 1942.

Morrill, Charles H., *The Trials of a Homesteader,* Palimpsest, 6: 351-358, Oct., 1925.

Mott, David C., *Charles Wesley Tolles,* Annals (3), 14: 621-632, April, 1925.

Murray, Janette Stevenson, *Lairds of North Tama,* Iowa Journal, 40: 227-260, July, 1942.

Murray, Janette Stevenson, *Women of North Tama,* Iowa Journal, 41: 287-318, July, 1943.

Murray, Ray, *When Men Were Men!,* Palimpsest, 27: 61-64, Feb., 1946.

Nossaman, Mrs. Sarah W., *Pioneering at Bonaparte and Near Pella,* Annals (3), 13: 441-453, Oct., 1922.

Nutting, William P., *Starting Life in Warren County,* Iowa Journal, 39: 180-199, April, 1941.

Olmstead, Agnes Briggs, *Recollections of a Pioneer Teacher of Hamilton County,* Annals (3), 28: 93-115, Oct., 1946.

Orvis, Melissa, *Letter from Iowa,* Palimpsest, 29: 121-126, April, 1948.

Parish, John C., *Iowa in the Days of Lucas,* Palimpsest, 29: 13-18, Jan., 1948.

Parish, John C., *A Study in Heads,* Palimpsest, 2: 322-327, Oct., 1921.

Parker, Addison M., *Grandfather's Adventure,* Palimpsest, 5: 9-15, Jan., 1924.

Parker, George F., *Iowa Pioneer Foundations,* 2 vols. SHSI. 1940.

Petersen, William J., *Builders of the Hawkeye State,* Palimpsest, 33: 129-160, May, 1952.

Petersen, William J., *Diseases and Doctors in Pioneer Iowa,* Iowa Journal, 49: 97-116, April, 1951.

Petersen, William J., *The First Iowa Thanksgiving*, Palimpsest, 25: 321-331, Nov., 1944.

Petersen, William J., *Frontiers of the Pioneers*, Palimpsest, 32: 55-56, Jan., 1951.

Petersen, William J., *In the Fields*, Palimpsest, 19: 275-285, July, 1938.

Petersen, William J., *The Pioneer Cabin*, Iowa Journal, 36: 387-409, Oct., 1938.

Petersen, William J., *The Story of Iowa*, 1: 352-381. Lewis Historical Co., New York. 1952.

Petersen, William J., *Town and Countryside in 1843*, Palimpsest, 24: 323-332, Oct., 1943.

Pioneer Life in Palo Alto County, Memoirs of E. May Lacey Crowder, Iowa Journal, 46: 156-198, April, 1948.

Pioneers, The, Palimpsest, 8: 1-54, Jan., 1927.

Pioneers, The, Palimpsest, 32: 1-56, Jan., 1951.

Robeson, George F., *The Early Iowans*, Palimpsest, 4: 285-300, Sept., 1923.

Robeson, George F., *Hard Times in Early Iowa*, Palimpsest, 5: 157-171, May, 1924.

Roddis, Louis H., *A Cherokee County Pioneer*, Iowa Journal, 27: 457-469, July, 1929.

Sabin, Henry, and E. L. Sabin, *The Making of Iowa*, Ch. XXI, A. Flanagan Co., Chicago. 1900.

Sanders, Cyrus, Journal of, Iowa Journal, 37: 52-88, Jan., 1939.

Savage, William, *Iowa Pioneer, Diarist, and Painter of Birds*, Annals (3), 19: 83-114, 189-220, Oct., 1933, Jan., 1934; 20: 140-150, Oct., 1935, 459-471, Oct., 1936, 535-543, Jan., 1937.

Seashore, Carl E., *Pioneering in Iowa*, Palimpsest, 22: 178-183, June, 1941.

Seerley, Homer H., *In Retrospect*, Palimpsest. 5: 258-260, July, 1924.

Shambaugh, Benj. F., *The Iowa Pioneers*, Palimpsest, 8: 1-4, Jan., 1927.

Shambaugh, Benj. F., *The Iowa Pioneers*, Palimpsest, 32: 1-4, Jan., 1951.

Shepard, Hugh H., *Background of a Pioneer*, Palimpsest, 27: 176-188, June, 1946.

Sherman, Roy V., *Pioneer Politics*, Palimpsest, 8: 47-50, Jan., 1927.

Snyder, Charles E., *The Eads of Argyle*, Iowa Journal, 42: 73-90, Jan., 1944.

Some Letters of James Mathews and Caroline Mathews Stone, Iowa Journal, 45: 311-320, July, 1947.

Taylor, Mary D., *A Farmers' Wives' Society in Pioneer Days*, Annals (3), 13: 22-31, July, 1921.

Throne, Mildred, *Letters from Taylor County, 1868-1880*, Iowa Journal, 46: 378-402, Oct., 1948.

Throne, Mildred, *The Memories of Aristarchus Cone*, Iowa Journal, 49: 51-72, Jan., 1951.

Titus, Lydia A., *From New York to Iowa*, Palimpsest, 2: 311-321, Oct., 1921.

Tjernagel, P. G., *Erik Kjyten*, Palimpsest, 12: 160-166, April 1931.

Tjernagel, P. G., and H. M. Tjernagel, *Who Was Nagelsen*, Palimpsest, 13: 261-273, July, 1932.

Tjernagel, N., *Pioneer Foods and Water Supply*, Annals (3), 31: 276-299, April, 1952.

Trachsel, Herman H., *The Hairy Nation*, Palimpsest, 8: 393-406, Dec., 1927.

Tweito, Thomas E., *Iowa in the Fifties*, Palimpsest, 24: 377-383, Dec., 1943.
Van Arsdale, Mrs. P. V., *A Pioneer Story*, Annals (3), 13: 279-303, April, 1922.
Wick, B. L., *Pioneers of the Norway Community*, Annals (3), 29: 366-378, July, 1948.
Wilson, Ben H., *Amelia Smith Hay*, Palimpsest, 28: 218-222, July, 1947.
Wing, Amelia Murdock, *Early Days in Clayton County*, Annals (3), 27: 257-296, April, 1946.
Wright, Henry W., *Iowa—As I Knew It*, Annals (3), 29: 379-396, July, 1948.

The Iowa Scene: 1833-1838

Briggs, John E., *A Commonplace Calendar*, Palimpsest, 19: 39, 40, 69-72, 117-120, 156-160, 200-204, 234-240, 286-292, 333-340, 390-396, 438-444, 478-484, 515-524, Jan. to Dec., 1938.
Harvey, R. E., *Faith and Works in the Black Hawk Purchase*, Annals (3). 21: 241-282, April, 1938.
Iowa in 1838, Palimpsest, 19: 1-524, Jan. to Dec., 1938.
Parish, John C., *Iowa in the Days of Lucas*, Palimpsest, 29: 13-18, Jan., 1948.
Petersen, William J., *Cultural Aspirations*, Palimpsest, 19: 161-172, May, 1938.
Petersen, William J., *Land of Promise*, Palimpsest, 18: 65-77, March, 1937.
Petersen, William J., *Life in the Iowa District*, Palimpsest, 18: 113-127, April, 1937.
The Settlers Came, 1833, Palimpsest, 14: 41-100, Feb., 1933.
A Trip into the Indian Country, 1838, Annals (3), 22: 248-253, Jan., 1940.

Pioneer Homes

Dubell, Susan I., *A Pioneer Home*, Palimpsest, 12: 445-453, Dec., 1931.
Duffield, George C., *An Iowa Settler's Homestead*, Annals (3), 6: 206-215, Oct., 1903.
Dusey, Frank W., *Two-story House Moved on Flat Cars*, Annals (3), 30: 135-141, Oct., 1949.
Fishburn, Jesse J., *Octagon Place*, Palimpsest, 29: 33-38, Feb., 1948.
Gallaher, Ruth A., *Around the Fireplace*, Palimpsest, 8: 18-23, Jan., 1927.
Gallaher, Ruth A., *Around the Fireplace*, Palimpsest, 32: 18-23, Jan., 1951.
Gallaher, Ruth A., *Indian Corn as a Substitute*, Palimpsest, 27: 189-192, June, 1946.
Jordan, Philip D., *The Stew Pan and the Spider*, Palimpsest, 24: 130-140. April, 1943.
Jordan, Philip D., *With Dyed Garments*, Palimpsest, 25: 82-89, March, 1944.
Ludwig, Mary Culbertson, *A Man and His Garden*, Palimpsest, 29: 204-213, July, 1948.
Macbride, Thomas H., *In Cabins and Sod-Houses*. SHSI. 1928.
Mahan, Bruce E., and Ruth A. Gallaher, *Stories of Iowa for Boys and Girls*. 171-230. Macmillan, New York. 1929.

Petersen, William J., *The Pioneer Cabin*, Iowa Journal, 36: 387-409, Oct., 1938.

Schmidt, G. Perle, *Old Flower Gardens*, Palimpsest, 12:189-197, May, 1931.

Sharp, Mildred J., *Early Cabins in Iowa*, Palimpsest, 2: 16-29, Jan., 1921.

Swisher, Jacob A., *Claim and Cabin*, Palimpsest, 8: 9-13, Jan., 1927.

Swisher, Jacob A., *Claim and Cabin*, Palimpsest, 32: 9-13, Jan., 1951.

Tjernagel, N., *Pioneer Iowa Homes*, Annals (3), 31: 146-151, Oct., 1951.

White, Charles A., *The Early Homes and Home-Makers of Iowa*, Annals (3), 4: 179-195, Oct., 1899.

Wilkinson, W. S., *A Pioneer Settlement in Madison County*, Annals (3), 6: 447-454, July, 1904.

See also Annals (1), 1:45; 2: 250, 251, 321; 3: 405, 437, 463; 6: 107, 108; 7: 36, 255-257; 10: 82, 83; 11: 415-417; Iowa Journal, 8: 347.

MARRIAGE AND DIVORCE

Brigham, Johnson, *The Wedding of James Harlan*, Palimpsest, 3: 101-105, April, 1922.

Gallaher, Ruth A., *Legal and Political Status of Women in Iowa*. SHSI. 1918.

Johnson, William S., *A Romance of the Forties*, Palimpsest, 1: 65-74, Sept., 1920.

Petersen, William J., *Some Beginnings in Iowa*, Iowa Journal, 28: 43, 44, Jan., 1930.

Trachsel, Herman H., *Due Process of Marriage*, Palimpsest, 8: 353-357, Oct., 1927.

CHILD LIFE IN EARLY IOWA

Brown, Harriet Connor, *Schoolday Memories*, Palimpsest, 30: 107-124, April, 1949.

Cyrus Bussey's Boyhood, Iowa Journal, 30: 513-531, Oct., 1932.

Duffield, George C., *Youthtime in Frontier Iowa*, Annals (3), 7: 347-360, April, 1906.

Felton, Oliver J., *Pioneer Life in Jones County*, Iowa Journal, 29: 233-281, April, 1931.

Gallaher, Ruth A., *Wanted—A Servant Girl*, Palimpsest, 7: 116-119, April, 1926.

Garland, Hamlin, *Boy Life in the West—Winter*, Midland Monthly, 1: 113-122, Feb., 1894.

Hoover, Herbert, *Boyhood in Iowa*, Palimpsest, 9: 269-276, July, 1928.

Hoover, Herbert, *Boyhood in Iowa*, Palimpsest, 29: 225-233, Aug., 1948.

Hoover, Herbert, *Boyhood in Iowa*, Palimpsest, 32: 409-416, Nov., 1951.

Hoover, Herbert, *Iowa Through Eyes of a Ten-Year-Old*, Annals (3), 27: 231-235, Jan., 1946.

Huftalen, Sarah Gillespie, *School Days of the Seventies*, Palimpsest, 28: 122-128, April, 1947.

Irwin, John R., *A Youngster Mingles With the Great*, Annals (3), 29: 608-
    613, April, 1949.
Petersen, Harold D., *Boyhood at Fort Dodge*, Palimpsest, 24: 186-204, June,
    1943.
Stuart, Granville, *Boyhood on the Frontier*, Palimpsest, 7: 213-229, July,
    1926.
Williams, Ira A., *Lost in an Iowa Blizzard*, Palimpsest, 2: 1-15, Jan., 1921.
Witter, D. R., *Two Lost Boys*, Palimpsest, 18: 312-316, Sept., 1937.

The Land and Its Owners

CLAIM ASSOCIATIONS

Battell, Fred C., *In Defense of Claims*, Palimpsest, 20: 77-84, March, 1939.
Donnel, William M., *The Majors War*, Palimpsest, 5: 261-269, July, 1924.
Early Land Claims in Des Moines County, Iowa Journal, 10: 255-260, April,
    1912.
Lokken, Roscoe L., *Iowa: Public Land Disposal*, 65-96. SHSI. 1942.
Malbin, Gladys, *Samuel H. McCrory*, Palimpsest, 20: 85-92, March, 1939.
Shambaugh, Benj. F., *Constitution and Records of the Claim Association of
    Johnson County, Iowa*. SHSI. 1894.
Shambaugh, Benj. F., *Frontier Land Clubs or Claim Associations*. Reprinted
    from the Annual Report of the American Historical Association, 1900,
    1: 67-84.
Shambaugh, Benj. F., *The Constitutions of Iowa*. SHSI. 1934.
Shambaugh, Benj. F., *History of the Constitutions of Iowa*, 30-65. Historical
    Department, Des Moines. 1902.
Swisher, Jacob A., *Claim and Cabin*, Palimpsest, 8: 9-13, Jan., 1927.
Swisher, Jacob A., *Claim and Cabin*, Palimpsest, 32: 9-13, Jan., 1951.
Thieves Beware (Constitution and By-Laws of the Grand River Vigilance
    Committee), Palimpsest, 13: 487-494, Dec., 1932.

SURVEYING IN IOWA

Cook, Ira, *Government Surveying in Early Iowa*, Annals (3), 2: 603-613,
    Jan., 1897.
Frémont, John C., *Pathfinding in Iowa*, Palimpsest, 9: 176-184, May, 1928.
Gallaher, Ruth A., *J. N. Nicollet Map Maker*, Palimpsest, 26: 289-302, Oct.,
    1945.
Ingalsbe, J. L., *Northwestern Iowa in 1855*, Iowa Journal, 18: 271-300, April,
    1920.
Lokken, Roscoe L., *Iowa: Public Land Disposal*, 13-64. SHSI. 1942.
Nicollet, Joseph N., *The Nicollet Boundaries*, Palimpsest, 9: 170-175, May,
    1928.
*Original Field Notes of William Austin Burt of the Survey of the Fifth
    Principal Meridian (Now in) Iowa, November, 1836*, Annals (3), 20:
    83-122, Oct., 1935.

Survey of the Iowa-Minnesota Boundary Line, Annals (3), 16: 483-503, Jan., 1929.

Swisher, Jacob A., *Township Surveys in the Iowa Country,* Iowa Journal, 35: 3-21, Jan., 1937.

Swisher, Jacob A., *With Rod and Chain,* Palimpsest, 18: 78-87, March, 1937.

Willard Barrows' Defense of His Original Survey of Salt Creek Township, Davis County, Iowa, Annals (3), 18: 544-549, Jan., 1933.

LAND SALES AND LAND TITLES

Johnson, Jack T., *Iowa City Lot Sales,* Palimpsest, 21: 242-246, Aug., 1940.

Letters of J. W. Denison, Iowa Journal, 31: 87-126, 274-304, Jan., April, 1933.

Lokken, Roscoe L., *Iowa: Public Land Disposal.* SHSI. 1942.

Parish, John C., *George Wallace Jones,* 151-156. SHSI. 1912.

Pelzer, Louis, *Augustus Caesar Dodge,* 47-62. SHSI. 1908.

Pelzer, Louis, *The Private Land Claims of the Old Northwest Territory,* Iowa Journal, 12: 373-393, July, 1914.

Reid, Harvey, *Thomas Cox,* 34-39. SHSI. 1909.

Roberts, Elizabeth Sperry, *An Iowa Land "Bargain" a Century Ago—A Letter,* Annals (3), 25: 113-116, Oct., 1943.

Scanlan, P. L., and Marian Scanlan, *Basil Giard and His Land Claim in Iowa,* Iowa Journal, 30: 219-247, April, 1932.

Shambaugh, Benj. F., *The Old Stone Capitol Remembers.* SHSI. 1939.

Swisher, Jacob A., *The First Land Sales,* Palimpsest, 19: 469-477, Nov., 1938.

Swisher, Jacob A., *Land for Sale,* Palimpsest, 27: 271-284, Sept., 1946.

Tweito, Thomas E., *The Osage Land Sale,* Palimpsest, 21: 157-164, May, 1940.

Van der Zee, Jacob, *The Oldest Land Titles in the State of Iowa,* Iowa Journal, 13: 238-249, April, 1915.

THE DES MOINES RIVER LAND GRANT

Des Moines River Grant. The Orr report, March 31, 1874, on the bill to indemnify holders of lands within the grant with a history of the whole matter since 1846. — *House Committee Reports,* 43rd Congress, 1st Session, Vol. 2 (Serial No. 1624), Report 344.

Frémont, John C., *Early Reports Concerning the Des Moines River,* Iowa Journal, 16: 108-120, Jan., 1918.

Frémont, John C., *Pathfinding in Iowa,* Palimpsest, 9: 176-184, May, 1928.

Gatch, C. H., *The Des Moines River Land Grant,* Annals (3), 1: 354-370, 466-492, 536-552, April, July, Oct., 1894, 629-641, Jan., 1895.

Negus, Charles, *The River of the Mounds,* Annals (1), 11: 481-501, July, 1873; 12: 253-274, Oct., 1874.

Swisher, Jacob A., *The Des Moines River Improvement Project,* Iowa Journal, 35: 142-180, April, 1937.

Swisher, Jacob A., *A Plan That Failed,* Palimpsest, 16: 273-288, Sept., 1935.

Van der Zee, Jacob, *Episodes in the Early History of the Des Moines Valley*, Iowa Journal, 14: 311-347, July, 1916.

Van der Zee, Jacob, *The Opening of the Des Moines Valley to Settlement*, Iowa Journal, 14: 479-558, Oct., 1916.

Immigration

THE COMING OF THE IMMIGRANTS

Aldrich, Charles, *Come to Hamilton County*, Palimpsest, 15: 275-286, Aug., 1934.

Bishop, J. C., *Letters of Jerome Carskaddan, 1853-1854*, Iowa Journal, 48: 247-266, July, 1950.

Bywater, Archimedes, *Bywater Odyssey*, Palimpsest, 18: 213-225, July, 1937.

Cammack, Eleanore, *From Indiana to Iowa*, Annals (3), 29: 400-405, July, 1948.

Cruikshank, Charles W., *The Making of a Pioneer*, Iowa Journal, 45: 290-310, July, 1947.

Foreman, Grant, *English Emigrants in Iowa*, Iowa Journal, 44: 385-420, Oct., 1946.

Fulton, A. R., *An Invitation to Immigrants*, Palimpsest, 18: 226-242, July, 1937.

Gallaher, Ruth A., *From Connecticut to Iowa*, Palimpsest, 22: 65-78, March, 1941.

Gallaher, Ruth A., *The Handcart Expeditions*, Palimpsest, 3: 214-226, July, 1922.

Galland, Isaac, *Galland's Iowa Emigrant, 1840*, (a reprint), Annals (3), 12: 481-509, Jan., 1921.

Galland's Iowa Emigrant. A reprint with an historical introduction by William J. Petersen. SHSI. 1950.

Goodwin, Cardinal, *The American Occupation of Iowa, 1833 to 1860*, Iowa Journal, 17: 83-102, Jan., 1919.

Goodwin, Cardinal, *The Movement of American Settlers into Wisconsin and Minnesota*, Iowa Journal, 17: 406-428, July, 1919.

Hansen, Marcus L., *Official Encouragement of Immigration to Iowa*, Iowa Journal, 19: 159-195, April, 1921.

Herriott, Frank I., *Some of Iowa's Stock*, Annals (3), 7: 38-64, April, 1905.

Herriott, Frank I., *Whence Came the Pioneers of Iowa?*, Annals (3), 7: 367-379, 446-465, April, July, 1906.

Johnson, Hildegard Binder, *German Forty-Eighters in Davenport*, Iowa Journal, 44: 3-53, Jan., 1946.

Jordan, Philip D., *Westward to Iowa*, Palimpsest, 30: 209-216, July, 1949.

Keck, Inez, *A. J. Whisman, Pioneer*, Palimpsest, 6: 337-345, Oct., 1925.

Kirkpatrick, Charles D., *Buying a Farm in 1866*, Palimpsest, 6: 346-350, Oct., 1925.

Lyon, Bessie L., *Gunda's Coffee Pot*, Palimpsest, 13: 416-425, Oct., 1932.

Lyon, Bessie L., *Prospecting for a New Home*, Palimpsest, 6: 225-232, July, 1925.

Mahan, Bruce E., *By Boat and Covered Wagon*, Palimpsest, 8: 5-8, Jan., 1927.

Mahan, Bruce E., *By Boat and Covered Wagon*, Palimpsest, 32: 5-8, Jan., 1951.

Mahan, Bruce E., *The Way to Iowa*, Palimpsest, 2: 301-310, Oct., 1921.

Morrill, Charles H., *The Trials of a Homesteader*, Palimpsest, 6: 351-358, Oct., 1925.

Mullin, Frank A., *Gleanings of an Editor*, Palimpsest, 6: 250-261, July, 1925.

Nibley, Preston, *Exodus to Greatness: The Story of the Mormon Migration*. Deseret News Press, Salt Lake City. 1947.

Peckham, Edward L., *A Journey Out West*, Palimpsest, 6: 233-249, July, 1925.

Petersen, William J., *Come to the Turkey Valley*, Palimpsest, 24: 352-364, Nov., 1943.

Petersen, William J., *Population Advance to the Upper Mississippi Valley: 1830-1860*, Iowa Journal, 32: 312-353, Oct., 1934.

Petersen, William J., *Steamboating on the Upper Mississippi*, 296-380. SHSI. 1937.

Petersen, William J., *To the Land of Black Hawk*, Palimpsest, 14: 53-68, Feb., 1933.

Petersen, William J., *Town and Countryside in 1843*, Palimpsest, 24: 323-332, Oct., 1943.

Petersen, William J., *The Story of Iowa*, 2: 923-948. Lewis Historical Co., New York. 1952.

Plumbe, John, *Sketches of Iowa and Wisconsin, Taken During a Residence of Three Years in Those Territories (a reprint)*, Annals (3), 14: 481-531, 595-619, Jan., April, 1925.

Plumbe, John, *Sketches of Iowa and Wisconsin*. A reprint with historical introduction by William J. Petersen. SHSI. 1948.

Richman, Irving B., *Ioway to Iowa*, 160-171. SHSI. 1931.

Shepard, Hugh H., *On the Way to Iowa*, Palimpsest, 27: 170-175, June, 1946.

Smith, Ophia D., *A Trip to Iowa in 1841*, Palimpsest, 17: 329-341, Oct., 1936.

Swartzendruber, J. F., *An Amish Migration*, Palimpsest, 17: 342-357, Oct., 1936.

Throne, Mildred, *Letters of John Larrabee, 1849*, Iowa Journal, 47: 247-274, July, 1949.

Throne, Mildred, *The Memories of Aristarchus Cone*, Iowa Journal, 49: 51-72, Jan., 1951.

Tjernagel, N., *Immigrants Trying Experiences*, Annals (3), 31: 64-71, July, 1951.

Van der Zee, Jacob, *The Mormon Trails in Iowa*, Iowa Journal, 12: 3-16, Jan., 1914.

Wittke, Carl, *We Who Built America*. Prentice-Hall, New York. 1939.

See also various nationalities and religious groups.

ENGLISH IN IOWA

Black, Jean Phyllis, *A Guide for Englishmen*, Palimpsest, 25: 289-297, Oct., 1944.

Foreman, Grant, *English Emigrants in Iowa*, Iowa Journal, 44: 385-420, Oct., 1946.

Gallaher, Ruth A., *The English Community in Iowa*, Palimpsest, 2: 80-94, March, 1921.

Hickman, C. Addison, *Barlow Hall*, Palimpsest, 22: 301-309, Oct., 1941.

Van der Zee, Jacob, *The British in Iowa*. SHSI. 1922.

GERMANS IN IOWA

Christensen, Thomas P., *A German Forty-eighter in Iowa*, Annals (3), 26: 245-253, April, 1945.

Eiboeck, Joseph, *Die Deutschen von Iowa*. Iowa Staats-Anzeiger, Des Moines. 1900.

Emery, Charles W., *The Iowa Germans in the Election of 1860*, Annals (3), 22: 421-453, Oct., 1940.

Faust, Albert B., *The German Element in the United States*. Houghton Mifflin, Boston. 1909.

Herriott, Frank I., *A Neglected Factor in the Anti-Slavery Triumph in Iowa in 1854*, Jahrbuch der Deutsch-Amerikanischen Gesellschaft von Illinois, 18-19: 174-352.

Jennings, Rosa Schreurs, *A Scrap of Americana*, Annals (3), 29: 290-297, April, 1948.

Johnson, Hildegard Binder, *German Forty-Eighters in Davenport*, Iowa Journal, 44: 3-53, Jan., 1946.

Schnuecker, George, *Die Ostfriesen in Amerika: Eine Illustrierte Geschichte Ihrer Kolonien biz zur Gegenwart*. Central Publishing House, Cleveland. 1917.

Schulz-Behrend, George, *Communia, Iowa, A Nineteenth-Century German-American Utopia*, Iowa Journal, 48: 27-54, Jan., 1950.

See also Amana.

HOLLANDERS IN IOWA

Cole, Cyrenus, *A Bit of Holland in America*, Midland Monthly, 3: 115-128, Feb., 1895.

Cole, Cyrenus, *I Remember, I Remember*. SHSI. 1936.

Cole, Cyrenus, *Iowa Through the Years*, 196-198. SHSI. 1940.

Lucas, Henry S., *The Beginnings of Dutch Immigration to Iowa, 1845-1847*, Iowa Journal, 22: 483-531, Oct., 1924.

Lucas, Henry S., *A Document Relating to Dutch Immigration in Iowa in 1846*, Iowa Journal, 21: 457-465, July, 1923.

Lucas, Henry S., *The Political Activities of the Dutch Immigrants from 1847 to the Civil War*, Iowa Journal, 26: 171-203, April, 1928.

Scholte, Leonora, *A Stranger in a Strange Land*, Iowa Journal, 37: 115-203, April, 1939.

Van der Zee, Jacob, *The Hollanders of Iowa*. SHSI. 1912.

Van der Zee, Jacob (tr.), *The Coming of the Hollanders to Iowa,* Iowa Journal, 9: 528-574, Oct., 1911.

Van der Zee, Jacob (tr.), *Diary of a Journey from the Netherlands to Pella, Iowa, in 1849,* Iowa Journal, 10: 363-382, July, 1912.

Van der Zee, Jacob (tr.), *An Eminent Foreigner's Visit to the Dutch Colonies of Iowa in 1873,* Iowa Journal, 11: 221-247, April, 1913.

SCANDINAVIANS IN IOWA

Blegen, Theodore C., *Norwegian Migration to America, 1825-1860.* Norwegian-American Historical Association, Northfield, Minn. 1931.

Blegen, Theodore C., *Norwegian Migration to America: The American Transition.* Norwegian-American Historical Association, Northfield, Minn. 1940.

Christensen, Thomas P., *Dansk-Amerikansk Historie.* Holst Printing Co., Cedar Rapids. 1927.

Dahlberg, Robert N., and Charles L. Dahlberg, *Pehr Dahlberg and the First Swedish Settlement in Iowa,* Annals (3), 16: 323-330, July, 1928.

Estrem, Andrew, *An Early Norse Settlement in Iowa,* Iowa Journal, 39: 387-402, Oct., 1941.

Flom, George T., *The Coming of the Norwegians to Iowa,* Iowa Journal, 3: 347-383, July, 1905.

Flom, George T., *The Danish Contingent in the Population of Early Iowa,* Iowa Journal, 4: 220-244, April, 1906.

Flom, George T., *The Early Swedish Immigration to Iowa,* Iowa Journal, 3: 583-615, Oct., 1905.

Flom, George T., *The Growth of the Scandinavian Factor in the Population of Iowa,* Iowa Journal, 4: 267-285, April, 1906.

Flom, George T., *The Scandinavian Factor in the American Population,* Iowa Journal, 3: 57-91, Jan., 1905.

Lyon, Bessie L., *Gunda's Coffee Pot,* Palimpsest, 13: 416-425, Oct., 1932.

McIntosh, Lois A., *Biography of a Church,* Palimpsest, 29: 129-144, May, 1948.

Petersen, William J., *The Story of Iowa,* 2: 930-936. Lewis Historical Co., New York. 1952.

Seashore, Carl E., *Pioneering in Iowa,* Palimpsest, 22: 178-183, June, 1941.

Stephenson, George M., *The Religious Aspects of Swedish Immigration.* University of Minnesota Press, Minneapolis. 1932.

Storing, James A., *Palestine Settlement,* Palimpsest, 21: 151-156, May, 1940.

Tjernagel, P. G., *Erik Kjyten,* Palimpsest, 12: 160-166, April, 1931.

Tjernagel, P. G., and H. M. Tjernagel, *Who Was Nagelsen,* Palimpsest, 13: 261-273, July, 1932.

Wick, Barthinius L., *The Earliest Scandinavian Settlement in Iowa,* Historical Record, 16: 21-29, Jan., 1900.

Wick, Barthinius L., *Early Cedar Rapids Swedish Churches,* Annals (3), 29: 468-472, Oct., 1948.

Bohemians (Cechs) in Iowa

Brewer, Luther A., and Barthinius L. Wick, *History of Linn County, Iowa*, 1: 121-126. Pioneer Publishing Co., Chicago. 1911.

Capek, Thomas, *Cechs (Bohemians) in America*. Houghton Mifflin, Boston. 1920.

Capek, Thomas, and Anna V. Capek, *Bohemian (Cech) Bibliography*. Fleming H. Revell, New York. 1918.

Evans, Ramona, *Dvorak at Spillville*, Palimpsest, 11: 113-118, March, 1930.

Griffith, Martha Eleanor, *The Czechs in Cedar Rapids*, Iowa Journal, 42: 114-161, April, 1944.

Griffith, Martha Eleanor, *The Czechs in Cedar Rapids (Part 2)*, Iowa Journal, 42: 266-315, July, 1944.

Merrill, Pauline Skorunka, *Pioneer Iowa Bohemians*, Annals (3), 26: 261-274, April, 1945.

Scots in Iowa

Mahan, Bruce E., *The Scotch Grove Trail*, Palimpsest, 4: 379-397, Nov., 1923.

Murray, Janette S., *The Gathering of the Clan*, Palimpsest, 17: 397-403, Dec., 1936.

Murray, Janette S., *Lairds of North Tama*, Iowa Journal, 40: 227-260, July, 1942.

Murray, Janette S., *Sabbath in the Kirk*, Palimpsest, 17: 404-409, Dec., 1936.

Murray, Janette S., *A Beloved Dominie*, Palimpsest, 17: 410-414, Dec., 1936. 1936.

Murray, Janette S., *Women of North Tama*, Iowa Journal, 41: 287-318, July, 1943.

Van der Zee, Jacob, *The British in Iowa*, 47, 48. SHSI. 1922.

Wilson, Margaret, *The Able McLaughlins* (novel). Harper & Brothers, New York. 1923.

Irish Immigrants

Colton, Kenneth E., *Parnell's Mission in Iowa*, Annals (3), 22: 312-327, April, 1940.

Van der Zee, Jacob, *The British in Iowa*, 42-44, SHSI. 1922.

Wittke, Carl, *We Who Built America*. Prentice-Hall, New York. 1939.

From Luxemburg

Given, Welker, *A Luxemburg Idyll in Early Iowa*. Privately printed.

Nennig, Elizabeth, *A Dubuque County Immigrant from the Grand Duchy of Luxemburg*, Annals (3), 19: 63-67, July, 1933.

The Hungarians and New Buda

Cole, Cyrenus, A History of the People of Iowa, 230-231. Torch Press, Cedar
   Rapids. 1921.
Cole, Cyrenus, Iowa Through the Years, 199-201. SHSI. 1940.
The Hungarians in Iowa, Annals (3), 30: 465-467, Oct., 1950.
Meyer, Marie E., Nicholas Fejervary, Palimpsest, 9: 189-198, June, 1928.
Wilson, Lillian M., Some Hungarian Patriots in Iowa, Iowa Journal, 11:
   479-516, Oct., 1913.

The Icarian Community

Gallaher, Ruth A., Icaria and the Icarians, Palimpsest, 2: 97-112, April, 1921.
Gray, Charles, The Icarian Community, Annals (3), 6: 107-114, July, 1903.
Huff, S. W., Icaria, Annals (1), 5: 848-853, April, 1867.
Ross, Marie M., Child of Icaria. Privately printed, New York. 1938.
Shaw, Albert, Icaria: A Chapter in the History of Communism. G. P. Put-
   nam's Sons, New York. 1884.
Teakle, Thomas, History and Constitution of the Icarian Community, Iowa
   Journal, 15: 214-286, April, 1917.
Wick, Barthinius L., The Icarian Community—Story of Etienne Cabet's
   Experiment in Communism, Midland Monthly, 3: 370-376, April, 1895.

Mutualistic Communities in Iowa

Albertson, Ralph, A Survey of Mutualistic Communities in America, Iowa
   Journal, 34: 375-444, Oct., 1936.
Johnson, Ava, Communism in Early Days, Annals (3), 30: 73-75, July, 1949.
Jordan, Philip D., The Iowa Pioneer Phalanx, Palimpsest, 16: 211-225, July,
   1935.
Schulz-Behrend, George, Communia, Iowa, A Nineteenth-Century German-
   American Utopia, Iowa Journal, 48: 27-54, Jan., 1950.
See also Amana, Icaria, New Melleray.

Travel

Guides to Iowa

Black, Jean Phyllis, A Guide for Englishmen, Palimpsest, 25: 289-297, Oct.,
   1944.
Galland, Isaac, Galland's Iowa Emigrant. Reprint with an historical intro-
   duction by William J. Petersen. SHSI. 1950.
Hoffmann, M. M., The First Gazetteer on Iowa, Annals (3), 18: 383-390,
   July, 1932.
Iowa: A Guide to the Hawkeye State. Viking, New York. 1938.
Johnson, Jack T., Guides to Iowa Territory, Palimpsest, 20: 65-76, March,
   1939.

Lea, Albert M., *Notes on The Wisconsin Territory: Particularly with Refer-*
ence to the Iowa District, or Black Hawk Purchase (1836). Reprinted
as *The Book That Gave to Iowa Its Name.* SHSI. 1936.

Mott, Frank L., *Literature of Iowa Pioneer Life.* SHSI. 1923.

Petersen, William J., *The Story of Iowa,* 1:272-283. Lewis Historical Co.,
New York. 1952.

Plumbe, John, Jr., *Sketches of Iowa and Wisconsin.* Reprint with an historical introduction by William J. Petersen. SHSI. 1948.

Wick, B. L., *Early Iowa Map Attracts Settlers,* Annals (3), 25: 135-136,
Oct., 1943.

Wright, Luella M., *Views and Reviews of Iowa,* Palimpsest, 27: 240-253,
Aug., 1946.

THROUGH EUROPEAN EYES

De Girardin, E., *A Trip to the Bad Lands,* Palimpsest, 8: 89-101, March,
1927.

Eastern Border of Iowa in 1823, The, Annals (3), 5: 601-616, Jan., 1903.

Latrobe, Charles J., *A River Trip in 1833,* Palimpsest, 2: 244-263, Aug.,
1921.

Nicollet, Joseph N., *The Missouri Slope,* Palimpsest, 8: 370-378, Nov., 1927.

A Peep at the Far West, Palimpsest, 21: 6-22, Jan., 1940.

Petersen, William J., *The Mississippi River Through Many Eyes,* Iowa
Journal, 46: 339-377, Oct., 1948.

Petersen, William J., *A Princely Visitor* (De Joinville), Palimpsest, 22:
325-343, Nov., 1941.

Petersen, William J., *The Voyage of the Virginia* (Beltrami), Palimpsest,
13: 297-317, Aug., 1932.

Rae, W. F., *Through English Eyes,* Palimpsest, 10: 412-418, Nov., 1929.

Swanson, Roy W., *Iowa of the Early Seventies as Seen by a Swedish
Traveler,* Iowa Journal, 27: 564-581, Oct., 1929.

Through European Eyes (Beltrami, Murray, Bremer, Stevenson), Palimpsest,
1: 144-165, Nov., 1920.

THROUGH AMERICAN EYES

Atwater, Caleb, *A Country Fit for Princes,* Palimpsest, 12: 144-159, April,
1931.

Blair, John Insley, *Attending a National Convention and Seeing Iowa,* Annals (3), 26: 23-44, July, 1944.

Catlin, George, *Artist at Large,* Palimpsest, 7: 337-376, Nov., 1926.

Clark, William, *A Trip Across the Plains in 1857,* Iowa Journal, 20: 163-
223, April, 1922.

Clement, Ernest W., *Jesse Clement: A Yankee Westernized,* Iowa Journal,
38: 233-281, July, 1940.

Clement, Jesse, *Gleanings from the Note Book of the Itinerating Editor,* Iowa
Journal, 38: 282-305, July, 1940.

Glimpses of Iowa (1861), Palimpsest, 17: 27-34, Jan., 1936.

Hayes, Stephen H., *Letters from the West in 1845*, Iowa Journal, 20: 3-69, Jan., 1922.

Jordan, Philip D., *Iowa in the World*, Palimpsest, 21: 278-285, Sept., 1940.

Jordan, Philip D., *A Prairie Tour in 1850*, Palimpsest, 22: 213-224, July, 1941.

Jordan, Philip D., *Thomas Gregg's Letters to the New York Express*, Annals (3), 18: 538-543, Jan., 1933.

London, Jack, *Tramping with Kelly Through Iowa*, Palimpsest, 7: 129-158, May, 1926.

Mott, David C., *John J. Audubon and His Visit to Iowa*, Annals (3), 16: 403-419, Oct., 1928.

Peckham, Edward L., *A Journey Out West*, Palimpsest, 6: 233-249, July, 1925.

Petersen, William J., *The Mississippi River Through Many Eyes*, Iowa Journal, 46: 339-377, Oct., 1948.

Petersen, William J., *The Story of Iowa*, 1: 272-283. Lewis Historical Co., New York. 1952.

Shepard, Hugh H., *On the Way to Iowa*, Palimpsest, 27: 170-175, June, 1946.

Tweito, Thomas E., *The Gem of the West*, Palimpsest, 23: 26-32, Jan., 1942.

Tweito, Thomas E., *A Journey of a Journalist*, Palimpsest, 20: 126-136, April, 1939.

Young, John A., *Traveling to the Middle West in 1838*, Annals (3), 19: 139-145, Oct., 1933.

EMIGRATION FROM IOWA

Brown, Clara S., *Midland Women in California*, Midland Monthly, 4: 393-410, Nov., 1895.

Burlingame, Merrill G., *The Contribution of Iowa to the Formation of the State Government in California in 1849*, Iowa Journal, 30: 182-218, April, 1932.

Cheney, J. W., *The Story of an Emigrant Train*, Annals (3), 12: 81-97, July, 1915.

Collins, Hubert E., *The Story of Mahlon Day Collins*, Iowa Journal, 28: 70-92, Jan., 1930.

Cresswell, John M., *Getting off from Iowa to California in the Spring of 1850*, Annals (3), 20: 71-73, July, 1935.

Deemer, Horace E., *The Part of Iowa Men in the Organization of Nebraska*, Annals (3), 9: 161-185, Oct., 1909.

Diary Kept by William Edmundson, of Oskaloosa, While Crossing the Western Plains in 1850, Annals (3), 8: 516-535, Oct., 1908.

Dodge, Nathan P., *Early Emigration Through and To Council Bluffs*, Annals (3), 18: 163-179, Jan., 1932.

Dutton, Jerome, *Across the Plains in 1850*, Annals (3), 9: 447-483, July-Oct., 1910.

Emigration from Iowa to Oregon in 1843, Iowa Journal, 10: 415-430, July, 1912.

Greene, Sam M., *Transplanted Iowans*, Annals (3), 29: 491-503, Jan., 1949.

Hall, Reeves, *Oregon Fever*, Palimpsest, 24: 93-104, March, 1943.

Hanford, Cornelius H., *Pioneers of Iowa and of the Pacific Northwest*, Annals (3), 10: 331-342, Jan.-April, 1912.

Harlan, *Journal of A. W., While Crossing the Plains in 1850*, Annals (3), 11: 32-62, April, 1913.

Herriott, Frank I., *Transplanting Iowa's Laws to Oregon*, Annals (3), 6: 455-463, July, 1904.

Iowa Journal of Education, *Going West Across Iowa*, Annals (3), 27: 43, July, 1945.

Iowans Assemble at Long Beach, Annals (3), 30: 464-465, Oct., 1950.

Jordan, Philip D., *Moses Sees the Elephant*, Palimpsest, 30: 217-228, July, 1949.

Lorch, Fred W., *Iowa and the California Gold Rush of 1849*, Iowa Journal, 30: 307-376, July, 1932.

Lyon, Bessie L., *Jasons of 1860*, Palimpsest, 17: 217-234, July, 1936.

Millsap, Kenneth F., *Romanzo Kingman's Pike's Peak Journal, 1859*, Iowa Journal, 48: 55-85, Jan., 1950.

Myers, Alice V., *Wagon Roads West, The Sawyers Expedition, 1865, 1866*, Annals (3), 23: 212-250, Jan., 1942.

Pearson, Benjamin F., *A Trip to Kansas and Return May 20, 1872, to June 27, 1872*, Annals (3), 20: 207-218, Jan., 1936.

Pruitt, O. J., *Bibi Camp and Trek Across the Plains*, Annals (3), 30: 551-553, Jan., 1951.

Smith, *Letter from Hon. Delazon*, Annals (3), 20: 527-534, Jan., 1937.

Spencer, Lafayette, *Journal of the Oregon Trail*, Annals (3), 8: 304-310, Jan., 1908.

Stimson, Fancher, *Overland Journey to California by Platte River Route and South Pass in 1850*, Annals (3), 13: 401-440, Oct., 1922.

Studley, Hiram W., *Letter Describing a March to Utah in 1859*, Annals (3), 13: 611-618, April, 1923.

Throne, Mildred, *Letters of a Forty-Niner* (Chauncey Swan), Iowa Journal, 47: 63-77, Jan., 1949.

Wyman, Walker D., *Council Bluffs and the Westward Movement*, Iowa Journal, 47: 99-118, April, 1949.

Territorial Government

THE OLD NORTHWEST TERRITORY

Bond, Beverley W., Jr., *The Civilization of the Old Northwest: A Study of Political, Social, and Economic Development, 1788-1812*. Macmillan, New York. 1934.

Bond, Beverley W., Jr., *The Foundations of Ohio*. Ohio State Archaeological and Historical Society, Columbus. 1941.

Buley, R. C., *The Old Northwest: Pioneer Period, 1815-1840.* 2 vols. Indiana Historical Society, Indianapolis. 1950.

Cole, Harry E., *Stagecoach and Tavern Tales of the Old Northwest.* Arthur H. Clark, Cleveland. 1930.

Hinsdale, B. A., *The Old Northwest; With a View of the Thirteen Colonies as Constituted by the Royal Charters.* T. MacCoun, New York. 1888.

Hubbart, Henry C., *The Older Middle West 1840-1880.* Appleton-Century, New York. 1936.

McCarty, Dwight G., *The Territorial Governors of the Old Northwest.* SHSI. 1910.

Petersen, William J., *The Story of Iowa,* 1: 287-291. Lewis Historical Co., New York. 1952.

THE LOUISIANA PURCHASE

Channing, Edward, *The Jeffersonian System,* 47-85. Harper & Brothers, New York. 1906.

Dean, Henry Clay, *The Philosophy of the History of the Louisiana Purchase,* Annals (1), 12: 161-190, July, 1874.

Hobby, C. M., *The Louisiana Purchase,* Iowa Historical Lectures, 1892, 53- 69. SHSI.

Hosmer, James K., *The History of the Louisiana Purchase.* Appleton, New York. 1902.

Ives, Ronald L., *Indefinite Boundaries Led to Disputes,* Annals (3), 29: Part 1, 132-137, Oct., 1947.

Kasson, John A., *The Expansion of the Republic West of the Mississippi,* Annals (3), 5: 177-198, Oct., 1901.

Muller, Edwin, *Our Lucky Louisiana Purchase,* Annals (3), 26: 129-134, Oct., 1944.

Pelzer, Louis, *Economic Factors in the Acquisition of Louisiana,* Proceedings of the Miss. Valley Hist. Assoc., 6: 109-128, 1912-1913.

Petersen, William J., *The Story of Iowa,* 1: 216-220. Lewis Historical Co., New York. 1952.

Salter, William, *The Louisiana Purchase in Correspondence of the Time,* Annals (3), 6: 401-415, July, 1904.

Salter, William, *Iowa: The First Free State in the Louisiana Purchase,* 50- 63. McClurg, Chicago. 1905.

Williams, Ora, *Rulers Over the Land That Is Iowa,* Annals (3), 29: 299- 306, April, 1948.

TERRITORIAL JURISDICTIONS IN THE IOWA COUNTRY BEFORE 1821

McCarty, Dwight G., *The Territorial Governors of the Old Northwest.* SHSI. 1910.

Petersen, William J., *Iowa in Louisiana,* Palimpsest, 15: 33-42, Feb., 1934.

Salter, William, *Iowa: The First Free State in the Louisiana Purchase,* 50- 123. McClurg, Chicago. 1905.

Salter, William, *Iowa in the Territory of Missouri*, Annals (3), 6: 248-265, Jan., 1904.

Shambaugh, Benj. F., *Documentary Material Relating to the History of Iowa*. 3 vols. SHSI. 1897-1901.

Shambaugh, Benj. F.. *Iowa History from 1699 to 1821*, Historical Record, 16: 29-46, Jan., 1900.

Iowa Under Michigan

Lea, Albert M., *The Expedition of 1835*, Palimpsest, 16: 105-134, April, 1935.

McCarty, Dwight G., *Territorial Governors of the Old Northwest*, 118-143. SHSI. 1910.

Petersen, William J., *Iowa in 1835*, Palimpsest, 16: 87-102, March, 1935.

Petersen, William J., *Iowa in Michigan*, Palimpsest, 15: 43-55, Feb., 1934.

Swisher, Jacob A., *Government Comes to Iowa*, Palimpsest, 15: 67-78, Feb., 1934.

Swisher, Jacob A., *Michigan Personalities*, Palimpsest, 15: 56-66, Feb., 1934.

Iowa Under Wisconsin

Colegrove, Kenneth W., *The Delegates to Congress from the Territory of Iowa*, Iowa Journal, 7: 230-265, April, 1909.

Gallaher, Ruth A., *Government in Iowa*, Palimpsest, 17: 79-96, March, 1936.

Iowa in 1837, Palimpsest, 18: 65-112, March, 1937.

McCarty, Dwight G., *Territorial Governors of the Old Northwest*, 144-155. SHSI. 1910.

Parish, John C., *George Wallace Jones*, 14-35. SHSI. 1912.

Pelzer, Louis, *Henry Dodge*, 128-144. SHSI. 1911.

Petersen, William J., *The Geography of Wisconsin Territory*, Palimpsest, 19: 12-21, Jan., 1938.

Petersen, William J., *The Story of Iowa*, 1: 302-312. Lewis Historical Co., New York. 1952.

Petersen, William J., *The Times in Review*, Palimpsest, 17: 97-114, March, 1936.

Shambaugh, Benj. F., *The Constitutions of Iowa*, 50-58. SHSI. 1934.

Shambaugh, Benj. F., *Documentary Material Relating to the History of Iowa*, 1: 45-100. 3 vols. SHSI. 1897-1901.

Shambaugh, Benj. F., *Messages and Proclamations of the Governors of Iowa*, 1: 1-70. 7 vols. SHSI. 1903-1905.

Swisher, Jacob A., *Creation of the Territory*, Palimpsest, 17: 69-78, March, 1936.

The Territory of Iowa

Briggs, John E., *The Birth of the Territory*, Palimpsest, 9: 8-29, Jan., 1928.

Colegrove, Kenneth W., *The Delegates to Congress from the Territory of Iowa*, Iowa Journal, 7: 230-265, April, 1909.

Cook, Claude R., *Territorial and State Organization*, Annals (3), 29: 599-607, April, 1949.

Gallaher, Ruth A., *Directory of Iowa Territorial Officials*, Iowa Journal, 35: 256-262, July, 1937.

Higgins, Ruth L., *The Development of Trans-Mississippi Political Geography*, Iowa Journal, 21: 397-456, July, 1923.

Horack, Frank E., *Government of Iowa*. Charles Scribner's Sons, New York. 1921.

Jackson, W. Turrentine, *The Army Engineers as Road Builders in Territorial Iowa*, Iowa Journal, 47: 15-33, Jan., 1949.

Parish, John C., *John Chambers*, 115-189. SHSI. 1909.

Parish, John C., *George Wallace Jones*, 23-24, 127-130. SHSI. 1912.

Parish, John C., *Robert Lucas*, 155-226. SHSI. 1907.

Petersen, William J., *The Birthday of the Territory*, Palimpsest, 19: 241-250, July, 1938.

Petersen, William J., *The Geography of Iowa Territory*, Palimpsest, 19: 264-274, July, 1938.

Petersen, William J., *Independence Day in 1845*, Palimpsest, 26: 193-201, July, 1945.

Petersen, William J., *Prologue to Statehood*, Palimpsest, 26: 353-369, Dec., 1945.

Petersen, William J., *Robert Lucas*, Palimpsest, 29: 1-12, Jan., 1948.

Petersen, William J., *The Story of Iowa*, 1: 310-335. Lewis Historical Co., New York. 1952.

Salter, William, *An Address in Commemoration of the Meeting of the First Legislative Assembly of the Territory of Iowa, November 12, 1838*, Annals (3), 4: 614-624, Jan., 1901.

Shambaugh, Benj. F., *The Constitutions of Iowa*, 59-98. SHSI. 1934.

Shambaugh, Benj. F., *Documentary Material Relating to the History of Iowa*, 1: 101-123. 3 vols. SHSI. 1897-1901.

Shambaugh, Benj. F., *The Origin of the Name Iowa*, Annals (3), 3: 641-644, Jan., 1899.

Swisher, Jacob A., *Iowa in 1844*, Palimpsest, 25: 141-155, May, 1944.

Swisher, Jacob A., *The Organic Act*, Palimpsest, 19: 205-214, June, 1938.

Swisher, Jacob A., *Territorial Governors*, Palimpsest, 16: 3-9, Jan., 1935.

Territorial Convention of 1837, The, Iowa Journal, 9: 385-407, July, 1911.

The Lucas-Conway Controversy

Conway, William B., *The Controversy between Secretary Conway and Governor Lucas*, Iowa Journal, 8: 229-264, April, 1910.

Conway, William B., *The Controversy between Secretary Conway and the Council*, Iowa Journal, 8: 211-228, April, 1910.

Johnson, Jack T., *The Man Who Would Be Governor* (Conway), Palimpsest, 19: 251-263, July, 1938.

Johnson, Jack T., *Mandatory Thrift*, Palimpsest, 19: 495-502, Dec., 1938.

Johnson, Jack T., *A Question of Dignity*, Palimpsest, 19: 445-452, Nov., 1938.

Parish, John C., *Robert Lucas*, 168-226. SHSI. 1907.

Parish, John C., *Robert Lucas*, Palimpsest, 3: 233-243, Aug., 1922.

Van Ek, Jacob, *The Pen Knife Quarrel*, Palimpsest, 5: 139-152, April, 1924.

THE LEGISLATURE OF THE TERRITORY OF IOWA

Briggs, John E., *History and Organization of the Legislature in Iowa*, Applied History, 3: 3-51.

Gallaher, Ruth A., *Guilty or Not Guilty*, Palimpsest, 19: 50-61, Feb., 1938.

Johnson, Jack T., *Parker for President*, Palimpsest, 20: 43-52, Feb., 1939.

Johnson, Jack T., *Second Legislative Assembly*, Palimpsest, 21: 33-44, Feb., 1940.

Kelso, Hugh E., *The Extra Session of 1840*, Palimpsest, 21: 197-208, July, 1940.

Swisher, Jacob A., *The First Territorial Assembly*, Palimpsest, 20: 33-42, Feb., 1939.

Swisher, J. A., *Iowa in 1844*, Palimpsest, 25: 141-155, May, 1944.

Swisher, Jacob A., *Legislation in 1841*, Palimpsest, 22: 97-111, April, 1941.

Swisher, Jacob A., *Legislation in 1842*, Palimpsest, 23: 57-69, Feb., 1942.

Taylor, Hawkins, *The First Territorial Legislature of Iowa*, Historical Record, 6: 516-522, July, 1890.

Upham, Cyril B., *The Speaker of the House of Representatives in Iowa*, Iowa Journal, 17: 3-82, Jan., 1919.

CAPITALS OF IOWA

Briggs, John E., *A Capital in Name Only*, Palimpsest, 8: 57-70, Feb., 1927.

Briggs, John E., *The Removal of the Capital from Iowa City to Des Moines*, Iowa Journal, 14: 56-95, Jan., 1916.

Briggs, Shirley A., *In the Lifetime of a Bur Oak*, Palimpsest, 18: 335-342, Oct., 1937.

Gallaher, Ruth A., *Two Facts and a Fiction*, Palimpsest, 28: 223-224, July, 1947.

Haefner, Marie, *The Capitol at Burlington*, Palimpsest, 18: 98-102, March, 1937.

Johnson, Jack T., *Iowa City Lot Sales*, Palimpsest, 21: 242-246, Aug., 1940.

Lathrop, Henry W., *The Capitals and Capitols of Iowa*, Historical Record, 4: 97-124, July, 1888.

Pelzer, Louis, *Iowa City: A Miniature Frontier of the Forties*, Iowa Journal, 29: 3-26, Jan., 1931.

Petersen, William J., *The Story of Iowa*, 1: 319-329. Lewis Historical Co., New York. 1952.

Plum, Harry G., *The "Old Stone Building,"* Historical Record, 12: 418-425, Jan., 1896.

Reid, Harvey, *Thomas Cox*, 89-105. SHSI. 1909.

Shambaugh, Benj. F., *Iowa City: A Contribution to the Early History of Iowa*. SHSI. 1893.

Shambaugh, Benj. F., *The Old Stone Capitol Remembers.* SHSI. 1939.
Sioux City Journal, *The National Capital in Iowa,* Annals (3), 26: 260, April, 1945.
Swisher, Jacob A., *The Capital on Wheels,* Palimpsest, 4: 151-169, May, 1923.
Swisher, Jacob A., *The Capitols at Des Moines,* Iowa Journal, 39: 52-87, Jan., 1941.
Swisher, Jacob A., *Old Zion Church,* Palimpsest, 13: 274-284, July, 1932.
Waring, Edmund H., *Old Zion Church, Burlington, Iowa,* Annals (3), 9: 524-534, July-Oct., 1910.

BOUNDARIES OF IOWA

Eriksson, Erik M., *The Boundaries of Iowa,* Iowa Journal, 25: 163-235, April, 1927.
Eriksson, Erik M., *The Boundaries of Iowa,* Palimpsest, 7: 54-62, Feb., 1926.
Gallaher, Ruth A., *An Editor Speaks,* Palimpsest, 26: 316-318, Oct., 1945.
Gallaher, Ruth A., *J. N. Nicollet Map Maker,* Palimpsest, 26: 289-302, Oct., 1945.
Gallaher, Ruth A., *Triangles,* Palimpsest, 26: 319-320, Oct., 1945.
Nicollet, Joseph N., *The Nicollet Boundaries,* Palimpsest, 9: 170-175, May, 1928.
Parish, John C., *John Chambers,* 143-161. SHSI. 1909.
Pelzer, Louis, *Augustus Caesar Dodge,* 112-127. SHSI. 1908.
Petersen, William J., *The Geography of Iowa Territory,* Palimpsest, 19: 264-274, July, 1938.
Shambaugh, Benj. F., *Maps Illustrative of the Boundary History of Iowa,* Iowa Journal, 2: 369-380, July, 1904.
Swisher, Jacob A., *Large State or Small,* Palimpsest, 26: 97-109, April, 1945.
Swisher, Jacob A., *Three "No Men,"* Palimpsest, 26: 321-331, Nov., 1945.

THE MISSOURI BOUNDARY DISPUTE

Burrows, J. M. D., *Rumors of War,* Palimpsest, 24: 71-72, Feb., 1943.
Duncan, Joseph G., *Harvey Boyd Duncan,* Iowa Journal, 40: 415-421, Oct., 1942.
Eriksson, Erik M., *The Honey War,* Palimpsest, 5: 339-350, Sept., 1924.
Hebard, Alfred, *The Border War Between Iowa and Missouri, on the Boundary Question,* Annals (3), 1: 651-657, Jan., 1895.
Landers, Frank E., *The Southern Boundary of Iowa,* Annals (3), 1: 641-651, Jan., 1895.
Lea, Albert M., *Iowa and the Missouri Boundary,* Historical Record, 2: 193-207, Jan., 1886.
Lea, Albert M., *Report Made by Albert Miller Lea on the Iowa-Missouri Boundary,* Iowa Journal, 33: 246-259, July, 1935.
Negus, Charles, *The Southern Boundary of Iowa,* Annals (1), 4: 743-753, Oct., 1866; 5: 786-793, Jan., 1867.
Parish, John C., *Robert Lucas,* 227-257. SHSI. 1907.

Pelzer, Louis, *Augustus Caesar Dodge*, 77-93. SHSI. 1908.
Rorer, David, *A Wolverine Among the Hawk-Eyes*, Annals (3), 14: 403-421, Oct., 1924.
Shambaugh, Benj. F., *Messages and Proclamations of the Governors of Iowa*, 1: 217-241. 7 vols. SHSI. 1903-1905.
State Boundary Disputes, Historical Record, 13: 13-27, Jan., 1897.
Wilson, Ben H., *The Southern Boundary*, Palimpsest, 19: 413-424, Oct., 1938.

State Government

THE CONSTITUTION OF 1844

Parish, John C., *John Chambers*, 143-161. SHSI. 1909.
Petersen, William J., *The Story of Iowa*, 1: 336-345. Lewis Historical Co., New York. 1952.
Shambaugh, Benj. F., *The Constitutions of Iowa*, 118-184. SHSI. 1934.
Shambaugh, Benj. F., *Documentary Material Relating to the History of Iowa*, 1: 150-184. 3 vols. SHSI. 1897-1901.
Shambaugh, Benj. F., *Fragments of the Debates of the Iowa Constitutional Conventions of 1844 and 1846*, 1-313. SHSI. 1900.
Shambaugh, Benj. F., *History of the Constitutions of Iowa*, 175-284. Historical Department, Des Moines. 1902.
Sly, John F., *Providing for a State Constitutional Convention*, Iowa Journal, 19: 3-43, Jan., 1921.
Swisher, Jacob A., *Constitution Making in 1844*, Palimpsest, 25: 311-320, Oct., 1944.
Swisher, Jacob A., *Three "No Men,"* Palimpsest, 26: 321-331, Nov., 1945.

THE CONSTITUTION OF 1846 AND THE ADMISSION OF IOWA

Briggs, John E., *Ripe for Statehood*, Palimpsest, 27: 129-141, May, 1946.
Burlingame, Merrill G., *The Contribution of Iowa to the Formation of the State Government of California in 1849*, Iowa Journal, 30: 182-218. April, 1932.
Clark, Dan E., *Arguments in Favor of the Admission of Iowa into the Union*, Iowa Journal, 14: 395-437, July, 1916.
Cook, Claude R., *Territorial and State Organization*, Annals (3), 29: 599-607, April, 1949.
English, Emory H., *As Iowa Approached Statehood*, Annals (3), 27: 207-216, Jan., 1946.
Macy, Jesse, *Institutional Beginnings in a Western State*, Annals (3), 3: 321-345, April-July, 1898.
Pelzer, Louis, *Augustus Caesar Dodge*, 112-127. SHSI. 1908.
Petersen, William J., *The Story of Iowa*, 1: 345-351. Lewis Historical Co., New York. 1952.
Shambaugh, Benj. F., *The Constitutions of Iowa*, 185-212. SHSI. 1934.

Shambaugh, Benj. F., *Documentary Material Relating to the History of Iowa*, 1: 123-131, 185-215. 3 vols. SHSI. 1897-1901.

Shambaugh, Benj. F., *Fragments of the Debates of the Iowa Constitutional Conventions of 1844 and 1846*, 317-401. SHSI. 1900.

Shambaugh, Benj. F., *History of the Constitutions of Iowa*, 285-328. Historical Department, Des Moines. 1902.

Sly, John F., *Providing for a State Constitutional Convention*, Iowa Journal, 19: 3-43, Jan., 1921.

Swisher, Jacob A., *Iowa Adopts a Constitution*, Palimpsest, 27: 193-203, July, 1946.

Swisher, Jacob A., *Selecting Convention Delegates*, Palimpsest, 27: 49-60, Feb., 1946.

Thornton, Harrison John, *State of the Union in 1846*, Palimpsest, 27: 1-18, Jan., 1946.

Williams, Ora, *Iowa, My Iowa, Free Iowa*, Annals (3), 27: 3-14, July, 1945.

Williams, Ora, *Steps to Statehood*, Annals (3), 27: 217-219, Jan., 1946.

The Constitution of 1857

The Constitution of Iowa. State of Iowa, Des Moines. 1931.

The Constitutional Convention of 1857, Historical Record, 12: 481-492, July, 1896.

Erbe, Carl H., *Constitutional Limitations on Indebtedness in Iowa*, Iowa Journal, 22: 363-417, July, 1924.

Erbe, Carl H., *Constitutional Provisions for the Suffrage in Iowa*, Iowa Journal, 22: 363-417, July, 1924.

Eriksson, Erik M., *The Framers of the Constitution of 1857*, Iowa Journal, 22: 52-88, Jan., 1924.

Harlan, Edgar R., *The Constitution of Iowa in Facsimile*, Annals (3), 14: 163-203, Jan., 1924.

Petersen, William J., *The Story of Iowa*, 1: 397-399. Lewis Historical Co., New York. 1952.

Shambaugh, Benj. F., *The Constitutions of Iowa*, 213-280, 299-344. SHSI. 1934.

Shambaugh, Benj. F., *Documentary Material Relating to the History of Iowa*, 1: 217-287. 3 vols. SHSI. 1897-1901.

Shambaugh, Benj. F., *History of the Constitutions of Iowa*, 329-352. Historical Department, Des Moines. 1902.

Sly, John F., *Providing for a State Constitutional Convention*, Iowa Journal, 19: 3-43, Jan., 1921.

Thorpe, Francis N., *The Political Value of State Constitutional History*, Iowa Journal, 1: 17-45, Jan., 1903.

Amendments to the Iowa Constitution

Brindley, John E., *The Legislative Reference Movement*, Iowa Journal, 7: 132-141, Jan., 1909.

Erbe, Carl H., *Amendment of the Iowa Constitution*, Iowa Journal, 23: 103-137, Jan., 1925.

Horack, Frank E., *Constitutional Amendments in the Commonwealth of Iowa*, Historical Record, 15: 449-475, April, 1899.

Horack, Frank E., *Recent Amendments to the Constitution of Iowa*, Iowa Journal, 3: 286-299, April, 1905.

Mott, David C., *Amendments to the Constitution of Iowa*, Annals (3), 14: 204-214, Jan., 1924.

Shambaugh, Benj. F., *The Constitutions of Iowa*, 281-296, 345-351. SHSI. 1934.

Van der Zee, Jacob, *Proposed Constitutional Amendments in Iowa—1836-1909*, Iowa Journal, 7: 266-283, April, 1909; 8: 171-210, April, 1910.

THE CODIFICATION OF IOWA LAW

Clark, Dan E., *Codification of Statute Law in Iowa*, Applied History, 3: 339-430. SHSI. 1916.

Powell, Clifford, *History of the Codes of Iowa Law*, Iowa Journal, 9: 493-527, Oct., 1911; 10: 3-69, 311-362, Jan., July, 1912; 11: 166-220, 364-443, April, July, 1913; 12: 17-33, Jan., 1914.

Swisher, Jacob A., *The Code of 1924*, Iowa Journal, 23: 58-77, Jan., 1925.

Van der Zee, Jacob, *A Review of the Work of the Iowa Code Commission*, Iowa Journal, 18: 477-533, Oct., 1920.

Van der Zee, Jacob, *Indexing the Compiled Code*, Iowa Journal, 18: 534-551, Oct., 1920.

THE EXECUTIVE DEPARTMENT

Barnett, James D., *The History of the Office of Governor in Wisconsin*, Iowa Journal, 3: 226-255, April, 1905.

Erbe, Carl H., *The Executive Department of Government as Provided by the Constitution of Iowa*, Iowa Journal, 23: 363-405, July, 1925.

Fleming, William H., *The Second Officer in the Government*, Annals (3), 13: 529-540, Jan., 1923.

Shambaugh, Benj. F., *Messages and Proclamations of the Governors of Iowa*. 7 vols. SHSI. 1903-1905.

Swisher, Jacob A., *The Executive Department*, Palimpsest, 30: 324-333, Oct., 1949.

Swisher, Jacob A., *The Executive Veto in Iowa*, Iowa Journal, 15: 155-213, April, 1917.

Swisher, Jacob A., *Early Iowa Governors*, Palimpsest, 16: 1-30, Jan., 1935.

Swisher, Jacob A., *The First State Governor*, Palimpsest, 27: 357-368, Dec., 1946.

For material on individual Governors of Iowa see Biographies of Iowans.

MISCELLANEOUS ADMINISTRATIVE DEPARTMENTS

Bodine, Marcy G., *The Administration of the Drivers' License Law in Iowa,* Iowa Journal, 40: 3-51, Jan., 1942.

Cook, Herbert C., *Administrative Functions of the Department of Public Instruction,* Iowa Journal, 27: 244-294, 339-407, April, July, 1929.

Haefner, John Henry, *Iowa State Department of Agriculture: Its Evolution,* Iowa Journal, 41: 113-175, April, 1943.

Hargrave, Roger J., *The Origin and Development of Comptrollership in Iowa,* Iowa Journal, 44: 339-384, Oct., 1946.

Interstate Commissioner's Journal, *Honor Judge Richard F. Mitchell,* Annals (3), 29: 64, July, 1947.

Kaloupek, Walter E., *The History and Administration of the Iowa Highway Safety Patrol,* Iowa Journal, 36: 339-386, Oct., 1938.

Powers, Samuel C. E., *The Iowa State Highway Commission,* Iowa Journal, 29: 42-103, Jan., 1931.

Scott, David C., *The Iowa State Tax Commission,* Studies in Iowa Government. No. 1. SHSI. 1950.

Shea, Robert W., *History and Administration of the Iowa Bureau of Criminal Investigation,* Iowa Journal, 34: 262-311, July, 1936.

Street, John Purcell, *Iowa Department of Public Instruction,* Annals (3), 30: 397-452, Oct., 1950.

Swisher, Jacob A., *Administrative Officers,* Palimpsest, 30: 334-340, Oct., 1949.

Willoughby, George Wilson, *Cooperation between the State and Federal Departments of Agriculture,* Iowa Journal, 41: 394-420, Oct., 1943.

Willoughby, George Wilson, *Iowa State Department of Agriculture: Its Administration,* Iowa Journal, 41: 225-286, July, 1943.

THE MILITIA IN IOWA

Erbe, Carl H., *The Militia Under the Constitution of Iowa,* Iowa Journal, 24: 270-289, April, 1926.

Hearst, Gladys Whitley, *The WAVES at Cedar Falls,* Palimpsest, 28: 367-380, Dec., 1947.

National Guard, The, Midland Monthly, 2: 404-425, Nov., 1894.

Ness, George T., Jr., *Iowa's Early West Pointers,* Annals (3), 29: 397-399, July, 1948.

Rockwood, Alan C., *A History of the Military Department of the State University of Iowa,* Iowa Journal, 21: 183-312, April, 1923.

Upham, Cyril E., *Historical Survey of the Militia in Iowa, 1838-1916,* Iowa Journal, 17: 299-405, July, 1919; 18: 3-93, 413-440, Jan., July, 1920.

Wilson, George, *George Wilson: First Territorial Adjutant of the Militia of Iowa,* Annals (3), 4: 563-576, Jan., 1901.

THE STATE LEGISLATURE AND LAW-MAKING

Briggs, John E., *History and Organization of the Legislature in Iowa*, Applied History, 3: 5-135. SHSI. 1916.

Clark, Dan E., *Codification of Statute Law in Iowa*, Applied History, 3: 399-430. SHSI. 1916.

English, Emory H., *Power-house and Training School*, Annals (3), 28: 205-211, Jan., 1947.

Erbe, Carl H., *The Legislative Department as Provided by the Constitution of Iowa*, Iowa Journal, 23: 217-303, April, 1925.

Horack, Frank E., *The Committee System*, Applied History, 3: 535-609. SHSI. 1916.

Horack, Frank E., *The Sifting Committee as a Legislative Expedient*, Iowa Journal, 32: 291-311, Oct., 1934.

Patton, O. K., *Interpretation and Construction of Statutes in Iowa*, Applied History, 3: 433-472. SHSI. 1916.

Patton, O. K., *Method of Statute Law-Making in Iowa*, Applied History, 3: 161-284. SHSI. 1916.

Pollock, Ivan L., *Some Abuses Connected with Statute Law-Making*, Applied History, 3: 613-687. SHSI. 1916.

Pollock, Ivan L., *Special Legislation in Iowa*, Iowa Journal, 15: 3-41, Jan., 1917.

Schaffter, Dorothy, *The Bicameral System in Practice*, Iowa Journal, 27: 82-128, 171-226, Jan., April, 1929.

Shambaugh, Benj. F., *Law-Making Powers of the Legislature in Iowa*, Applied History, 3: 139-158. SHSI. 1916.

Swisher, Jacob A., *The General Assembly of Iowa*, Palimpsest, 30: 314-323, Oct., 1949.

Swisher, Jacob A., *The First General Assembly of Iowa*, Iowa Journal, 45: 62-84, Jan., 1947.

Upham, Cyril B., *The President of the Senate in Iowa*, Iowa Journal, 17: 223-265, April, 1919.

Upham, Cyril B., *The Speaker of the House of Representatives in Iowa*, Iowa Journal, 17: 3-82, Jan., 1919.

Van der Zee, Jacob, *The Drafting of Statutes*, Applied History, 3: 475-531. SHSI. 1916.

Van der Zee, Jacob, *Form and Language of Statutes in Iowa*, Applied History, 3: 287-395. SHSI. 1916.

Williams, Ora, *An Era of Open Debate in Iowa*, Annals (3), 26: 159-172, Jan., 1945.

THE PIONEER LAWMAKERS' ASSOCIATION

Colton, Kenneth E., *Iowa Pioneer Lawmakers' Association*, Annals (3), 22: 597-624, April, 1941.

Colton, Kenneth E., *Pioneer Lawmakers Association*, Annals (3), 21: 563-603, April, 1939.

English, Emory H., *Iowa Pioneer Lawmakers Convene*, Annals (3), 30: 3-38, July, 1949.

English, Emory H., *Pioneer Lawmakers Honored*, Annals (3), 31: 1-35, July, 1951.

English, Emory H., *Pioneer Lawmakers in Session*, Annals (3), 29: 3-45, July, 1947.

English, Emory H., *Power-house and Training School*, Annals (3), 28: 205-211, Jan., 1947.

Missouri's New Constitution, Annals (3), 26: 204, Jan., 1945.

Mott, David C., *Pioneer Lawmakers Association*, Annals (3), 19: 563-591, April, 1935; 20: 563-602, April, 1937.

Titus, George M., *An Iowa International Suggestion, The Monetary Problem*, Annals (3), 24: 297, April, 1943.

Williams, Ora, *Iowa Pioneer Lawmakers Association*. (Portraits of Former Justice Horace E. Deemer and Gen. Mathew A. Tinley), Annals (3), 24: 259-297, April, 1943.

Williams, Ora, *Iowa Pioneer Lawmakers Association*, Annals (3), 25: 61-79, July, 1943.

RECENT LEGISLATION IN IOWA

Briggs, John E., and Cyril B. Upham, *The Legislation of the Thirty-eighth General Assembly of Iowa*, Iowa Journal, 17: 471-612, Oct., 1919.

Briggs, John E., *The Legislation of the Thirty-ninth General Assembly of Iowa*, Iowa Journal, 19: 489-666, Oct., 1921.

Briggs, John E., and Jacob Van Ek, *The Legislation of the Fortieth General Assembly of Iowa*, Iowa Journal, 21: 507-676, Oct., 1923.

Horack, Frank E., *The Work of the Thirty-fourth General Assembly of Iowa*, Iowa Journal, 9: 475-492, Oct., 1911.

Horack, Frank E., *The Work of the Thirty-fifth General Assembly of Iowa*, Iowa Journal, 11: 546-600, Oct., 1913.

Horack, Frank E., *The Legislation of the Thirty-sixth General Assembly of Iowa*, Iowa Journal, 13: 475-528, Oct., 1915.

Horack, Frank E., *The Legislation of the Thirty-seventh General Assembly of Iowa*, Iowa Journal, 15: 503-570, Oct., 1917.

Swisher, Jacob A., *A Century of School Legislation in Iowa*, Iowa Journal, 44: 174-204, April, 1946.

Swisher, Jacob A., *The Legislation of the Forty-first General Assembly of Iowa*, Iowa Journal, 23: 507-625, Oct., 1925.

Swisher, Jacob A., and Dorothy Schaffter, *The Legislation of the Forty-second General Assembly of Iowa*, Iowa Journal, 25: 499-630, Oct., 1927.

Swisher, Jacob A., *The Legislation of the Forty-third General Assembly of Iowa*, Iowa Monograph Series, No. 1. SHSI. 1929.

Swisher, Jacob A., *The Legislation of the Forty-fourth General Assembly of Iowa*, Iowa Journal, 30: 3-114, Jan., 1932.

Swisher, Jacob A., and Ruth A. Gallaher, *The Legislation of the Forty-fifth General Assembly of Iowa*, Iowa Monograph Series, No. 5. SHSI. 1933.

Swisher, Jacob A., *The Legislation of the Forty-fifth General Assembly of Iowa: Extra Session*, Iowa Monograph Series, No. 7. SHSI. 1934.

Swisher, Jacob A., *The Legislation of the Forty-sixth General Assembly of Iowa*, Iowa Journal, 34: 3-97, Jan., 1936.

Swisher, Jacob A., *The Legislation of the Forty-sixth General Assembly of Iowa: Extra Session*, Iowa Journal, 35, 206-211, April, 1937.

Swisher, Jacob A., and Jack T. Johnson, *The Legislation of the Forty-seventh General Assembly of Iowa*, Iowa Journal, 35: 347-470, Oct., 1937.

Swisher, Jacob A., and Russell M. Ross, *The Legislation of the Fifty-third General Assembly of Iowa*. SHSI. Jan., 1951.

Van Ek, Jacob, *The Legislation of the Extra Session of the Fortieth General Assembly of Iowa*, Iowa Journal, 23: 78-102, Jan., 1925.

Administration of Justice

FRONTIER JUSTICE

Babbitt, Charles H., *At the End of Their Rope*, Palimpsest, 6: 405-408, Dec., 1925.

Black, Paul W., *Attempted Lynchings in Iowa*, Annals (3), 11: 260-285, Jan., 1914.

Black, Paul W., *Lynchings in Iowa*, Iowa Journal, 10: 151-254, April, 1912.

Grahame, Orville F., *The Vigilance Committees*, Palimpsest, 6: 359-370, Oct., 1925.

Parish, John C., *White Beans for Hanging*, Palimpsest, 1: 9-28, July, 1920.

Parker, James E., *Pioneer Protection from Horse Thieves*, Annals (3), 6: 59-62, April, 1903.

Price, Eliphalet, *The Execution of Patrick O'Connor*, Palimpsest, 1: 86-97, Sept., 1920.

Robeson, George F., *Justice in Early Iowa*, Palimpsest, 5: 102-113, March, 1924.

Robeson, George F., *Rough Justice*, Palimpsest, 8: 51-54, Jan., 1927.

Robeson, George F., *Rough Justice*, Palimpsest, 32: 51-54, Jan., 1951.

Tjernagel, N., *The Last Horse Robbery*, Palimpsest, 12: 373-380, Oct., 1931.

See also references under Stories of Crime and the Bellevue War.

STORIES OF CRIME

Briggs, John E., *Pioneer Gangsters*, Palimpsest, 21: 73-90, March, 1940.

Eriksson, Erik M., *The Boyd Wilkinson Case*, Palimpsest, 6: 95-104, March, 1925.

Gallaher, Ruth A., *A Race Riot on the Mississippi*, Palimpsest, 2: 369-378, Dec., 1921.

Jordan, Philip D., *The Adair Train Robbery*, Palimpsest, 17: 49-66, Feb., 1936.

Jordan, Philip D., *The Case of the Gold Carrier*, Palimpsest, 30: 229-236, July, 1949.

Mantz, H. J., *Audubon County's "Troublesome Gang,"* Annals (3), 30: 269-278, April, 1950.

McMurry, Donald L., *The Pacific City Fight,* Palimpsest, 2: 182-189, June, 1921.

Quick, Herbert, *The Hawkeye* (novel). Bobbs-Merrill, Indianapolis. 1923.

Smith, Frederic C., *The Green Goods Case,* Iowa Journal, 38: 163-181, April, 1940.

Swisher, Jacob A., *The Jones County Calf Case,* Palimpsest, 7: 197-208, July, 1926.

Teeters, Wilber J., *Science Fights Crime,* Palimpsest, 30: 79-92, March, 1949.

Tweito, Thomas E., *Mississippi Pirates,* Palimpsest, 23: 185-188, June, 1942.

Wallace, Jocelyn, *An Iowa Doone Band* (Rainsbargers), Palimpsest, 4: 267-280, Aug., 1923.

See also Frontier Justice.

ADMINISTRATION OF CRIMINAL LAW

Black, Paul W., *Attempted Lynchings in Iowa,* Annals (3), 11: 260-285, Jan., 1914.

Black, Paul W., *Lynchings in Iowa,* Iowa Journal, 10: 151-254, April, 1912.

Briggs, John E., *A Penitentiary for Iowa,* Palimpsest, 20: 400-410, Dec., 1939.

Brookman, Donald W., *Prison Labor in Iowa,* Iowa Journal, 32: 124-165, April, 1934.

Fox, Dorus M., *Is the Gallows as Efficacious as Imprisonment for the Prevention of Murder?,* Midland Monthly, 3: 290-295, March, 1895.

Haynes, Fred E., *County Jails in Iowa,* Iowa Journal, 44: 61-85, Jan., 1946.

Haynes, Fred E., *Friend of the Friendless,* Palimpsest, 29: 214-224, July, 1948.

Haynes, Fred E., *The Warden's Theories,* Palimpsest, 23: 330-336, Oct., 1942.

Haynes, Fred E., *Warden Haynes,* Palimpsest, 23: 305-316, Oct., 1942.

The Iowa Sheriff. 1929 to date. Iowa State Sheriffs' Association, Des Moines.

Kern, Jean B., *Warden and Warrior,* Palimpsest, 29: 182-192, June, 1948.

Robinson, Gifford S., *Penal Reforms,* Iowa Journal, 3: 529-561, Oct., 1905.

Shea, Robert W., *History and Administration of the Iowa Bureau of Criminal Investigation,* Iowa Journal, 34: 262-311, July, 1936.

THE BELLEVUE WAR

Black, Paul W., *Lynchings in Iowa,* Iowa Journal, 10: 151-254, April, 1912.

Briggs, John E., *Pioneer Gangsters,* Palimpsest, 21: 73-90, March, 1940.

Parish, John C., *White Beans for Hanging,* Palimpsest, 1: 9-28, July, 1920.

Reid, Harvey, *Thomas Cox,* 122-167. SHSI. 1909.

COURTS AND LAWYERS OF IOWA

Allen, Ethan P., *Appeals from the Supreme Court of Iowa to the Supreme Court of the United States,* Iowa Journal, 31: 211-273, April, 1933.

Bicknell, A. D., *The Early Courts of Iowa—The County Court—The Circuit Court,* Historical Record, 17: 262-277, April, 1901.

Briggs, John E., *An Eloquent Plea* (David Rorer), Palimpsest, 26: 270-274, Sept., 1945.

Briggs, John E., *A Rare Man* (David Rorer), Palimpsest, 26: 257-269, Sept., 1945.

Centennial of Iowa Federal Court, Annals (3), 30: 225-227, Jan., 1950.

Corlett, Leroy E., *History of the Mahaska County Bar,* Annals (3), 29: 511-543, Jan., 1949.

Clark, Dan E., *Judicial Districting in Iowa,* Iowa Journal, 5: 455-492, Oct., 1907.

Elliott, Gordon L., *The Circuit Courts of Iowa,* Annals (3), 23: 126-137, Oct., 1941.

English, Emory H., *Centennial of Federal Court in Iowa,* Annals (3), 30: 237-259, April, 1950.

Erbe, Carl H., *The Judicial Department of Government as Provided by the Constitution of Iowa,* Iowa Journal, 23: 406-474, July, 1925.

Glass, Remley J., *The Law Came to Fayette County,* Annals (3), 27: 171-199, Jan., 1946.

Glass, Remley J., *The Pioneer Bench and Bar of the Twelfth Judicial District of Iowa,* Annals (3), 23: 3-34, July, 1941.

Glass, Remley J., *Some Northern Iowa Judicial History,* Annals (3), 20: 403-419, Oct., 1936.

Halloran, John J., *Pioneer Bench and Bar,* Annals (3), 25: 43-58, July, 1943.

Heiserman, J. E., *The Legal Institute Program,* Annals (3), 30: 68-72, July, 1949.

Johnson, Jack T., *A Judge Well Met* (Joseph Williams), Palimpsest, 19: 370-378, Sept., 1938.

Jordan, Philip D., *The Case of the Gold Carrier,* Palimpsest, 30: 229-236, July, 1949.

Kendrick, W. R. C., *Historical Data of the Iowa Bar,* Annals (3), 29: 454-467, Oct., 1948.

Lauderdale, Maude, *How Justice Came to Webster County,* Annals (3), 30: 561-603, April, 1951.

Mahan, Bruce E., *Judge Joseph Williams,* Palimpsest, 5: 85-101, March, 1924.

McNeely, Lee, *Northern Judicial District of Iowa,* Annals (3), 30: 105-122, Oct., 1949.

Montzheimer, O. H., *Judicial Districts in Northwestern Iowa,* Annals (3), 20: 483-496, Jan., 1937.

Nourse, C. C., *Beginning Fifty Years of Practice at the Iowa Bar,* Annals (3), 8: 481-495, Oct., 1908.

Parvin, Theodore S., *The Early Bar of Iowa,* Iowa Historical Lectures, 1894, 70-92. SHSI.

Petersen, William J., *The Legal Profession,* Palimpsest, 19: 425-437, Oct., 1938.

Petersen, William J., *The Story of Iowa,* 2: 820-844. Lewis Historical Co., New York. 1952.

Petersen, William J., *Thomas S. Wilson*, Palimpsest, 19: 379-389, Sept., 1938.

Reed, Nicholas F., *Southern Judicial District of Iowa*, Annals (3), 30: 123-134, Oct., 1949.

Robeson, George F., *Justice in Early Iowa*, Palimpsest, 5: 102-113, March, 1924.

Silwold, Henry, *A Bit of Judicial History Pertaining to Jasper County, Iowa*, Annals (3), 18: 518-537, Jan., 1933.

Snyder, Charles E., *Two Sons of New York in Iowa*, Annals (3), 25: 147-173, Jan., 1944.

Stiles, Edward H., *Recollections and Sketches of Notable Lawyers and Public Men of Early Iowa.* Homestead, Des Moines. 1916.

Swisher, Jacob A., *The Jones County Calf Case*, Palimpsest, 7: 197-208, July, 1926.

Swisher, Jacob A., *A Just Man* (Charles Mason), Palimpsest, 19: 360-369, Sept., 1938.

Swisher, Jacob A., *An Adams in Iowa*, Palimpsest, 29: 39-48, Feb., 1948.

Swisher, Jacob A., *Eminence at the Bar* (David Rorer), Palimpsest, 26: 275-288, Sept., 1945.

Swisher, Jacob A., *The Judiciary*, Palimpsest, 30: 341-344, Oct., 1949.

Traer, J. F., *Bench, Bar and Court in Benton County*, Annals (3), 30: 279-293, April, 1950.

Wilson, Thomas S., *Address at the Opening of the Supreme Court-Room*, Historical Record, 3: 457-468, April, 1887.

Wright, George G., *The Pioneer Bar of Iowa*, Historical Record, 12: 401-418, Jan., 1896.

For references on Austin Adams, Caleb Baldwin, Charles Baldwin, Alexander Brown, Henry Clay Caldwell, Henry Clay Dean, John F. Dillon, John J. Dyer, James Grant, Jonathan C. Hall, Orlando C. Howe, John Johns, Edward Johnstone, James M. Love, Charles Mason, J. Scott Richman, David Rorer, Stephen Whicher, Joseph Williams, Thomas S. Wilson, and George G. Wright see Biographies of Iowans. See also Supreme Court of Iowa.

THE SUPREME COURT OF IOWA

Allen, Ethan P., *Appeals from the Supreme Court of Iowa to the Supreme Court of the United States*, Iowa Journal, 31: 211-273, April, 1933.

Johnson, Jack T., *A Judge Well Met* (Joseph Williams), Palimpsest, 19: 370-378, Sept., 1938.

Johnson, Jack T., *The Supreme Court in Session*, Palimpsest, 20: 191-195, June, 1939.

McLaughlin, Wm. M., *Judge Joseph Williams*, Annals (3), 25: 87-98, Oct., 1943.

Norem, Enoch A., *The Clear Lake Outlet Feud*, Palimpsest, 24: 173-185, June, 1943.

Parish, John C., *An Early Fugitive Slave Case West of the Mississippi River*, Iowa Journal, 6: 88-95, Jan., 1908.

Petersen, William J., *The Story of Iowa*, 2: 820-844. Lewis Historical Co., New York. 1952.

Petersen, William J., *Thomas S. Wilson*, Palimpsest, 19: 379-389, Sept., 1938.

Robeson, George F., *Justice in Early Iowa*, Palimpsest, 5: 102-113, March, 1924.

Snyder, Rev. Chas. E., *Statesmen and Politicians in Early Iowa*, Annals (3), 27: 15-36, July, 1945.

Swisher, Jacob A., *The Case of Ralph*, Palimpsest, 7: 33-43, Feb., 1926.

Swisher, Jacob A., *The Judiciary*, Palimpsest, 30: 341-344, Oct., 1949.

Swisher, Jacob A., *The Judiciary of the Territory of Iowa*, Iowa Journal. 20: 224-275, April, 1922.

Williams, Ora, *Iowa's Supreme Court* (illustrated), Annals (3), 26: 3-22, 138-154, July, Oct., 1944.

Suffrage, Parties, and Elections

POLITICAL CAMPAIGNS IN IOWA

Aman, John A., *Views of Three Iowa Newspapers on the League of Nations 1919-1920*, Iowa Journal, 39: 227-285, July, 1941.

Blanchard, B. W., *A Typical Midland State Convention*, Midland Monthly, 2: 230-242, Sept., 1894.

Braden, Waldo W., *The Cummins-Cannon Controversy of 1909*, Iowa Journal, 49: 211-220, July, 1951.

Brigham, Johnson, *Glimpses of Iowa Statesmen*, Iowa Journal, 32: 99-123, April, 1934.

Cone, Carl B., *Clinton Politics in 1903*, Palimpsest, 23: 264-272, Aug., 1942.

Gallaher, Ruth A., *Leaders*, Palimpsest, 26: 349-352, Nov., 1945.

Hall, Reeves, *The Election of 1843*, Palimpsest, 24: 301-312, Oct., 1943.

Herriott, Frank I., *A Neglected Factor in the Anti-Slavery Triumph in Iowa in 1854*, Jahrbuch der Deutsch-Amerikanischen Gesellschaft von Illinois, 18-19: 174-352.

How Dowell Went to Congress, Annals (3), 31: 311-313, April, 1952.

Johnson, Jack T., *The Campaign of 1840*, Palimpsest, 21: 229-241, Aug., 1940.

Johnson, Jack T., *The Election of 1842*, Palimpsest, 23: 241-252, Aug., 1942.

Johnson, Jack T., *The First State Election*, Palimpsest, 27: 257-270, Sept., 1946.

Johnson, Jack T., *Frontier Democracy*, Palimpsest, 19: 341-349, Sept., 1938.

Johnson, Jack T., *No Convention in 1840*, Palimpsest, 21: 309-317, Oct., 1940.

Kern, Jean B., *The Political Career of Horace Boies*, Iowa Journal, 47: 215-246, July, 1949.

Lucas, Henry S., *The Political Activities of the Dutch Immigrants from 1847 to the Civil War*, Iowa Journal, 26: 171-203, April, 1928.

Meyers, F. W., *Incidents in a Political Campaign*, Midland Monthly, 1: 169-176, Feb., 1894.

Millsap, Kenneth F., *The Election of 1860 in Iowa*, Iowa Journal, 48: 97-120, April, 1950.

Mott, David C., *Iowa Political Conventions and Platforms*, Annals (3), 14: 33-58, 101-145, July, Oct., 1923.

Pelzer, Louis, *The Election of Francis Gehon in 1839*, Iowa Journal, 5: 534-543, Oct., 1907.

Pelzer, Louis, *Seward and Douglas in Iowa*, Palimpsest, 7: 297-308, Oct., 1926.

Petersen, William J., *The Political Potpourri*, Palimpsest, 17: 271-279, Aug., 1936.

Petersen, William J., *The Political Scene*, Palimpsest, 16: 238-244, Aug., 1935; 18: 252-261, Aug., 1937.

Petersen, William J., *The Story of Iowa*, 1: 382-410. Lewis Historical Co., New York. 1952.

Petersen, William J., *Stumping Iowa in 1860*, Palimpsest, 31, 468-483, Dec., 1950.

Peterson, Henry John, *The Regulation by Law of Elections in the Territory of Iowa*, Iowa Journal, 5: 493-533, Oct., 1907.

Roll, Charles, *Political Trends in Iowa History*, Iowa Journal, 26: 499-519, Oct., 1928.

Schmidt, Louis B., *The Miller-Thompson Election Contest*, Iowa Journal, 12: 34-127, Jan., 1914.

Sherman, Roy V., *Pioneer Politics*, Palimpsest, 8: 47-50, Jan., 1927.

Sherman, Roy V., *Pioneer Politics*, Palimpsest, 32: 47-50, Jan., 1951.

Snyder, Charles, *Curtis Bates*, Iowa Journal, 44: 291-313, July, 1946.

Snyder, Charles, *Forgotten Men—Thomas McKnight*, Iowa Journal, 43: 254-282, July, 1945.

Snyder, Charles E., *Forgotten Men—James L. Thompson*, Iowa Journal, 43: 357-369, Oct., 1945.

Swisher, Jacob A., *The Campaign of 1883*, Palimpsest, 7: 321-334, Oct., 1926.

Swisher, Jacob A., *Politics in 1844*, Palimpsest, 25: 249-256, Aug., 1944.

Throne, Mildred, *Electing an Iowa Governor, 1871: Cyrus Clay Carpenter*, Iowa Journal, 48: 335-370, Oct., 1950.

Van Ek, Jacob, *A Contested Election*, Palimpsest, 4: 78-89, March, 1923.

Williams, Ora, *Gue, Russell, Thorington*, Annals (3), 28: 139-148, Oct., 1946.

Wilson, Ben Hur, *The Little Giant*, Palimpsest, 26: 218-224, July, 1945.

Wright, Luella M., *Henry A. and George D. Perkins in the Campaign of 1860*, Iowa Journal, 42: 162-191, April, 1944.

THE WHIG PARTY IN IOWA

Clark, Dan E., *History of Senatorial Elections in Iowa*, Chs. I-III. SHSI. 1912.

Gannaway, John W., *The Development of Party Organization in Iowa*, Iowa Journal, 1: 493-524, Oct., 1903.

Johnson, Jack T., *A Whig of Many Parts* (W. H. Wallace), Palimpsest, 19: 462-468, Nov., 1938.

Pelzer, Louis, *The History and Principles of the Whigs of the Territory of Iowa*, Iowa Journal, 5: 46-90, Jan., 1907.

Schmidt, Louis B., *History of Congressional Elections in Iowa*, Iowa Journal, 10: 463-502, Oct., 1912; 11: 38-67, Jan., 1913.

The Democratic Party in Iowa

Clark, Dan E., *History of Senatorial Elections in Iowa*, SHSI. 1912.

Gannaway, John W., *The Development of Party Organization in Iowa*, Iowa Journal, 1: 493-524, Oct., 1923.

Denison, John D., *Iowa Democracy: A History of Politics and Personalities of the Democratic Party 1846-1938.* 4 vols. Democratic Historical Association. 1939.

Herriott, Frank I., *A Neglected Factor in the Anti-Slavery Triumph in Iowa in 1854.* Jahrbuch der Deutsch-Amerikanischen Gesellschaft von Illinois, 18-19: 174-352.

Kern, Jean B., *The Political Career of Horace Boies*, Iowa Journal, 47: 215-246, July, 1949.

Letters Written by John P. Irish to George F. Parker, Iowa Journal, 31: 421-512, July, 1933.

Petersen, William J., *The Political Potpourri*, Palimpsest, 17: 271-279, Aug., 1936.

Petersen, William J., *The Political Scene*, Palimpsest, 16: 238-244, Aug., 1935; 18: 252-261, Aug., 1937.

Petersen, William J., *The Story of Iowa*, 1: 382-410. Lewis Historical Co., New York. 1952.

Schmidt, Louis B., *History of Congressional Elections in Iowa*, Iowa Journal, 10: 463-502, Oct., 1912; 11: 38-67, Jan., 1913.

The Republican Party in Iowa

Beall, Walter H., *A Mass Convention*, Palimpsest, 13: 285-295, July, 1932.

Clark, Dan E., *The History of Liquor Legislation in Iowa*, Iowa Journal, 6: 55-87, 339-374, 503-608, Jan., July, Oct., 1908.

Clark, Dan E., *History of Senatorial Elections in Iowa.* SHSI. 1912.

Clarkson, James S., *The Stampede from General Weaver in the Republican Convention of 1875*, Annals (3), 10: 561-569, Jan., 1913.

Cole, Cyrenus, *Iowa Through the Years.* SHSI. 1940.

Funk, A. B., *The Republican National Convention of 1884*, Annals (3), 22: 392-404, July, 1940.

Gallaher, Ruth A., *A Colored Convention*, Palimpsest, 2: 178-181, June, 1921.

Garretson, O. A., *A Lincoln Pole Raising*, Palimpsest, 6: 109-116, April, 1925.

Herriott, Frank I., A Neglected Factor in the Anti-Slavery Triumph in Iowa in 1854, Jahrbuch der Deutsch-Amerikanischen Gesellschaft von Illinois, 18-19: 174-352.

Meyers, F. W., Campaigning with Jackson, Palimpsest, 9: 371-382, Oct., 1928.

Mott, David C., The Pivotal Convention of 1883, Annals (3), 26: 254-260, April, 1945.

Pelzer, Louis, The History of Political Parties in Iowa from 1857 to 1860, Iowa Journal, 7: 179-229, April, 1909.

Pelzer, Louis, The Origin and Organization of the Republican Party in Iowa, Iowa Journal, 4: 487-525, Oct., 1906.

Petersen, William J., The Story of Iowa, 1: 382-410. Lewis Historical Co., New York. 1952.

Roberts, George E., The Origin and History of the Iowa Idea, Iowa Journal, 2: 69-82, Jan., 1904.

Robeson, George F., John Johns of Webster County, Palimpsest, 5: 424-430, Nov., 1924.

Swisher, J. A., A Convention Stampeded, Palimpsest, 9: 349-356, Oct., 1928.

Swisher, J. A., Grant's Des Moines Speech, Palimpsest, 6: 409-421, Dec., 1925.

Throne, Mildred, Electing an Iowa Governor, 1871: Cyrus Clay Carpenter, Iowa Journal, 48: 335-370, Oct., 1950.

THIRD PARTIES IN IOWA POLITICS

Aldrich, Charles, The Repeal of the Granger Law in Iowa, Iowa Journal, 3: 256-270, April, 1905.

Anderson, Walfred A., The Granger Movement in the Middle West with Special Reference to Iowa, Iowa Journal, 22: 3-51, Jan., 1924.

Clark, Dan E., The History of Liquor Legislation in Iowa, Iowa Journal, 6: 55-87, 339-374, 503-608, Jan., July, Oct., 1908.

Cross, Ira, The Origin, Principles, and History of the American Party, Iowa Journal, 4: 526-553, Oct., 1906.

Gardner, Charles M., The Grange—Friend of the Farmer: 1867-1947. National Grange, Washington. 1949.

Haynes, Fred E., Forward Movements in Politics Since the Civil War, Iowa Journal, 11: 147-165, April, 1913.

Haynes, Fred E., Third Party Movements Since the Civil War. SHSI. 1916.

Nixon, Herman C., The Economic Basis of the Populist Movement in Iowa, Iowa Journal, 21: 373-396, July, 1923.

Nixon, Herman C., The Populist Movement in Iowa, Iowa Journal, 24: 3-107, Jan., 1926.

Nydegger, Walter E., The Election of 1892 in Iowa, Iowa Journal, 25: 359-449, July, 1927.

Robeson, George F., Restless Farmers, Palimpsest, 14: 404-410, Nov., 1933.

Roll, Charles, Political Trends in Iowa History, Iowa Journal, 26: 499-519, Oct., 1928.

Ruggles, Clyde O., *The Economic Basis of the Greenback Movement in Iowa and Wisconsin*, Proceedings of the Mississippi Valley Historical Association, 1912-1913, 6: 142-165.

Schmidt, Louis B., *Some Significant Aspects of the Agrarian Revolution in the United States*, Iowa Journal, 18: 371-395, July, 1920.

ELECTION MACHINERY IN IOWA

Benton, Edward M., *Soldier Voting in Iowa*, Iowa Journal, 29: 27-41, Jan., 1931.

Crossley, James J., *The Regulation of Primary Elections by Law*, Iowa Journal, 1: 165-192, April, 1903.

English, Emory H., *Evolution in Iowa Voting Practices*, Annals (3), 29: 249-281, April, 1948.

Erbe, Carl H., *Constitutional Provisions for the Suffrage in Iowa*, Iowa Journal, 22: 163-216, April, 1924.

Horack, Frank E., *The Operation of the Primary Election Law in Iowa*, Iowa Journal, 19: 94-124, Jan., 1921.

Horack, Frank E., *Primary Elections in Iowa*, Applied History, 1: 259-300. SHSI. 1912.

Johnson, Jack T., *The First State Election*, Palimpsest, 27: 257-270, Sept., 1946.

Martin, Ethyl E., *A Bribery Episode in the First Election of United States Senators in Iowa*, Iowa Journal, 7: 483-502, Oct., 1909.

Robeson, George F., *The County and Elections*, Applied History, 4: 585-601. SHSI. 1925.

Sherman, Roy V., *The Municipal Electorate in Iowa*, Applied History, 5: 79-146. SHSI. 1930.

Swisher, Jacob A., *Government and the Voter*, Palimpsest, 30: 305-313, Oct., 1949.

Titus, George M., *Battle for Primary Elections*, Annals (3), 29: 163-175, Jan., 1948.

SOLDIER VOTING IN IOWA

Aldrich, Charles, *Voting with the Soldiers in 1864*, Annals (3), 6: 618-623, Jan., 1905.

Benton, Edward M., *Soldier Voting in Iowa*, Iowa Journal, 29: 27-41, Jan., 1931.

McMurry, Donald L., *The Soldier Vote in Iowa in the Election of 1888*, Iowa Journal, 18: 335-356, July, 1920.

WOMAN SUFFRAGE IN IOWA

Clarkson, Mrs. James S., *Evolution of the Politics of Iowa*, Midland Monthly, 8: 61-67, July, 1897.

Erbe, Carl H., *Constitutional Provisions for the Suffrage in Iowa*, Iowa Journal, 22: 163-216, April, 1924.

Gallaher, Ruth A., *Legal and Political Status of Women in Iowa*. SHSI. 1918.

Horack, Frank E., *Equal Suffrage in Iowa*, Applied History, 2: 275-314. SHSI. 1914.

Iowa Suffrage Memorial Commission, Annals (3), 14: 357-365, July, 1924.

Jordan, Philip D., *The Bloomers in Iowa*, Palimpsest, 20: 295-309, Sept., 1939.

McCowen, Jennie, *Women in Iowa*, Annals (2), 3: 96-113, Oct., 1884.

Political Equality in Iowa, Annals (3), 26: 197, Jan., 1945.

Iowa and National Affairs

TERRITORIAL DELEGATES

Chapman, W. W., Letters of, Annals (3), 22: 328-339, April, 1940.

Colegrove, Kenneth W., *The Delegates to Congress from the Territory of Iowa*, Iowa Journal, 7: 230-265, April, 1909.

Colton, Kenneth E., *W. W. Chapman, Delegate to Congress from Iowa Territory*, Annals (3), 21: 283-295, April, 1938.

Johnson, Jack T., *Pioneer and Politician*, Palimpsest, 19: 350-359, Sept., 1938.

Johnson, Jack T., *Sponsor of Iowa Territory*, Palimpsest, 19: 121-132, April, 1938.

Parish, John C., *George Wallace Jones*, 14-35. SHSI. 1912.

Pelzer, Louis, *Augustus Caesar Dodge*, 63-127. SHSI. 1908.

Swisher, Jacob A., *Iowa Delegates to Congress*, Palimpsest, 27: 19-29, Jan., 1946.

UNITED STATES SENATORS FROM IOWA

Clark, Dan E., *History of Senatorial Elections in Iowa*. SHSI. 1912.

Francis, Leslie E., *Last Legislative Election of An Iowa U. S. Senator*, Annals (3), 31: 263-275, April, 1952.

Gallaher, Ruth A., *Deadlock on Senators*, Palimpsest, 28: 1-11, Jan., 1947.

Senator Kenyon An Idealist, Annals (3), 31: 313-316, April, 1952.

Snyder, Chas. E., *Statesmen and Politicians in Early Iowa*, Annals (3), 27: 15-36, July, 1945.

For references on William B. Allison, Albert B. Cummins, Augustus Caesar Dodge, Jonathan P. Dolliver, John H. Gear, James W. Grimes, James Harlan, James B. Howell, George W. Jones, Samuel J. Kirkwood, James F. Wilson, and George G. Wright, see Biographies of Iowans.

REPRESENTATIVES IN CONGRESS

Pierce, Paul S., *Congressional Districting in Iowa*, Iowa Journal, 1: 334-361, July, 1903.

Price, Hiram, *Recollections of Iowa Men and Affairs*, Annals (3), 1: 1-14, April, 1893.

Schaffter, Dorothy, *In the House*, Palimpsest, 11: 16-29, Jan., 1930.

Schmidt, Louis B., *History of Congressional Elections in Iowa*, Iowa Journal, 10: 463-502, Oct., 1912; 11: 38-67, Jan., 1913.

Wilcox, Francis O., *Congressional Redistricting in Iowa*, Iowa Journal, 29: 461-517, Oct., 1931.

For references on various Representatives see Biographies of Iowans.

IOWA AND THE SUPREME COURT

Allen, Ethan P., *Appeals from the Supreme Court of Iowa to the Supreme Court of the United States*, Iowa Journal, 31: 211-273, April, 1933.

Petersen, William J., *Chouteau v. Molony*, Palimpsest, 12: 434-440, Nov., 1931.

See also Samuel Freeman Miller in Biographies of Iowans, Des Moines River Land Grant, and Missouri Boundary Dispute.

PRESIDENTS IN IOWA

Kern, Jean B., *Wilson in Iowa*, Palimpsest, 29: 310-316, Oct., 1948.

Petersen, William J., *The Presidential Parade*, Palimpsest, 29: 317-320, Oct., 1948.

Smith, Frederic C., *Teddy Roosevelt in Iowa*, Palimpsest, 29: 296-302, Oct., 1948.

Swisher, Jacob A., *Grant's Des Moines Speech*, Palimpsest, 6: 409-421, Dec., 1925.

Swisher, Jacob A., *Taft in Iowa*, Palimpsest, 29: 303-309, Oct., 1948.

Swisher, Jacob A., *Theodore Roosevelt in Iowa*, Palimpsest, 13: 397-409, Oct., 1932.

Throne, Mildred, *McKinley in Iowa*, Palimpsest, 29: 289-295, Oct., 1948.

PRESIDENTIAL CANDIDATES FROM IOWA

Eriksson, Erik M., *Presidential Hopes*, Palimpsest, 6: 284-294, Aug., 1925.

Haynes, Fred E., *James Baird Weaver*. SHSI. 1919.

Haynes, Fred E., *Third Party Movements Since the Civil War*. SHSI. 1916.

Hoover, Herbert, *Boyhood in Iowa*, Palimpsest, 9: 269-276, July, 1928.

Hoover, Herbert, *Boyhood in Iowa*, Palimpsest, 29: 225-233, Aug., 1948; 32: 409-416, Nov., 1951.

Hoover, Herbert, *The Meaning of America*, Palimpsest, 32: 433-438, Nov., 1951.

Petersen, William J., *Great Journeys from Little Homes*, Palimpsest, 29: 255-256, Aug., 1948; 32: 439, 440, Nov., 1951.

Swisher, Jacob A., *Bert Hoover*, Palimpsest, 9: 263-268, July, 1928.

Swisher, Jacob A., *Bert Hoover*, Palimpsest, 29: 234-240, Aug., 1948.

Throne, Mildred, *Hoover in Iowa*, Palimpsest, 32: 417-432, Nov., 1951.

White, Edward A., *A Woman Promotes the Presidential Candidacy of Senator Allison, 1888,* Iowa Journal, 48: 221-246, July, 1950.

See also William Boyd Allison and James Baird Weaver in Biographies of Iowans.

IOWANS IN THE CABINET

Ainsworth, Peter, *The Meredith Publications,* Palimpsest, 11: 256-265, June, 1930.

Evans, Ramona, *In the Cabinet,* Palimpsest, 11: 38-45, Jan., 1930.

Ross, Earle D., *Charles Mason and Federal Aid to Agriculture,* Palimpsest, 28: 12-24, Jan., 1947.

Ross, Earle D., *A Yankee-Hawkeye,* Palimpsest, 28: 353-366, Dec., 1947.

For references on James Harlan, Frank Hatton, Herbert C. Hoover, E. T. Meredith, Samuel J. Kirkwood, Henry A. Wallace, and James Wilson see Biographies of Iowans.

IOWANS AND THE DIPLOMATIC SERVICE

An Iowa Consulate Coat of Arms, Annals (3), 30: 147-149, Oct., 1949.

Briggs, John E., *Iowa and the Diplomatic Service,* Iowa Journal, 19: 321-365, July, 1921.

Briggs, John E., *Kasson and the First International Postal Conference,* Iowa Journal, 19: 366-388, July, 1921.

Wagner, Dorothy, *Near Foreign Chancelleries,* Palimpsest, 11: 46-54, Jan., 1930.

Wead, Eunice, *Kasson Letters—Austria and Germany,* Annals (3), 30: 260-268, April, 1950.

Younger, Edward E., *John A. Kasson at Vienna and Berlin,* Iowa Journal, 45: 175-203, April, 1947.

For references on S. H. M. Byers and Augustus C. Dodge see Biographies of Iowans.

Local Government

THE COUNTIES OF IOWA

Brainard, John M., *Opening an Iowa County,* Annals (3), 2: 260-277, Jan., 1896.

Briggs, John E., *County Evolution in 1839,* Palimpsest, 20: 93-104, March, 1939.

Briggs, John E., *New Counties in 1843,* Palimpsest, 24: 365-376, Dec., 1943.

Call, Ambrose A., *Indians Repelled in Kossuth,* Annals (3), 31: 81-90, Oct., 1951.

Childs, C. C., *Names of Iowa Counties,* Historical Record, 4: 32-37, Jan., 1888.

Cook, Luella E., *Histories of Iowa Counties,* Iowa Journal, 36: 115-151, April, 1938.

Crosby, James O., *The County Judge System*, Annals (3), 10: 42-48, April, 1911.

Fleming, William H., *Floyd County Named for William Floyd*, Annals (3), 12: 615-617, April, 1921.

Garver, Frank H., *Boundary History of the Counties of Iowa*, Iowa Journal, 7: 3-131, Jan., 1909.

Garver, Frank H., *A Critical Study of the Definition and Alteration of County Boundaries in Iowa and of the Laws by Which They Were Established*, Iowa Journal, 7: 402-443, July, 1909.

Garver, Frank H., *History of the Establishment of Counties in Iowa*, Iowa Journal, 6: 375-456, July, 1908.

Harpel, Almeda B., *Counties of Iowa*, Annals (3), 13: 619, April, 1923.

Lauderdale, Maude, *The Webster County Bar*, Annals (3), 31: 91-144, Oct., 1951.

Louis, John J., *Shelby County--A Sociological Study*, Iowa Journal, 2: 83-101, 218-255, Jan., April, 1904.

Morris, Emmet L., *Iowa Today*, 45-54. School Necessities Co., Marquette, Iowa. 1931.

Pollock, Ivan L., *Historical Background of the County in Iowa*, Iowa Journal, 23: 3-57, Jan., 1925.

Swisher, Jacob A., *History of the Organization of Counties in Iowa*, Iowa Journal, 20: 483-576, Oct., 1922.

Swisher, Jacob A., *Seven New Counties*, Palimpsest, 19: 22-30, Jan., 1938.

Wilson, Ben H., *Henry County Beginnings*, Palimpsest, 20: 313-344, Oct., 1939.

See also County Government and Administration in Iowa.

RIVALRY FOR COUNTY SEATS

Ferguson, William R., *A County Seat Scrap*, Palimpsest, 22: 247-256, Aug., 1941.

Glass, Remley J., *A County Seat Lost and Found*, Annals (3), 27: 158-161, Oct., 1945.

Sly, Blanche C., *Magnolia*, Palimpsest, 2: 290-297, Sept., 1921.

Swisher, Jacob A., *A Transient County Seat*, Palimpsest, 7: 390-397, Dec., 1926.

Swisher, Jacob A., *The Location of County Seats in Iowa*, Iowa Journal, 22: 89-128, 217-294, 323-362, Jan., April, July, 1924.

Swisher, Jacob A., *Twixt Rockingham and Davenport*, Palimpsest, 19: 62-68, Feb., 1938.

COUNTY GOVERNMENT AND ADMINISTRATION

Fullbrook, Earl S., *County Welfare Work*, Applied History, 4: 363-415. SHSI. 1925.

Fullbrook, Earl S., *County Administration of Health*, Applied History, 4: 576-584. SHSI. 1925.

Haynes, Fred Emory, *County Jails in Iowa*, Iowa Journal, 44: 61-85, Jan., 1946.

Jackson, William A., *The County Sheriff*, Applied History, 4: 240-279. SHSI. 1925.

Lauderdale, Maude, *The Webster County Bar*, Annals (3), 31: 91-144, Oct., 1951.

Leggett, Richard C., *A Courthouse at a Bargain*, Annals (3), 27: 37-43, July, 1945.

McVicker, James R., *The Administration of Justice in the County*, Applied History, 4: 320-362. SHSI. 1925.

McVicker, James R., *The Clerk of the District Court*, Applied History, 4: 167-202. SHSI. 1925.

McVicker, James R., *The County Attorney*, Applied History, 4: 203-239. SHSI. 1925.

Pollock, Ivan L., *The Administration of Highways in the County*, Applied History, 4: 416-471. SHSI. 1925.

Pollock, Ivan L., *Administration of Taxation and Finance in the County*, Applied History, 4: 472-533. SHSI. 1925.

Porter, Kirk H., *Definition of the County in Iowa*, Applied History, 4: 1-18. SHSI. 1925.

Porter, Kirk H., *Reorganization of County Government in Iowa*, Applied History, 4: 602-625. SHSI. 1925.

Robeson, George F., *The County and Elections*, Applied History, 4: 585-601. SHSI. 1925.

Sherman, Jay J., *The County Coroner*, Applied History, 4: 280-293. SHSI. 1925.

Sherman, Jay J., *The County Superintendent of Schools*, Applied History, 4: 294-319. SHSI. 1925.

Sherman, Jay J., *Drainage Districts in Iowa*, Applied History, 4: 534-575. SHSI. 1925.

Van Ek, Jacob, *The County Board of Supervisors*, Applied History, 4: 19-76. SHSI. 1925.

Van Ek, Jacob, *The County Auditor*, Applied History, 4: 77-113. SHSI. 1925.

Van Ek, Jacob, *The County Recorder*, Applied History, 4: 145-166. SHSI. 1925.

Van Ek, Jacob, *The County Treasurer*, Applied History, 4: 114-144. SHSI. 1925.

See also Counties of Iowa.

MUNICIPAL GOVERNMENT AND ADMINISTRATION

Aumann, Francis R., *Municipal Administration of Justice*, Applied History, 6: 145-221. SHSI. 1930.

Brown, Roy E., *Municipal Administration of Public Safety*, Applied History, 6: 225-311. SHSI. 1930.

Gallaher, Ruth A., *The Administration of Municipal Finance*, Applied History, 6: 3-142. SHSI. 1930.

Gallaher, Ruth A., *The City Engineer*, Applied History, 5: 465-480. SHSI. 1930.

Gallaher, Ruth A., *The City Solicitor*, Applied History, 5: 437-461. SHSI. 1930.

Gallaher, Ruth A., *Municipalities and Associated Activities*, Applied History, 6: 559-567. SHSI. 1930.

Hargrave, William M., *Municipal Administration of Public Health*, Applied History, 6: 513-556. SHSI. 1930.

Knepper, David W., *The Municipal Assessor in Iowa*, Applied History, 5: 379-416. SHSI. 1930.

Manning, John W., *Municipal Planning and Zoning*, Applied History, 6: 447-510. SHSI. 1930.

Marshall, Cecil F., *Police Administration in Davenport*, Iowa Journal, 31: 339-440, July, 1933.

Maxwell, Bertram W., *Municipal Boards and Commissions*, Applied History, 5: 497-519. SHSI. 1930.

Pfiffner, John M., *The City Manager in Iowa*, Applied History, 5: 331-355, SHSI. 1930.

Pfiffner, John M., *The City Manager Plan in Iowa*, Iowa Journal, 26: 520-590, Oct., 1928; 27: 3-81, Jan., 1929.

Pfiffner, John M., *The Mayor in Iowa*, Applied History, 5: 255-327. SHSI. 1930.

Robeson, George F., *The Government of Special Charter Cities in Iowa*. SHSI. 1923.

Robeson, George F., *Special Municipal Charters in Iowa 1836-1858*, Iowa Journal, 18: 163-270, April, 1920.

Sherman, Roy V., *The Municipal Electorate in Iowa*, Applied History, 5: 79-146. SHSI. 1930.

Swisher, Jacob A., *The City Clerk*, Applied History, 5: 359-375. SHSI. 1930.

Swisher, Jacob A., *The Creation and Dissolution of Municipal Corporations*, Applied History, 5: 3-18. SHSI. 1930.

Swisher, Jacob A., *The League of Iowa Municipalities*, Applied History, 6: 571-576. SHSI. 1930.

Swisher, Jacob A., *Legal Status of Municipalities*, Applied History, 5: 21-75. SHSI. 1930.

Swisher, Jacob A., *Municipal Administration of Public Works*, Applied History, 6: 315-369. SHSI. 1930.

Swisher, Jacob A., *The Municipal Treasurer*, Applied History, 5: 419-433. SHSI. 1930.

Swisher, Jacob A., *Other City Officials*, Applied History, 5: 483-494. SHSI. 1930.

Trachsel, Herman H., *The City Council*, Applied History, 5: 149-251. SHSI. 1930.

Trachsel, Herman H., *Municipal Administration of Public Utilities*, Applied History, 6: 373-443. SHSI. 1930.

Special Charter Towns

Petersen, William J., *A Chartered Town* (Dubuque), Palimpsest, 21: 366-378, Nov., 1940.

Petersen, William J., *A Town Incorporated* (Davenport), Palimpsest, 20: 264-272, Aug., 1939.

Petersen, William J., *The Wheels of Government* (Muscatine), Palimpsest, 20: 355-368, Nov., 1939.

Robeson, George F., *The Government of Special Charter Cities in Iowa.* SHSI. 1923.

Swisher, Jacob A., *Beginnings of Salem,* Palimpsest, 21: 140-150, May, 1940.

Swisher, Jacob A., *Chartered Towns* (Burlington and Fort Madison), Palimpsest, 19: 31-35, Jan., 1938.

Townships in Iowa

Aurner, Clarence R., *The Establishment and Organization of Townships in Johnson County,* Iowa Journal, 9: 155-195, April, 1911.

Aurner, Clarence R., *History of Township Government in Iowa.* SHSI. 1914.

Mitchell, Thomas, *Mitchell's Early Settlement,* Annals (3), 31: 72-73, July, 1951.

Smith, Gordon, *Six Miles Square,* Palimpsest, 26: 119-128, April, 1945.

Wick, B. L., *Early Iowa Map Attracts Settlers,* Annals (3), 25: 135-136, Oct., 1943.

Wilson, Ben Hur, *High Water in Canaan,* Palimpsest, 25: 78-81, March, 1944.

Cities and Towns

Towns of Iowa

Aldrich, Charles, *Come to Hamilton County* (Webster City), Palimpsest, 15: 275-286, Aug., 1934.

Barnhart, Cornelia Mallett, *Osceola and Oskaloosa,* Palimpsest, 28: 300-309, Oct., 1947.

Braden, Waldo W., *The YMA of Mount Pleasant,* Palimpsest, 29: 76-86, March, 1948.

Chase, Edwin P., *Forty Years of Main Street* (Atlantic), Iowa Journal, 34: 227-261, July, 1936.

Craig, James Thomas, *Oelwein Secures the C. G. W. Shops, 1894,* Annals (3), 24: Part I, 211-236, Jan., 1943.

Donovan, Josephine B., *Old O'Brien,* Palimpsest, 5: 23-33, Jan., 1924.

Eriksson, Erik M., *The Name of Odebolt,* Palimpsest, 10: 432-441, Dec., 1929.

Evans, S. B., *The Blotting Out of an Iowa Town* (Iowaville), Annals (3), 8: 57-59. April, 1907.

Farquhar, Catharine Grace Barbour, *Tabor and Tabor College,* Iowa Journal, 41: 337-393, Oct., 1943.

Garretson, O. A., *Lowell*, Palimpsest, 9: 437-449, Dec., 1928.

Garretson, O. A., *Pilot Grove*, Palimpsest, 3: 390-399, Dec., 1922.

Gingerich, Melvin, *The Washington Chautauqua*, Palimpsest, 26: 370-376, Dec., 1945.

Glass, Remley J., *Iowa-Minnesota Townsite Towns*, Annals (3), 28: 69-70, July, 1946.

Green, John A., *The Development of Stone City*, Annals (3), 20: 304-308, April, 1936.

Haefner, Marie, *Rivalry Among the River Towns*, Palimpsest, 18: 160-174, May, 1937.

Holy, T. C., *J. I. Cavett of Vandalia*, Palimpsest, 23: 158-174, May, 1942.

Horack, Katharine, *The Quest of a Prairie Home*, Palimpsest, 5: 249-257, July, 1924.

Jewett, W. H., *Marion, Iowa*, Midland Monthly, 6: 2-9, Aug., 1896.

Jewett, W. H., *A Typical Iowa Town: The City of Maquoketa*, Midland Monthly, 6: 1-18, Sept., 1896.

Johnson, Jack T., *Napoleon on the Frontier*, Palimpsest, 20: 114-125, April, 1939.

Johnston, Clarence S., *The Ottumwa Courier*, Palimpsest, 21: 401-406, Oct., 1950.

Kelly, Harry E., *Lytle City*, Palimpsest, 17: 9-26, Jan., 1936.

Koop, Theodore F., *Bowen's Prairie*, Palimpsest, 9: 202-218, June, 1928.

Lovell, Miriam Fay, *The Monticello Friday Club*, Palimpsest, 24: 59-70, Feb., 1943.

Ludwig, Mary C., *Beginnings at Morning Sun*, Palimpsest, 30: 142-148, May, 1949.

Ludwig, Mary C., *Namer of Towns*, Palimpsest, 29: 161-173, June, 1948.

Lyon, Bessie L., *The Passing of Homer*, Palimpsest, 3: 381-389, Dec., 1922.

Mahan, Bruce E., *The Scotch Grove Trail*, Palimpsest, 4: 379-397, Nov., 1923.

Mann, T. E., *Union Grove*, Palimpsest, 26: 28-32, Jan., 1945.

Meyer, Marie E., *River Towns*, Palimpsest, 7: 381-389, Dec., 1926.

Mott, David C., *Abandoned Towns, Villages and Post Offices of Iowa*, Annals (3), 17: 435-465, 513-543, 578-599, Oct., 1930, Jan., April, 1931; 18: 42-69, 117-148, 189-220, July, Oct., 1931, Jan., 1932.

Perkins, H. E., *New Chicago*, Annals (3), 19: 42-54, July, 1933.

Quigley, Iola B., *McGregor Sketches*, Palimpsest, 12: 1-37, Jan., 1931.

Rischmueller, Marian Carroll, *The Ringlings of McGregor*, Palimpsest, 25: 179-192, June, 1944.

Rischmueller, Marian Carroll, *McGregor Sand Artist*, Palimpsest, 26: 129-147, May, 1945.

Seashore, Carl E., *The Dayton Swedish Settlement*, Palimpsest, 22: 347-356, Nov., 1941.

Smith, Milo P., *Recollections of Marengo*, Annals (3), 12: 429-445, Oct., 1920.

Stevens, Ruth W., *Musical Ottumwa*, Palimpsest, 28: 172-183, June, 1947.

Storing, James A., *A Town That Moved*, Palimpsest, 20: 53-64, Feb., 1939.

Storing, James A., *Palestine Settlement*, Palimpsest, 21: 151-156, May, 1940.

Sweet, Oney Fred, *An Iowa County Seat* (Hampton), Iowa Journal, 38: 339-407, Oct., 1940.

Swisher, Jacob A., *Beginnings of Salem,* Palimpsest, 21: 140-150, May, 1940

Swisher, Jacob A., *Hopeville,* Palimpsest, 26: 303-315, Oct., 1945.

Swisher, Jacob A., *The Rise and Fall of Buxton,* Palimpsest, 26: 179-192, June, 1945.

Swisher, Jacob A., *Willson Alexander Scott,* Palimpsest, 28: 225-238, Aug. 1947.

Taylor, Loren, *The Colesburg Pottery,* Palimpsest, 29: 65-75, March, 1948.

Trachsel, Herman H., *Proximity,* Palimpsest, 9: 106-108, March, 1928.

Tweito, Thomas E., *The Osage Land Sale,* Palimpsest, 21: 157-164, May, 1940.

Wilson, Ben H., *Henry County Beginnings,* Palimpsest, 20: 313-344, Oct., 1939.

BURLINGTON

Brown, Harriet Connor, *Burlington Backgrounds,* Palimpsest, 30: 97-106, April, 1949.

Brown, Harriet Connor, *A Town Looks Back,* Palimpsest, 30: 125-134, April, 1949.

Ekdale, Edith Harper, *The Grand Opera House,* Palimpsest, 28: 184-192, June, 1947.

Haefner, Marie, *The Capitol at Burlington,* Palimpsest, 18: 98-102, March, 1937.

Installation of the Edward Ames Temple Memorial Tablet, Annals (3), 11: 225-226, July-Oct., 1913.

Jordan, Philip D., *Westward to Iowa,* Palimpsest, 30: 209-216, July, 1949.

Lathrop, Henry W., *The Capitals and Capitols of Iowa,* Historical Record, 4: 97-124, July, 1888.

Pelzer, Louis, *Early Burlington,* Palimpsest, 15: 225-254, July, 1934.

Petersen, William J., *The Burlington Comes,* Palimpsest, 14: 381-395, Nov., 1933.

Phillips, Semira A., *Semi-Centennial Celebration,* Historical Record, 13: 27-43, Jan., 1897.

Ross, William R., *The Beginnings of Burlington,* Palimpsest, 2: 351-365, Nov., 1921.

Salter, William, *Iowa: The First Free State in the Louisiana Purchase.* McClurg, Chicago. 1905.

Snyder, Charles E., *Unitarianism in Iowa,* Palimpsest, 30: 345-376, Nov., 1949.

Swisher, Jacob A., *Chartered Towns,* Palimpsest, 19: 31-35, Jan., 1938.

Swisher, Jacob A., *Old Zion Church,* Palimpsest, 13: 274-284, July, 1932.

Thornton, Harrison John, *Origins of Iowa Masonry,* Palimpsest, 25: 161-172, June, 1944.

Two Burlington Churches Occupied, Annals (3), 29: 473-476, Oct., 1948.

Waring, Edmund H., *Old Zion Church, Burlington, Iowa,* Annals (3), 9: 524-534, July-Oct., 1910.

Wilson, Ben H., *The Burlington Road*, Palimpsest, 16: 305-334, Oct., 1935.
Wilson, Ben H., *Abram Tuston Hay*, Palimpsest, 28: 193-206, July, 1947.
Wilson, Ben H., *Lincoln at Burlington*, Palimpsest, 24: 313-322, Oct., 1943.
See also histories of Des Moines County.

Cedar Falls

Aldrich, Bess Streeter, *Miss Bishop* (novel). Appleton-Century, New York. 1933.
Aldrich, Bess Streeter, *Song of Years* (novel). Appleton-Century, New York. 1939.
Barnhart, Cornelia Mallett, *The Old Pottery Shop*, Palimpsest, 28: 239-246, Aug., 1947.
Hearst, Gladys Whitley, *The WAVES at Cedar Falls*, Palimpsest, 28: 367-380, Dec., 1947.
Schmidt, G. Perle, *A Magic Lantern Lecture*, Palimpsest, 26: 110-118, April, 1945.
Wright, D. Sands, *Iowa State Normal School*, Palimpsest, 13: 1-40, Jan., 1932.
Wright, Luella M., *The Cedar Falls Parlor Reading Circle*, Iowa Journal, 34: 339-374, Oct., 1936.
Wright, Luella M., *The Pioneer Greys*, Palimpsest, 22: 1-32, Jan., 1941.
Wright, Luella M., *Victory and Mourning*, Palimpsest, 21: 101-132, April, 1940.
See also histories of Black Hawk County.

Cedar Rapids

Carroll, George R., *Pioneer Life in and around Cedar Rapids, Iowa, from 1839 to 1849*. Times Printing and Binding House, Cedar Rapids. 1895.
Cole, Cyrenus, *I Remember, I Remember*. SHSI. 1936.
Eriksson, Erik M., *Baseball Beginnings*, Palimpsest, 8: 329-338, Oct., 1927.
Griffith, Martha Eleanor, *The Czechs in Cedar Rapids*, Iowa Journal, 42: 114-161, April, 1944.
Griffith, Martha Eleanor, *The Czechs in Cedar Rapids, (Part 2)*, Iowa Journal, 42: 266-315, July, 1944.
Holiday Souvenir Supplement to the Cedar Rapids Iowa Evening Gazette. Gazette Co., Cedar Rapids. 1889.
Laurance, Charles A., *Pioneer Days in Cedar Rapids: 1860-1880*. Laurance Press, Cedar Rapids. 1936.
Murray, Janette Stevenson and Murray, Frederick Gray, *The Story of Cedar Rapids*. Stratford House, New York, 1950.
Thornton, Harrison J., *The History of the Quaker Oats Company*. University of Chicago Press, Chicago. 1933.
Proceedings of the Historical Society of Linn County, Iowa (Albert N. Harbert, editor). 2 vols. Published by the Society, Cedar Rapids. 1905, 1907.

Wick, B. L., *Early Cedar Rapids, Swedish Churches*, Annals (3), 29: 468-472, Oct., 1948.
See also histories of Linn County.

COUNCIL BLUFFS

Babbitt, Charles H., *Early Days in Council Bluffs*. B. S. Adams Press, Washington, Iowa. 1916.

Babbitt, Charles H., *The Old Pottawattamie Mill*, Palimpsest, 6: 319-334, Sept., 1925.

Branch, E. Douglas, *Railroads Came to Council Bluffs*, Palimpsest, 10: 201-229, June, 1929.

Dodge, N. P., *Early Emigration Through and To Council Bluffs*, Annals (3), 18: 163-179, Jan., 1932.

Gallaher, Ruth A., *An Adventure in Faith*, Palimpsest, 13: 93-105, March, 1932.

Holt, Edgar A., *A Voyage of the Omaha*, Palimpsest, 6: 128-136, April, 1925.

Jordan, Philip D., *The Bloomers in Iowa*, Palimpsest, 20: 295-309, Sept., 1939.

McMurry, Donald L., *The Pacific City Fight*, Palimpsest, 2: 182-189, June, 1921.

McMurtrie, Douglas C., *The First Printing at Council Bluffs*, Annals (3), 18: 3-11, July, 1931.

McMurtrie, Douglas C., *Two Early Issues of the Council Bluffs Press*, Annals (3), 18: 83-86, Oct., 1931.

Peckham, Edward L., *A Journey Out West*, Palimpsest, 6: 233-249, July, 1925.

Petersen, William J., *Steamboating on the Upper Mississippi*, 81-89. SHSI. 1937.

Phillips, E. Bryant, *Early Street Railways in Council Bluffs*, Iowa Journal, 48: 121-132, April, 1950.

Sioux City Journal, *The National Capital in Iowa*, Annals (3), 26: 260, April, 1945.

Swisher, J. A., *Chief Waubonsie*, Palimpsest, 29: 353-361, Dec., 1946.

Weaver, James B., *James Depew Edmundson*, Palimpsest, 14: 1-38, Jan., 1933.

Wyman, Helen B., *Potter Christ*, Palimpsest, 14: 334-346, Sept., 1933.

Wyman, Walker D., *Council Bluffs and the Westward Movement*, Iowa Journal, 47: 99-118, April, 1949.
See also histories of Pottawattamie County.

DAVENPORT

Barnhart, Cornelia Mallett, *Phoebe W. Sudlow*, Palimpsest, 28: 25-32, Jan., 1947.

Bowers, Luther F., *The Iowa Sun*, Palimpsest, 19: 313-322, Aug., 1938.

Burrows, J. M. D., *Rumors of War*, Palimpsest, 24: 71-72, Feb., 1943.

Christensen, Thomas P., *An Industrial History of Scott County, Iowa*, Annals (3), 22: 87-127, Oct., 1939, 259-311, 345-391, April, July, 1940.

Downer, Harry E., *History of Davenport and Scott County, Iowa*. 2 vols. S. J. Clarke, Chicago. 1910.

Gallaher, Ruth A., *Guilty or Not Guilty*, Palimpsest, 19: 50-61, Feb., 1938.

Harrison, Hugh, *The Davenport Democrat*, Palimpsest, 31: 417-420, Oct., 1950.

Hoeltje, Hubert H., *Emerson at Davenport*, Palimpsest, 7: 265-276, Sept., 1926.

Johnson, Hildegard Binder, *German Forty-Eighters in Davenport*, Iowa Journal, 44: 3-53, Jan., 1946.

Johnson, Hildegard Binder, *List of Lectures and Debates Given Before the Davenport Turngemeinde*, Iowa Journal, 44: 54-60, Jan., 1946.

Kern, Jean B., *First Municipal Gallery*, Palimpsest, 30: 8-14, Jan., 1949.

Leysen, Ralph J., *The Davenport Times*, Palimpsest, 31: 407-411, Oct., 1950.

Lincoln and the Bridge Case, Palimpsest, 3: 142-154, May, 1922.

Marshall, Cecil F., *Police Administration in Davenport*, Iowa Journal, 31: 339-420, July, 1933.

Meyer, Marie E., *Charles A. Ficke, Public Citizen*, Annals (3), 21: 483-500, Jan., 1939.

Meyer, Marie E., *Nicholas Fejérváry*, Palimpsest, 9: 189-198, June, 1928.

Parish, John C., *The First Mississippi Bridge*, Palimpsest, 3: 133-141, May, 1922.

Petersen, William J., *Beginnings of Davenport*, Palimpsest, 20: 241-280, Aug., 1939.

Petersen, William J., *A Princely Visitor*, Palimpsest, 22: 325-343, Nov., 1941.

Petersen, William J., *The Rock Island Comes*, Palimpsest, 14: 285-300, Aug., 1933.

Ross, Earle D., *George Barnard Sargent—Western Promoter*, Iowa Journal, 45: 115-132, April, 1947.

Sanders, Alfred, *An Indian Ceremony*, Palimpsest, 2: 379-381, Dec., 1921.

Schick, Joseph S., *The Early Theater in Davenport*, Palimpsest, 31: 1-44, Jan., 1950.

Schick, Joseph S., *The Early Theater in Eastern Iowa*. University of Chicago Press, Chicago. 1939.

Snyder, Charles E., *Antoine LeClaire, The First Proprietor of Davenport*, Annals (3), 23: 79-117, Oct., 1941.

Snyder, Charles E., *Army Camp and Orphans Home*, Annals (3), 29: 307-314, April, 1948.

Swisher, Jacob A., *Twixt Rockingham and Davenport*, Palimpsest, 19: 62-68, Feb., 1938.

Wilkie, Franc B., *Davenport: Past and Present*. Luse, Lane & Co., Davenport. 1858.

See also histories of Scott County.

Des Moines

Brief of Laws Relating to the New State Capitol, Annals (3), 15: 130-138, Oct., 1925.

Briggs, John E., The Removal of the Capital from Iowa City to Des Moines, Iowa Journal, 14: 56-95, Jan., 1916.

Brigham, Johnson, History of Des Moines and Polk County. 2 vols. S. J. Clarke, Chicago. 1911.

Brigham, Johnson, Kasson's Long Fight for the New Capitol, Annals (3), 10: 81-89, July, 1911.

Clark, Dan E., Some Episodes in the Early History of Des Moines, Iowa Journal, 13: 175-237, April, 1915.

Clark, Ernest E., Architecture in Iowa's Capital City, Midland Monthly, 10: 110-120, 205-213, Aug., Sept., 1898.

Dey, Peter A., Recollections of the Old Capitol and the New, Annals (3), 7: 81-101, July, 1905.

Dey, Peter A., Robert S. Finkbine and His Associates in the Erection of the Iowa Capitol, Annals (3), 5: 209-218, Oct., 1901.

Dunlap, Flora, Roadside Settlement of Des Moines, Annals (3), 21: 161-189, Jan., 1938.

Harlan, Edgar R., A Decade of Improvement, Annals (3), 14: 3-31, July, 1923.

Harlan, Edgar R., Proposed Improvement of the Iowa State Capitol Grounds, Annals (3), 11: 96-114, July-Oct., 1913.

Hartford of the West, The, Midland Monthly, 10: 353-367, Oct., 1898.

Harvey, Rev. R. E., Des Moines M. E. Conference Growth, Annals (3), 25: 282-317, April, 1944.

Harvey, Rev. R. E., Reopening a Closed Chapter (Historical Sketch of the Des Moines Conference of the M. E. Church, 1832-1860), Annals (3), 25: 192-228, Jan., 1944.

Hill, Raymond S., The Princess Theater of Des Moines, Iowa Journal, 49: 1-22, Jan., 1951.

Howard, Lawrence C., The Des Moines Negro and His Contribution to American Life, Annals (3), 30: 211-221, Jan., 1950.

Huntington, Ida M., Willson Alexander Scott, Annals (3), 13: 243-262, April, 1922.

Johnson, Jack T., Peter Anthony Dey, 156-172. SHSI. 1939.

Kasson, John A., The Fight for the New Capitol, Annals (3), 4: 241-262, Jan., 1900.

Kern, Jean B., The Des Moines Art Center, Palimpsest, 30: 23-32, Jan., 1949.

Keyes, Charles Rollin, Calvin Webb Keyes, Iowa Centenarian, Annals (3), 13: 193-216, Jan., 1922.

Lathrop, Henry W., The Capitals and Capitols of Iowa, Historical Record, 4: 97-124, July, 1888.

McGlothlen, W. F., Des Moines' Street Transit, Annals (3), 31: 223-228, Jan., 1952.

McLaughlin, Wm. M., Pioneer Park and Its Pioneer, Annals (3), 30: 453-457, Oct., 1950.

Mills, George, The Des Moines Register, Palimpsest, 30: 273-304, Sept., 1949.

Mott, David C., *The Pivotal Convention of 1883*, Annals (3), 26: 254-260, April, 1945.

Nelson, Howard J., *The Economic Development of Des Moines*, Iowa Journal, 48: 193-220, July, 1950.

Rice, Henry T., *Telegraphy First Used Here in 1862*, Annals (3), 30: 294-301, April, 1950.

Seeburger, Vernon R., *Fort Des Moines and Des Moines*, Annals (3), 25: 20-31, July, 1943.

Swisher, Jacob A., *The Capitols at Des Moines*, Iowa Journal, 39: 52-87, Jan., 1941.

Three Fort Des Moines—100th Anniversary of Establishment of Military Post at Des Moines, Annals (3), 25: 3-7, July, 1943.

Williams, Ora, *Des Moines' First Hundred Years*, Annals (3), 25: 7-20, July, 1943.

See also histories of Polk County. For references on Peter A. Dey, John A. Kasson, Calvin Webb Keyes, and Willson Alexander Scott see Biographies of Iowans.

Dubuque

Battell, Frederic C., *The Du Buque Visitor and Its Press*, Iowa Journal, 47: 193-214, July, 1949.

Catlin, George, *The Lead Mines of Dubuque*, Palimpsest, 7: 346-348, Nov., 1926.

Gallaher, Ruth A., *The First Bank in Iowa*, Palimpsest, 18: 103-112, March, 1937.

Gallaher, Ruth A., *The First Church in Iowa*, Palimpsest, 7: 1-10, Jan., 1926.

Grahame, Pauline P., *The Rockdale Flood*, Palimpsest, 10: 233-242, July, 1929.

Kelm, William E., *The People's Theater*, Palimpsest, 9: 89-105, March, 1928.

Kintzle, Clarence A., *The Julien Theater*, Palimpsest, 15: 139-158, April, 1934.

Langworthy, Lucius H., *Dubuque: Its History, Mines, Indian Legends, etc.* Dubuque Literary Institute, Dubuque. 1855. Reprinted in the Iowa Journal, 8: 366-422, July, 1910.

Letters of Joseph T. Fales, Annals (3), 21: 462-471, Oct., 1938.

Mahan, Bruce E., *The Iowa Thespians*, Palimpsest, 4: 14-24, Jan., 1923.

Mullin, Frank A., *Gleanings of an Editor*, Palimpsest, 6: 250-261, July, 1925.

Murray, Charles A., *Through European Eyes*, Palimpsest, 1: 144-165, Nov., 1920.

Parish, John C., *The Langworthys of Early Dubuque and Their Contributions to Local History*, Iowa Journal, 8: 315-355, July, 1910. (With autobiographical sketches of Lucius H., Solon M., and Edward Langworthy).

Parish, John C., *Three Men and a Press*, Palimpsest, 1: 56-60, Aug., 1920.

Petersen, William J., *The Beginnings of Dubuque*, Palimpsest, 21: 345-392, Nov., 1940.

Petersen, William J., *Chouteau v. Molony*, Palimpsest, 12: 434-440, Nov., 1931.

Petersen, William J., *Du Buque Visitor,* Palimpsest, 17: 117-128, April, 1936.

Petersen, William J., *Regulating the Lead Miners,* Palimpsest, 17: 185-200, June, 1936.

Petersen, William J., *Some Beginnings in Iowa,* Iowa Journal, 28: 3-54, Jan., 1930.

Petersen, William J., *Steamboats Dubuque,* Palimpsest, 10: 398-411, Nov., 1929.

Pickard, Josiah L., *Dubuque in Territorial Days,* Historical Record, 15: 542-555, Oct., 1899.

Price, Eliphalet, *Dubuque in Early Times,* Historical Record, 11: 225-231, Jan., 1895.

Price, Eliphalet, *The Execution of O'Connor,* Palimpsest, 1: 86-97, Sept., 1920.

Quaife, M. M., *John P. Sheldon,* Palimpsest, 17: 201-214, June, 1936.

Schoolcraft, Henry R., *Dubuque in 1820, August 7th,* Historical Record, 16: 100-106, July, 1900.

Shoup, Samantha W., *Literary Dubuque,* Midland Monthly, 3: 340-348, April, 1895.

Sullivan, Roger, and Swisher, J. A., *The Dubuque Shot Tower,* Palimpsest, 30: 377-388, Dec., 1949.

Van der Zee, Jacob, *Early History of Lead Mining in the Iowa Country,* Iowa Journal, 13: 3-52, Jan., 1915.

See also histories of Dubuque County.

Fort Dodge

Gallaher, Ruth A., *The Cardiff Giant,* Palimpsest, 2: 269-281, Sept., 1921.

Keeney, Charles C., *A Prospect of Fort Dodge,* Palimpsest, 13: 106-130, March, 1932.

Peterson, Harold D., *Boyhood at Fort Dodge,* Palimpsest, 24: 186-204, June, 1943.

Peterson, Harold D., *Wahkonsa,* Palimpsest, 23: 121-135, April, 1942.

Ruggles, W. Oakley, *Early Recollections of Fort Dodge,* Iowa Journal, 49: 168-184, April, 1951.

See also histories of Webster County.

Fort Madison

Briggs, John E., *The Fort Madison Patriot,* Palimpsest, 19: 98-105, March, 1938.

Briggs, John E., *A Penitentiary for Iowa,* Palimpsest, 20: 400-410, Dec., 1939.

Haynes, Fred E., *Warden Haynes,* Palimpsest, 23: 305-316, Oct., 1942.

Jordan, Philip D., *James Gardiner Edwards,* Palimpsest, 19: 106-116, March, 1938.

Kern, Jean B., *Warden and Warrior,* Palimpsest, 29: 182-192, June, 1948.

Schlicher, Raymond J., *Commemorating Emancipation,* Palimpsest, 28: 150-157, May, 1947.

Swisher, Jacob A., *Chartered Towns*, Palimpsest, 19: 31-35, Jan., 1938.
See also histories of Lee County. For references on the fort see Old Fort
Madison.

Iowa City

Briggs, John E., *The Removal of the Capital from Iowa City to Des Moines*,
Iowa Journal, 14: 56-95, Jan., 1916.
Briggs, John E., *Ripe for Statehood*, Palimpsest, 27: 129-141, May, 1946.
Cone, Carl B., *Hello Central*, Palimpsest, 24: 73-81, March, 1943.
Cone, Carl B., *Ole Bull and the Fire*, Palimpsest, 24: 154-160, May, 1943.
Eriksson, Erik M., *The Boyd Wilkinson Case*, Palimpsest, 6: 95-104, March,
1925.
Gallaher, Ruth A., *Methodists in Conference*, Palimpsest, 25: 225-233, Aug.,
1944.
Gallaher, Ruth A., *One More River to Cross*, Palimpsest, 8: 102-118, March,
1927.
Hall, Reeves, *Oregon Fever*, Palimpsest, 24: 93-104, March, 1943.
Heffner, Joseph S., *History of the Congregational Church of Iowa City*, Iowa
Journal, 15: 70-112, Jan., 1917.
Hoffman, M. M., *John Francis Rague—Pioneer Architect of Iowa*, Annals
(3), 19: 444-448, Oct., 1934.
Kuhns, Frederick I., *Diary of S. S. Howell, 1868*, Iowa Journal, 49: 143-
167, April, 1951.
Lathrop, Henry W., *The Capitals and Capitols of Iowa*, Historical Record,
4: 97-124, July, 1888.
Ludwig, Mary Culbertson, *Take a Letter*, Palimpsest, 29: 87-96, March, 1948.
Pelzer, Louis, *Iowa City: A Miniature Frontier of the Forties*, Iowa Journal,
29: 3-26, Jan., 1931.
Petersen, William J., *Iowa City Municipal Airport*, Palimpsest, 11: 404-414,
Sept., 1930.
Petersen, William J., *The State Centennial Stamp*, Palimpsest, 28: 65-77,
March, 1947.
Reizenstein, Jacob E., *Kirkwood Elected Road Supervisor*, Annals (3), 26:
305-306, April, 1945.
Rogers, Frances L., *An Old Autograph Album*, Palimpsest, 28: 247-256,
Aug., 1947.
Shambaugh, Benj. F., *The Founding of Iowa City*, Palimpsest, 20: 137-176,
May, 1939.
Shambaugh, Benj. F., *Iowa City: A Contribution to the Early History of
Iowa*. SHSI. 1893.
Shambaugh, Benj. F., *The Old Stone Capitol Remembers*. SHSI. 1939.
Swisher, Jacob A., *Air Mail in the Twenties*, Palimpsest, 26: 12-20, Jan.,
1945.
Swisher, Jacob A., *The Iowa City Centennial*, Iowa Journal, 37: 363-378,
Oct., 1939.
Swisher, Jacob A., *Plum Grove*, Palimpsest, 29: 19-32, Jan., 1948.

Thornton, Harrison John, *Birth of the Grand Lodge*, Palimpsest, 25: 173-178, June, 1944.

Thornton, Harrison John, *Locating the State University of Iowa*, Iowa Journal, 47: 50-62, Jan., 1949.

Throne, Mildred, *Letters of a Forty-Niner*, Iowa Journal, 47: 63-77, Jan., 1949.

Van der Zee, Jacob, *History of Presbyterianism in Iowa City*, Iowa Journal, 13: 529-580, Oct., 1915.

Van der Zee, Jacob, *One Hundred Years of Presbyterianism in Iowa City, Iowa, 1840-1940*. Iowa City Presbyterian Church, Iowa City. 1941.

See also histories of Johnson County.

KEOKUK

Davis, Caleb F., and James C. Davis, *The Autobiographies of an Iowa Father and Son*, Annals (3), 19: 483-538, Jan., 1935.

Lorch, Fred W., *Albert Bigelow Paine's Visit to Keokuk in 1910*, Iowa Journal, 42: 192-197, April, 1944.

Petersen, William J., *Crossroads of Empire*, Palimpsest, 32: 377-379, Oct., 1951.

Petersen, William J., *The Keokuk Packet Company*, Iowa Journal, 50: 193-208, July, 1952.

Smith, Frederic C., *The Estes House Hospital*, Palimpsest, 10: 341-350, Sept., 1929.

Smith, Frederic C., *Keokuk in Big League Baseball*, Palimpsest, 27: 204-216, July, 1946.

Smith, Frederic C., *The Gate City of Iowa*, Palimpsest, 32: 380-408, Oct., 1951.

Smith, Frederic C., *The Keokuk Lantern Club*, Palimpsest, 27: 116-125, April, 1946.

Snyder, Charles E., *Unitarianism in Iowa*, Palimpsest, 30: 345-376, Nov., 1949.

Wilson, Ben H., *Planked from Keokuk*, Palimpsest, 27: 369-380, Dec., 1946.

See also histories of Lee County. For references on Samuel Ryan Curtis and Mrs. Annie Turner Wittenmyer see Biographies of Iowans.

MASON CITY

Carlson, Gretchen, *Mason City Junior College*, Palimpsest, 11: 462-470, Oct., 1930.

Hall, W. Earl, *The Mason City Globe-Gazette*, Palimpsest, 31: 421-424, Oct., 1950.

Main, W. F., *Mason City in Retrospect*, Palimpsest, 29: 362-372, Dec., 1948.

Williams, Ira A., *Lost in an Iowa Blizzard*, Palimpsest, 2: 1-15, Jan., 1921.

For references on Mason City attorneys see Courts and Lawyers of Iowa. See also histories of Cerro Gordo County.

Muscatine

Bell, Edith M., *The Bloomington Herald*, Palimpsest, 21: 331-344, Oct., 1940.
Erwin, A. T., *Suel Foster*, Palimpsest, 24: 105-115, April, 1943.
Fishburn, Jesse J., *Ben Hershey—Lumber Baron*, Palimpsest, 28: 289-299, Oct., 1947.
Fishburn, Jesse J., *Octagon Place*, Palimpsest, 29: 33-38, Feb., 1948.
Fox, James, *Crum and the Standard*, Palimpsest, 21: 318-330, Oct., 1940.
Haefner, Marie, *Argonauts of the Mississippi*, Palimpsest, 13: 473-486, Dec., 1932.
Mott, David C., *Suel Foster*, Annals (3), 20: 497-509, Jan., 1937.
Petersen, William J., *Beginnings of Muscatine*, Palimpsest, 20: 345-384, Nov., 1939.
Richman, Irving B., *Congregational Life in Muscatine, 1843-1893*, Iowa Journal, 21: 347-372, July, 1923.
Russell, Walter, *The Muscatine Journal*, Palimpsest, 31: 412-416, Oct., 1950.
Walton, J. P., *Pioneer Papers*. Muscatine. 1899.
See also histories of Muscatine County.

Sioux City

Briggs, John E., *The Sioux City Corn Palaces*, Palimpsest, 3: 313-326, Oct., 1922.
Catlin, George, *The Grave of Sergeant Floyd*, Palimpsest, 7: 337-341, Nov., 1926.
Downing, J. Hyatt, *Sioux City* (novel). G. P. Putnam's Sons, New York. 1940.
Eriksson, Erik M., *Sioux City and the Black Hills Gold Rush 1874-1877*, Iowa Journal, 20: 319-347, July, 1922.
Garver, F. H., *Tents for Lewis and Clark*. Palimpsest, 25: 90-96, March, 1944.
Garver, Frank H., *Reminiscences of John H. Charles*, Annals (3), 8: 401-432, July, 1908.
Haefner, Marie, *The Boom in Sioux City*, Palimpsest, 21: 54-64, Feb., 1940.
Haefner, Marie, *Yankee Magic*, Palimpsest, 21: 45-53, Feb., 1940.
Hall, Reeves, *Rickenbacker Wins*, Palimpsest, 23: 381-394, Dec., 1942.
Hickman, C. Addison, *Barlow Hall*, Palimpsest, 22: 301-309, Oct., 1941.
Hickman, C. Addison, *The Sioux City Elevated*, Palimpsest, 22: 119-128, April, 1941.
Hickman, C. Addison, *Sioux City Frontier Guards*, Palimpsest, 23: 136-144, April, 1942.
Hoyt, Mabel F., *History of Community House, Sioux City, Iowa*, Annals (3), 21: 190-209, Jan., 1938.
Immigration,—Sioux City and Community House, Annals (3), 21: 226-234, Jan., 1938.
Kern, Jean B., *WPA Project Ten Years Later*, Palimpsest, 30: 15-22, Jan., 1949.
Kirby, Chester H., *The World's Series of 1891*, Palimpsest, 3: 364-373, Nov., 1922.

Myers, Alice V., *Wagon Roads West: The Sawyers Expeditions of 1865,
1866*, Annals (3), 23: 212-250, Jan., 1942.

Perkins, George D., Palimpsest, 5: 273-317, Aug., 1924.

Petersen, William J., *George C. Haddock*, Palimpsest, 14: 233-248, June,
1933.

Swisher, J. A., *War Eagle*, Palimpsest, 30: 33-41, Feb., 1949.

Taylor, Landon, *Pioneer Ministry*, Palimpsest, 25, 1-32, Jan., 1944.

Tweito, Thomas E., *A College in a Cornfield*, Palimpsest, 25: 340-352,
Nov., 1944.

Tweito, Thomas E., *A Destined Land*, Palimpsest, 29: 155-160, May, 1948.

Tweito, Thomas E., *Frontier Journalism*, Palimpsest, 32: 441-456, Dec., 1951.

See also histories of Woodbury County.

WATERLOO

Grahame, Russell C., *Voyages of the Black Hawk*. Palimpsest, 9: 157-169,
May, 1928.

Petersen, William J., *The Dairy Cattle Congress*, Palimpsest, 15: 357-386,
Nov., 1934.

Wilson, Ellis E., *Buffalo Wallows and Trails in Black Hawk County*, Annals
(3), 18: 181-188, Jan., 1932.

See also histories of Black Hawk County.

Iowa and the Civil War

THE NEGRO IN IOWA

Bergmann, Leola Nelson, *The Negro in Iowa*, Iowa Journal, 46: 3-90, Jan.,
1948.

Brown, Mabel E., *Dusky Lading*, Palimpsest, 9: 242-248, July, 1928.

Byrkit, Christian S., *A Derailment on the Railway Invisible*, Annals (3),
14: 95-100, Oct., 1923.

Calkin, Homer L., *A Slaveowner in Iowa*, Palimpsest, 22: 344-346, Nov.,
1941.

Coffin, Nathan E., *The Case of Archie P. Webb, A Free Negro*, Annals (3),
11: 200-214, July- Oct., 1913.

Frazee, George, *The Iowa Fugitive Slave Case*, Annals (3), 4: 118-137,
July, 1899.

Frazee, George, *An Iowa Fugitive Slave Case—1850*, Annals (3), 6: 9-45,
April, 1903.

Gallaher, Ruth A., *A Race Riot on the Mississippi*, Palimpsest, 2: 369-378,
Dec., 1921.

Gallaher, Ruth A., *Slavery in Iowa*, Palimpsest, 28: 158-160, May, 1947.

Hill, G. W. E., *Underground Railroad Adventures*, Midland Monthly, 3:
173-180, Feb., 1895.

Howard, Lawrence C., *The Des Moines Negro and His Contribution to
American Life*, Annals (3), 30: 211-221, Jan., 1950.

An Iowa Fugitive Slave Case, Annals (3), 2: 531-539, Oct., 1896.

Jones, Mrs. Laurence C., *The Desire for Freedom*, Palimpsest, 8: 153-162,
    May, 1927.
Jones, Louis T., *The Quakers of Iowa*, 191-197. SHSI. 1914.
Mahan, Bruce E., *The Passing of a Slave*, Palimpsest, 3: 227-230, July, 1922.
Parish, John C., *An Early Fugitive Slave Case West of the Mississippi River*,
    Iowa Journal, 6: 88-95, Jan., 1908.
Pelzer, Louis, *The Negro and Slavery in Early Iowa*, Iowa Journal, 2: 471-
    484, Oct., 1904.
Petersen, William J., *The Story of Iowa*, 1: 411-420. Lewis Historical Co.,
    New York. 1952.
Reed, Charles D., *George Washington Carver, Mystic Scientist*, Annals (3),
    24: Part 1, 248-253, Jan., 1943.
Schlicher, Raymond J., *Commemorating Emancipation*, Palimpsest, 28: 150-
    157, May, 1947.
Snyder, Charles E., *John Emerson, Owner of Dred Scott*, Annals (3), 21:
    441-461, Oct., 1938.
Stiles, Cassius C., *John Ross Miller*, Annals (3), 19: 384-386, July, 1934.
Swisher, Jacob A., *The Case of Ralph*, Palimpsest, 7: 33-43, Feb., 1926.
Van Ek, Jacob, *Underground Railroad in Iowa*, Palimpsest, 2: 129-143,
    May, 1921.
Wick, Barthinius L., *Delia Webster*, Annals (3), 18: 228-231, Jan., 1932.
Wick, Barthinius L., *Peter Rice*, Palimpsest, 23: 204-208, June, 1942.
Williams, Ora, *Underground Railroad Signals*, Annals (3), 27: 297-303,
    April, 1946.
See also John Brown in Iowa.

JOHN BROWN IN IOWA

Caskie, George E., *Trial of John Brown*, Annals (3), 9: 359-379, April,
    1910.
Coppoc, J. L., *John Brown and His Cause*, Midland Monthly, 4: 317-325,
    Oct., 1895.
Garretson, O. A., *Travelling on the Underground Railroad in Iowa*, Iowa
    Journal, 22: 418-543, July, 1924.
Gue, Benjamin F., *John Brown and His Iowa Friends*, Midland Monthly,
    7: 103-113, 267-277, Feb., March, 1897.
Harris, Ransom L., *John Brown and His Followers in Iowa*, Midland Monthly,
    2: 262-268, Oct., 1894.
Lloyd, Frederick, *John Brown Among the Pedee Quakers*, Annals (1), 4:
    665-670, 712-719, 759-764, April, July, Oct., 1866.
Payne, Charles E., *Josiah Bushnell Grinnell*, 99-115. SHSI. 1938.
Richman, Irving B., *John Brown Among the Quakers, and Other Sketches*,
    11-59. Historical Department, Des Moines. 1904.
Richman, Irving B., *John Brown's Band*, Palimpsest, 9: 249-255, July, 1928.
Smith, Narcissa M., *Reminiscences of John Brown*, Midland Monthly, 4:
    231-236, Sept., 1895.
Williams, Ora, *Underground Railroad Signals*, Annals (3), 27: 297-303,
    April, 1946.

Barclay Coppoc — Follower of John Brown

Brown, Owen, *The Escape*, Palimpsest, 9: 405-426, Nov., 1928.
Coppoc Boys, The, Palimpsest, 9: 385-436, Nov., 1928.
Grahame, Pauline P., *At Harper's Ferry*, Palimpsest, 9: 392-404, Nov., 1928.
Grahame, Pauline P., *Springdale Recruits*, Palimpsest, 9: 385-391, Nov., 1928.
Jones, Louis T., *The Quakers of Iowa*, 194-197. SHSI. 1914.
Richman, Irving B., *John Brown Among the Quakers, and Other Sketches*, 49-56. Historical Department, Des Moines. 1904.
Teakle, Thomas, *Rendition Foiled*, Palimpsest, 9: 427-433, Nov., 1928.
Teakle, Thomas, *The Rendition of Barclay Coppoc*, Iowa Journal, 10: 503-566, Oct., 1912.

Lincoln and Iowa

Aldrich, Charles, *At Lincoln's First Inauguration*, Annals (3), 8: 43-50, April, 1907.
Emery, Charles W., *The Iowa Germans in the Election of 1860*, Annals (3), 22: 421-454, Oct., 1940.
Garretson, O. A., *A Lincoln Pole Raising*, Palimpsest, 6: 109-116, April, 1925.
Harlan, Edgar R., *The Lincoln Mass of American People*, Annals (3), 17: 563-577, April, 1931.
Harlan, Edgar R., *Lincoln's Iowa Lands*, Annals (3), 15: 621-623, April, 1927.
Herriott, Frank I., *Iowa and the First Nomination of Abraham Lincoln*, Annals (3), 8: 81-115, 186-220, July, Oct., 1907.
Herriott, Frank I., *Memories of the Chicago Convention of 1860*, Annals (3), 12: 446-466, Oct., 1920.
Herriott, Frank I., *Republican Presidential Preliminaries in Iowa—1859-1860*, Annals (3), 9: 241-283, Jan., 1910.
Herriott, Frank I., *The Republican State Convention*, Annals (3), 9: 401-446, July-Oct., 1910.
Lincoln and the Bridge Case, Palimpsest, 3: 142-154, May, 1922.
Lytle, Harry J., *Lincoln Admirers*, Palimpsest, 30: 269-272, Aug., 1949.
Lytle, Harry J., *Words of Lincoln*, Palimpsest, 30: 257-268, Aug., 1949.
Palmer, F. W., *Death of President Lincoln*, Annals (3), 4: 403-414, July, 1900.
Parish, John C., *The First Mississippi Bridge*, Palimpsest, 3: 133-141, May, 1922.
Petersen, William J., *Lincoln and Iowa*, Palimpsest, 30: 241-256, Aug., 1949.
Petersen, William J., *The Story of Iowa*, 1: 382-453. Lewis Historical Co., New York. 1952.
Swisher, Jacob A., *Lincoln in Iowa*, Iowa Journal, 43: 69-84, Jan., 1945.
The Visit of Abraham Lincoln to Council Bluffs, Annals (3), 4: 460-463, July, 1900.
Wilson, Ben H., *Lincoln at Burlington*, Palimpsest, 24: 313-322, Oct., 1943.
Wright, Luella M., *Victory and Mourning*, Palimpsest, 21: 101-132, April, 1940.

THE CIVIL WAR — IN GENERAL

Adjutant General of Iowa, *Annual Report, 1861-1865.* State of Iowa, Des Moines.

Briggs, John E., *The Lure of Hope,* Palimpsest, 24: 267-268, Aug., 1943.

Briggs, John E., *Iowa Old and New,* 244-260. University Publishing Co., Lincoln, Nebr. 1939.

Brigham, Johnson, *Iowa—Its History and Its Foremost Citizens,* 1: 293-396. 3 vols. S. J. Clarke, Chicago. 1915. Also in a 2 vol. edition.

Byers, Samuel H. M., *Iowa in War Times.* W. D. Condit, Des Moines. 1888.

Ingersoll, Lurton D., *Iowa and the Rebellion.* Lippincott, Philadelphia. 1866.

Michael, William H., *Iowa and the Navy During the War of the Rebellion,* Historical Record, 10: 160-181, Oct., 1894.

Petersen, William J., *The Story of Iowa,* 1: 421-495. Lewis Historical Co., New York. 1952.

Pollock, Ivan L., *The Iowa Civil War Loan,* Iowa and War, No. 3, Sept., 1917. SHSI.

Pollock, Ivan L., *The Iowa War Loan of 1861,* Iowa Journal, 15: 467-502, Oct., 1917.

Pollock, Ivan L., *State Finances in Iowa During the Civil War,* Iowa Journal, 16: 53-107, Jan., 1918.

Roster and Record of Iowa Soldiers in the War of the Rebellion. 6 vols. State of Iowa, Des Moines. 1908-1911.

Swisher, Jacob A., *Remember Our Heroes,* Palimpsest, 23: 189-203, June, 1942.

Thornton, Harrison John, *The State University of Iowa and the Civil War,* Annals (3), 30: 198-209, Jan., 1950.

Upham, Cyril B., *Iowa and War,* Iowa and War, No. 5, Nov., 1917. SHSI.

MILITARY ADMINISTRATION IN THE CIVIL WAR

Briggs, John E., *The Enlistment of Iowa Troops During the Civil War,* Iowa Journal, 15: 323-392, July, 1917.

Briggs, John E., *Enlistments from Iowa During the Civil War,* Iowa and War, No. 2, Aug., 1917. SHSI.

Bryant, Thomas J., *A War Time Militia Company,* Iowa Journal, 10: 403-414, July, 1912.

Clark, Dan E., *Border Defense in Iowa During the Civil War,* Iowa and War, No. 10, April, 1918. SHSI.

Gist, W. W., *The Ages of the Soldiers in the Civil War,* Iowa Journal, 16: 387-399, July, 1918.

Swisher, Jacob A., *Camp Life in Other Days,* Palimpsest, 22: 310-324, Oct., 1941.

Upham, Cyril B., *Arms and Equipment for the Iowa Troops in the Civil War,* Iowa Journal, 16: 3-52, Jan., 1918.

Upham, Cyril B., *Equipment of the Iowa Troops in the Civil War,* Iowa and War, No. 4, Oct., 1917. SHSI.

MILITARY LEADERS

Aldrich, Charles, *Captain Thomas Drummond*, Annals (3), 2: 203-211, July-Oct., 1895.

Allison, Senator William B., *Young Men Saved the Union in 1861-1865*, Annals (3), 26: 68-69, July, 1944.

Briggs, John E., *George Windle Read*, Palimpsest, 11: 172-179, April, 1930.

Briggs, John E., *Hanson Edward Ely*, Palimpsest, 11: 180-190, April, 1930.

Briggs, John E., *William Peters Hepburn*, 48-87. SHSI. 1919.

Bussey, Cyrus, *Cyrus Bussey's Boyhood: An Autobiographical Sketch*, Iowa Journal, 30: 513-531, Oct., 1932.

Carlson, Gretchen, *Francis Jay Herron*, Palimpsest, 11: 141-150, April, 1930.

Carpenter, Cyrus C., *Major-General G. M. Dodge*, Annals (3), 1: 161-180, 302-328, Oct., 1893, Jan., 1894.

Clark, Charles A., *Congressional Medals of Honor and Iowa Soldiers*, Annals (3), 7: 102-114, July, 1905.

Clark, J. S., *General Lyon and the Fight for Missouri*, Midland Monthly, 8: 111-120, Aug., 1897.

Colton, Kenneth E., *Frontier War Problems: The Letters of Samuel Ryan Curtis*, Annals (3), 24: 298-314, April, 1943.

Colton, Kenneth E., *The Irrepressible Conflict of 1861, The Letters of Samuel Ryan Curtis*, Annals (3), 24: 14-58, July, 1942.

Colton, Kenneth E., *With Fremont in Missouri, in 1861. The Letters of Samuel Ryan Curtis*, Annals (3), 24: 105-167, Oct., 1942.

Dodge, Grenville M., *Colonel William H. Kinsman*, Annals (3), 5: 241-250, Jan., 1902.

Dodge, Grenville M., *Gen. James A. Williamson*, Annals (3), 6: 161-184, Oct., 1903.

Dodge, Grenville M., *Historical Address*, Annals (3), 4: 577-594, Jan., 1901.

Dodge, Grenville M., *Some Characteristics of Gen. U. S. Grant*, Annals (3), 10: 570-589, Jan., 1913.

Dugan, Ruth E., *Grenville Mellen Dodge*, Palimpsest, 11: 160-171, April, 1930.

Eaton, Willard L., *Gen. A. K. Eaton*, Annals (3), 5: 33-37, April, 1901.

Gallaher, Ruth A., *Benjamin Stone Roberts*, Palimpsest, 1: 75-85, Sept., 1920.

Gallaher, Ruth A., *Samuel Ryan Curtis*, Iowa Journal, 25: 331-358, July, 1927.

Gallaher, Ruth A., *Samuel Ryan Curtis*, Palimpsest, 11: 129-140, April, 1930.

Gill, Adelaide M., *Frederick Steele*, Palimpsest, 11: 151-159, April, 1930.

Hammond, William A., *Recollections of Gen. Nathaniel Lyon*, Annals (3), 4: 415-436, July, 1900.

An Iowa Emancipator, Annals (3), 30: 302-305, April, 1950.

Keyes, Charles Rollin, *Major-General Lewis Addison Grant*, Annals (3), 12: 511-532, Jan., 1921.

Lacey, John F., *General Samuel A. Rice at Jenkins' Ferry*, Annals (3), 2: 32-44, April, 1895.

Lacey, John F., *Major-General Frederick Steele*, Annals (3), 3: 424-438, April-July, 1898.

MacBride, Dorothy, *Lieutenant Jefferson Davis*, Palimpsest, 4: 346-357, Oct., 1923.

Mills, F. M., *Colonel N. W. Mills of the Second Iowa Infantry*, Annals (3), 13: 375-381, July, 1922.

Perkins, J. R., *Trails, Rails, and War*. Bobbs-Merrill, Indianapolis. 1929.

Rebel Colonel and Yankee General, Annals (3), 30: 61-62, July, 1949.

Ross, General Leonard F., Historical Record, 4: 145-183, Oct., 1888.

Salter, William, *Major-General John M. Corse*, Annals (3), 2: 1-19, 105-145, 278-304, April, July, Oct., 1895, Jan., 1896.

Smith, David M., *The Civil War Diary of Colonel John Henry Smith*, Iowa Journal, 47: 140-170, April, 1949.

Steele, Alice M., *Iowa at West Point and Annapolis*, Annals (3), 6: 594-617, Jan., 1905.

Stiles, Edward H., *General Fitz Henry Warren*, Annals (3), 6: 481-497, Oct., 1904.

Stuart, Addison A., *Iowa Colonels and Regiments*. Mills & Co., Des Moines. 1865.

Swisher, Jacob A., *The Career of Cyrus Bussey*, Iowa Journal, 30: 532-558, Oct., 1932.

Thompson, General William, Historical Record, 6: 481-516, July, 1890.

Tyler, Loren S., *The Tyler Photographs of Iowa Military Men*, Annals (3), 10: 408-430, July, 1912.

Williams, Ora, *Sword of General Crocker*, Annals (3), 28: 61-68, July, 1946.

Wilson, Gen. James, Historical Record, 3: 481-496, July, 1887.

BATTLES AND CAMPAIGNS

Aldrich, Charles, *Incidents Connected with the History of the Thirty-second Iowa Infantry*, Iowa Journal, 4: 70-85, Jan., 1906.

Benson, Solon F., Henry H. Childers, and William H. Heath, *The Battle of Pleasant Hill, Louisiana*, Annals (3), 7: 481-522, Oct., 1906.

Boyd, C. F., *The Civil War Diary of C. F. Boyd, Fifteenth Iowa Infantry*, (Edited by Mildred Throne), Iowa Journal, 50: 239-270, July, 1952.

Briggs, John E., *In the Battle of Winchester*, Palimpsest, 6: 394-402, Nov., 1925.

Brown, Charles P., *Battle of Blue Mills*, Annals (3), 14: 287-294, April, 1924.

Bryant, Thomas J., *The Capture of General Marmaduke by James Dunlavy, an Iowa Private Cavalryman*, Iowa Journal, 11: 248-257, April, 1913.

Bussey, Cyrus, *The Battle of Athens, Missouri*, Annals (3), 5: 81-92, July, 1901.

Byers, Samuel H. M., *The Battle of Iuka*, Historical Record, 3: 543-552, Oct., 1887.

Cherry, Amos R., *Iowa Troops in the Sully Campaign*, Iowa Journal, 20: 364-366, 374-440, July, 1922.

Harbert, Albert N., *James M. Elson*, Historical Record, 13: 49-53, April, 1897.

Hall, Reeves, *A Year of Victory*, Palimpsest, 24: 255-266, Aug., 1943.

Hill, Josiah F., *Iowa Troops in the Sully Campaign*, Iowa Journal, 20: 364-366, 440-443, July, 1922.

Lyon, Bessie L., *Flashlights on Vicksburg*, Palimpsest, 8: 71-80, Feb., 1927.

Nicholson, William L., *The Engagement at Jenkin's Ferry*, Annals (3), 11: 505-519, Oct., 1914.

O'Connor, Henry, *With the First Iowa Infantry*, Palimpsest, 3: 53-61, Feb., 1922.

Parkhurst, Clint, *The Attack on Corinth*, Palimpsest, 3: 169-191, June, 1922.

Parkhurst, Clint, *A Few Martial Memories*, Palimpsest, 1: 111-128, Oct., 1920.

Parkhurst, Clint, *Our First View of Vicksburg*, Palimpsest, 3: 69-83, March, 1922.

Parkhurst, Clint, *The Siege of Corinth*, Palimpsest, 4: 1-13, Jan., 1923.

Parkhurst, Clint, *Yankees in Memphis*, Palimpsest, 21: 65-72, March, 1940.

Price, Hiram, *Paying the First Iowa*, Palimpsest, 3: 62-65, Feb., 1922.

Rhodes, Milton, *Captives in Dixie*, Palimpsest, 10: 243-266, July, 1929.

Rich, Joseph W., *The Battle of Shiloh*, Iowa Journal, 7: 503-581, Oct., 1909.

Rich, Joseph W., *The Color Bearer of the Twelfth Iowa Volunteer Infantry*, Iowa Journal, 6: 96-102, Jan., 1908.

Rich, Joseph W., *The Death of General Albert Sidney Johnston on the Battlefield of Shiloh*, Iowa Journal, 16: 275-281, April, 1918.

Rich, Joseph W., *General Lew. Wallace at Shiloh: How He Was Convinced of an Error After Forty Years*. Iowa Journal, 18: 301-308, April, 1920.

Stibbs, John H., *Andersonville and the Trial of Henry Wirz*, Iowa Journal, 9: 33-56, Jan., 1911.

Thompson, J. K. P., *Iowa at Vicksburg and the Vicksburg National Military Park*, Annals (3), 5: 272-292, Jan., 1902.

Wieneke, Henry J., *Iowa Troops in the Sully Campaigns*, Iowa Journal, 20: 364-374, July, 1922.

Wilkie, Franc B., *The Battle of Wilson's Creek*, Palimpsest, 9: 291-310, Aug., 1928.

Wilson, Peter, *in the Civil War*, Iowa Journal, 40: 153-203, April, 1942.

INCIDENTS IN THE CIVIL WAR

Aldrich, Charles, *The Song "Sherman's March to the Sea"*, Annals (3), 11: 215-217, July-Oct., 1913.

Aurner, Clarence R., *Chance*, Palimpsest, 13: 318-330, Aug., 1932.

Briggs, John E., *The Hornets' Nest*, Palimpsest, 10: 267-268, July, 1929.

Byers, Samuel H. M., *A Historic War Song*, Midland Monthly, 1: 48-56, Jan., 1894.

Child, Bert B., *Civil War Musicians*, Annals (3), 25: 122-128, Oct., 1943.

Cowman, Evangeline S., *In This Neglected Spot*, Palimpsest, 8: 132-137, April, 1927.

Gallaher, Ruth A., *S. H. M. Byers*, Palimpsest, 13: 429-469, Nov., 1932.

Garretson, O. A., *A Famous War Horse*, Palimpsest, 12: 354-358, Sept., 1931.

Garretson, O. A., *An Incident of the Civil War*, Palimpsest, 24: 348-351, Nov., 1943.

Harlan, James, *The Iowa Soldiers' and Sailors' Monument*, Midland Monthly, 5: 99-113, Feb., 1896.

Hawley, Charles A., *The Historical Background of the Attitude of the Jasper Colony Toward Slavery in the Civil War*, Iowa Journal, 34: 172-197, April, 1936.

Hawley, Charles A., *Whittier and Iowa*, Iowa Journal, 34: 115-143, April, 1936.

Hickman, C. Addison, *Sioux City Frontier Guards*, Palimpsest, 23: 136-144, April, 1942.

Mahan, Bruce E., *Border Troubles*, Palimpsest, 5: 189-233, June, 1924.

Moore, Samuel A., *Hostile Raids Into Davis County, Iowa*, Annals (3), 13: 362-374, July, 1922.

The Mothers of Warriors, Annals (3), 30: 146-147, Oct., 1949.

Palmetto Flag, The, Annals (3), 15: 47-66, July, 1925.

Rich, Ellen M., *The State University of Iowa and the Civil War*, Iowa and War, No. 8, Feb., 1918. SHSI.

Ross, Earle D., *Northern Sectionalism in the Civil War Era*, Iowa Journal, 30: 455-512, Oct., 1932.

Schmidt, Louis B., *The Influence of Wheat and Cotton on Anglo-American Relations During the Civil War*, Iowa Journal, 16: 400-439, July, 1918.

Snyder, Charles E., *Army Camp and Orphans Home*, Annals (3), 29: 307-314, April, 1948.

Temple, Seth J., *Camp McClellan During the Civil War*, Annals (3), 21: 17-55, July, 1937.

Trachsel, Herman H., *Jim Jackson's Raid*, Palimpsest, 8: 265-283, Aug., 1927.

Wright, Luella M., *The Pioneer Greys*, Palimpsest, 22: 1-32, Jan., 1941.

Wright, Luella M., *Victory and Mourning*, Palimpsest, 21: 101-132, April, 1940.

RELIEF WORK IN THE CIVIL WAR

Fullbrook, Earl S., *Relief Work in Iowa During the Civil War*, Iowa Journal, 16: 155-274, April, 1918.

Fullbrook, Earl S., *Sanitary Fairs—A Method of Raising Funds for Relief Work in Iowa*, Iowa and War, No. 6, Dec., 1917. SHSI.

Gallaher, Ruth A., *Annie Turner Wittenmyer*, Iowa Journal, 29: 518-569, Oct., 1931.

Gallaher, Ruth A., *The Wittenmyer Diet Kitchens*, Palimpsest, 12: 337-346, Sept., 1931.

Gallarno, George, *How Iowa Cared for Orphans of Her Soldiers of the Civil War*, Annals (3), 15: 163-193, Jan., 1926.

Haddock, Emma H., *Lucinda Humphrey Hay*, Historical Record, 10: 49-64, April, 1894.

Jordan, Philip D., *Forty Days with the Christian Commission: A Diary by William Salter*, Iowa Journal, 33: 123-154, April, 1935.

Smith, Frederic C., *The Estes House Hospital*, Palimpsest, 10: 341-350, Sept., 1929.

Throne, Mildred, *Diary of W. H. Turner, M. D., 1863*, Iowa Journal, 48: 267-282, July, 1950.

Wright, Luella M., *A 'Tater Patch for Soldiers*, Palimpsest, 22: 240-246, Aug., 1941.

REMINISCENCES AND PERSONAL RECORDS

Abernethy, Alonzo, *Incidents of an Iowa Soldier's Life, or Four Years in Dixie*, Annals (3), 12: 401-428, Oct., 1920.

Adventures of Geo. A. Tod, An Iowa Drummer Boy in Rebel Prisons at Cahawba and Andersonville, Iowa Journal, 49: 339-351, Oct., 1951.

Beall, Walter H., *With Gager in Georgia*, Palimpsest, 24: 41-58, Feb., 1943.

Byers, Samuel H. M., *How Men Fell in Battle*, Annals (3), 2: 438-449, July, 1896.

Calkin, Homer L., *Life in the Army*, Palimpsest, 23: 1-15, Jan., 1942.

Crosley, George W., *Some Reminiscences of an Iowa Soldier*, Annals (3), 10: 119-136, July, 1911.

Duckworth, William A., *Escape of Iowa Soldiers from Confederate Prison*, Annals (3), 9: 337-359, April, 1910.

Duckworth, William A., *A Republic Within the Confederacy and Other Recollections of 1864*, Annals (3), 11: 342-351, April, 1914.

English, Emory H., *Confederate Soldiers' Home Closed in Missouri*, Annals (3), 31: 308, April, 1952.

English, Emory H., *Desperate Battles Survived by Youth*, Annals (3), 26: 198-204, Jan., 1945.

Ezell, John S., *Excerpts from the Civil War Diary of Lt. Charles Alley, Company C, Fifth Iowa Cavalry*, Iowa Journal, 49: 241-256, July, 1951.

Gulick, William O., *The Journal and Letters of Corporal William O. Gulick*, Iowa Journal, 28: 194-267, 390-455, 543-603, April, July, Oct., 1930.

Hadley, Elbridge, D., *A Young Soldier's Career*, Annals (3), 13: 321-361, July, 1922.

Jackson, Luther W., *A Prisoner of War*, Annals (3), 19: 23-41, July, 1933.

Jordan, Philip D., *Forty Days with the Christian Commission: A Diary by William Salter*, Iowa Journal, 33: 123-154, April, 1935.

Longley, Charles L., *The Twenty-fourth Iowa Volunteers*, Annals (3), 1: 446-454, 553-565, July, Oct., 1894; 2: 44-56, April, 1895.

Lucas, Charles A., *A Soldier's Letters from the Field*, Historical Record, 16: 126-157, 172-196, July, Oct., 1900; 17: 217-253, 293-304, 348-351, 371-396, Jan., April, July, Oct., 1901; 18: 438-448, 463-496, 511-551, Jan., April, July, 1902.

Lyon, Bessie L., *Christian Soldier*, Palimpsest, 25: 50-64, Feb., 1944.

Morgan, John S., *Diary of John S. Morgan, Company G, Thirty-third Iowa Infantry*, Annals (3), 13: 483-508, 570-610, Jan., April, 1923.

Murray, Ray, *Lest We Forget*, Palimpsest, 29: 174-181, June, 1948.

Pearson, Benjamin F., *War Diary*, Annals (3), 15: 83-129, Oct., 1925.

Smith, Thad. L., *The Twenty-fourth Iowa Volunteers*, Annals (3), 1: 15-
37, 111-128, 180-196, April, July, Oct., 1893.
Sweney, Col. Joseph H., *Nursed a Wounded Brother*, Annals (3), 31: 177-
204, Jan., 1952.
Thomas, Benjamin F., *Off to the War*, Palimpsest, 22: 161-177, June, 1941.
Throne, Mildred, *The Civil War Diary of John Mackley*, Iowa Journal, 48:
141-168, April, 1950.
Throne, Mildred, *Diary of W. H. Turner, M. D., 1863*, Iowa Journal, 48:
267-282, July, 1950.
Throne, Mildred, *The Civil War Diary of C. F. Boyd, Fifteenth Iowa In-
fantry*, Iowa Journal, 50: 47-82, 155-184, 239-270, Jan., April, July,
1952.
Van Dyke, Ben, *Escape from the Hospital at Pleasant Hill, Louisiana*, Annals
(3), 7: 523-532, Oct., 1906.
Williams, Ora, *College Student and Soldier Boy*, Annals (3), 26: 45-54,
July, 1944.
Wilson, Peter, *Peter Wilson in the Civil War: The Training Period* (letters),
Iowa Journal, 40: 153-203, April, 1942.
Peter Wilson in the Civil War in Battle and on Parole, Iowa Journal, 40:
261-320, July, 1942.
Peter Wilson in the Civil War 1863-1865, Iowa Journal, 40: 339-414, Oct.,
1942.
Wortman, F. A., *A Pension Gone Astray*, Palimpsest, 27: 285-288, Sept.,
1946.

Southern Sentiment in Iowa

Abrams, Paul R., *The Assault Upon Josiah B. Grinnell by Lovell H. Rousseau*,
Iowa Journal, 10: 383-402, July, 1912.
Arena, Frank C., *Southern Sympathizers in Iowa During Civil War Days*,
Annals (3), 30: 486-538, Jan., 1951.
Clark, Dan E., *Samuel Jordan Kirkwood*, 270-271. SHSI. 1917.
Edmundson, J. D., *In Honor of the Flag*, Palimpsest, 6: 141-145, May, 1925.
Fulton, Charles J., *The Coalport Home Guards*, Annals (3), 14: 83-94,
Oct., 1923.
Mahan, Bruce E., *A Confederate Spy*, Palimpsest, 4: 33-52, Feb., 1923.
Parish, John C., *George Wallace Jones*, 60-67. SHSI. 1912.
Patton, R. A., *Washed Loyal*, Palimpsest, 7: 120-126, April, 1926.
Robeson, George F., *Henry Clay Dean*, Palimpsest, 5: 321-333, Sept., 1924.
Stiles, Cassius C., *The Skunk River War (Or Tally War)*, Annals (3), 19:
614-631, April, 1935.

The Grand Army of the Republic

Calkin, Homer L., *A Grand Rally*, Palimpsest, 22: 89-96, March, 1941.
In Honor of Iowa Soldiers, Annals (3), 27: 151-157, Oct., 1945.
Swisher, Jacob A., *The Iowa Department of the Grand Army of the Republic*.
SHSI. 1936.

Iowa and Foreign Wars

IOWA IN THE MEXICAN WAR

Cole, Cyrenus, A History of the People of Iowa, 178-180. Torch Press, Cedar Rapids. 1921.

Gallaher, Ruth A., Benjamin Stone Roberts, Palimpsest, 1: 75-85, Sept., 1920.

Gue, Benjamin F., History of Iowa, 1: 224-226. 4 vols. Century History Co., New York. 1903.

Murray, Ray, Lest We Forget, Palimpsest, 29: 174-181, June, 1948.

Swisher, Jacob A., Remember Our Heroes, Palimpsest, 23: 189-203, June, 1942.

Upham, Cyril B., The Mexican War, Iowa and War, No. 12, June, 1918. SHSI.

Williams, Ora, Forgetting Chapultepec, Annals (3), 28: 81-92, Oct., 1946.

IOWA IN THE SPANISH-AMERICAN WAR

Blanchard, B. W., The Torpedo-Boat Ericsson, Midland Monthly, 2: 85-88, Aug., 1894.

Bloomfield Military Company in 1898, Annals (3), 18: 221-227, Jan., 1932.

Evans, Robley D., The Battleship Iowa, Annals (3), 5: 143-147, July, 1901.

Gallaher, Ruth A., The Iowa, Palimpsest, 4: 101-112, April, 1923.

Harbert, Albert N., The Iowa as a Defender, Historical Record, 14: 337-348, Oct., 1898.

Irving, Minna, The Queen of the Navy, Midland Monthly, 8: 99-105, Aug., 1897.

Mahan, Bruce E., The Fifty-first Iowa, Palimpsest, 6: 177-222, June, 1925.

Murray, Ray, Lest We Forget, Palimpsest, 29: 174-181, June, 1948.

Petersen, William J., Three Earlier Iowas, Palimpsest, 33: 93-96, March, 1952.

Swisher, Jacob A., Remember Our Heroes, Palimpsest, 23: 189-203, June, 1942.

Swisher, Jacob A., Robert Gordon Cousins, 99-101. SHSI. 1938.

Wilson, Ben H., The Ericsson, Palimpsest, 14: 177-210, May, 1933.

IOWA IN THE FIRST WORLD WAR

Aman, John A., Views of Three Iowa Newspapers on the League of Nations 1919-1920, Iowa Journal, 39: 227-285, July, 1941.

Cole, Cyrenus, A History of the People of Iowa, 536-542. Torch Press, Cedar Rapids. 1921.

Fullbrook, Earl S., The Red Cross in Iowa. 2 vols. SHSI. 1922.

Gallaher, Ruth A., An Iowa Flag, Iowa and War, No. 14, Aug., 1918. SHSI.

Hansen, Marcus L., Welfare Campaign in Iowa. SHSI. 1920.

Hansen, Marcus L., Welfare Work in Iowa. SHSI. 1921.

Hansen, Marcus L., The Writing of War History in Iowa, Iowa and War, No. 23, May, 1919. SHSI.

Harding, W. L., *Iowa War Proclamations*, Iowa and War, No. 13, July, 1918. SHSI.

Haynes, Fred E., *Social Work at Camp Dodge*, Iowa Journal, 16: 471-547, Oct., 1918.

Installation of a Memorial Tablet Commemorating the Services of the 351st Infantry, 88th Div., A. E. F., Annals (3), 13: 83-98, Oct., 1921.

Iowa Men and Women Lost in World War, Annals (3), 15: 358-376, July, 1926.

Murray, Ray, *Lest We Forget*, Palimpsest, 29: 174-181, June, 1948.

Murray, Ray, *Merle D. Hay*, Palimpsest, 24: 141-153, May, 1943.

Pollock, Ivan L., *The Food Administration in Iowa.* 2 vols. SHSI. 1923.

Rear Admiral George Collier Remey, Annals (3), 19: 403-405, Oct., 1934.

Shambaugh, Benj. F., *The History of Iowa's Part in the World War*, Iowa and War, No. 19, Jan., 1919. SHSI.

Shambaugh, Benj. F., *The State Historical Society of Iowa in War Times*, Iowa and War, No. 18, Dec., 1918. SHSI.

Shambaugh, Bertha M. H., *Organized Speaking in Iowa During the War*, Iowa and War, No. 17, Nov., 1918. SHSI.

Social Work at Camp Dodge, Iowa and War, No. 16, Oct., 1918. SHSI.

Stiles, Cassius C., *Bonds of the State of Iowa*, Annals (3), 16: 524-535, Jan., 1929.

Swisher, Jacob A., *MacArthur and Iowa Troops*, Palimpsest, 23: 209-223, July, 1942.

Swisher, Jacob A., *Remember Our Heroes*, Palimpsest, 23: 189-203, June, 1942.

Taber, John H., *The Story of the 168th Infantry.* 2 vols. SHSI. 1925.

Tentative Outline for a County War History, Iowa and War, No. 20, Feb., 1919. SHSI.

Tentative Outline for a State War History, Iowa and War, No. 21, March, 1919. SHSI.

Watson, Martha A., *A Visit to the American Cemeteries in Europe*, Annals (3), 14: 215-231, Jan., 1924.

Whitney, Nathaniel R., *The First Three Liberty Loans in Iowa*, Iowa and War, No. 15, Sept., 1918. SHSI.

Whitney, Nathaniel R., *The Sale of War Bonds in Iowa.* SHSI. 1923.

Wilson, Ellis E., *A Duffle Bag Diary of an American Red Cross Worker in France*, Annals (3), 22: 64-76, 128-170, 201-247, July, Oct., 1939, Jan., 1940.

IOWA IN THE SECOND WORLD WAR

Briggs, John E., *The Lure of Hope*, Palimpsest, 24: 267-268, Aug., 1943.

Colton, Kenneth E., *The Sun Rises for Japan*, Annals (3), 29: Part 1, 138-144, Oct., 1947.

Keyes, Charles Rollin, *Iowa and the League of Nations*, Annals (3), 28: 253-286, April, 1947.

Murray, Ray, *Lest We Forget*, Palimpsest, 29: 174-181, June, 1948.

Petersen, William J., *Iowa Editors and the Second World War*, Iowa Journal, 40: 115-152, April, 1942.

Petersen, William J., *Remember Pearl Harbor*, Palimpsest, 23: 33-46, Feb., 1942.

Petersen, William J., *The Battleship IOWA*, Palimpsest, 33: 65-96, March, 1952.

Swisher, Jacob A., *Remember Our Heroes*, Palimpsest, 23: 189-203, June, 1942.

Williams, Ora, *Iowa Fighting Power Afloat*, Annals (3), 24: Part 1, 195-199, Jan., 1943.

Williams, Ora, *Iowa Navy Afloat*, Annals (3), 27: 236-243, Jan., 1946.

Williams, Ora, *Iowans Honored in Naming Vessels*, Annals (3), 26: 55-60, July, 1944.

Education in Iowa

SCHOOLS AND EDUCATION IN EARLY IOWA

Aurner, Clarence R., *History of Education in Iowa*. 5 vols. SHSI. 1914-1920.

Aurner, Clarence R., *Mechanics' Institutions*, Iowa Journal, 19: 389-413, July, 1921.

Aurner, Clarence R., *Some Early Educational Leaders in Iowa*, Iowa Journal, 22: 532-568, Oct., 1924.

Barnhart, Cornelia Mallett, *Phoebe W. Sudlow*, Palimpsest, 28: 25-32, Jan., 1947.

Briggs, John E., *Iowa Old and New*, 389-420. University Publishing Co., Lincoln, Nebr. 1939.

Brigham, Johnson, *James Harlan*, 35-78. SHSI. 1913.

Brown, Harriet Connor, *Schoolday Memories*, Palimpsest, 30: 107-124, April, 1949.

Buffum, Hugh S., *Federal and State Aid to Education in Iowa*, Iowa Journal, 4: 554-598, Oct., 1906; 5: 3-45, 147-192, 311-325, Jan., April, July, 1907. Reprinted by the State University of Iowa.

Emhoff, Floy L., *A Pioneer School Teacher in Central Iowa: Alice Money Lawrence*, Iowa Journal, 33: 376-395, Oct., 1935.

Faville, F. F., and Albert M. Deyoe, *In Commemoration of Hon. Richard C. Barrett*, Annals (3), 12: 165-177, Oct., 1915.

Fulton, Charles J., *The Beginnings of Education in Iowa*, Iowa Journal, 23: 171-191, April, 1925.

Grahame, Orville F., *The First Iowa School*, Palimpsest, 5: 401-407, Nov., 1924.

Hawley, Charles A., *Excelsior*, Palimpsest, 16: 189-198, June, 1935.

Hilmer, Gertrude, *An Apostle of Free Education*, Palimpsest, 29: 49-63, Feb., 1948.

Hoeltje, Hubert H., *The Means of Education*, Palimpsest, 8: 34-37, Jan., 1927.

Hoeltje, Hubert H., *The Means of Education*, Palimpsest, 32, 34-37, Jan., 1951.

Huftalen, Sarah Gillespie, *School Days of the Seventies*, Palimpsest, 28: 122-128, April, 1947.

Jennings, Rosa Schreurs, *The Country School Teacher*, Annals (3), 31: 41-62, July, 1951.

Klingaman, O. E., *The Guthrie County High School*, Annals (3), 21: 119-126, Oct., 1937.

Logan, Lawrence A., *History of the Guthrie County High School*, Annals (3), 21: 83-118, Oct., 1937.

Olmstead, Agnes Briggs, *Recollections of a Pioneer Teacher of Hamilton County*, Annals (3), 28: 93-115, Oct., 1946.

Parker, Leonard F., *Teachers in Iowa Before 1858*, Iowa Historical Lectures, 1894, 27-69. SHSI.

Parvin, Theodore S., *Dr. Berryman Jennings, Iowa-Oregon*, Historical Record, 6: 385-391, Jan., 1890.

Parvin, Theodore S., *The Early Schools and Teachers of Iowa*, Annals (3), 3: 445-449, April-July, 1898.

Parvin, Theodore S., *Early Schools in Iowa*, Annals (2), 3: 3-16, Jan., 1884.

Parvin, Theodore S., *The Iowa School System*, Historical Record, 5: 249-255, April, 1889.

Parvin, Theodore S., *Thomas Hart Benton, Jr.*, Historical Record, 16: 1-14, Jan., 1900.

Parvin, Theodore S., *Who Taught "The First School in Iowa, and When and Where?"*, Historical Record, 5: 201-212, Jan., 1889.

Petersen, William J., *The Story of Iowa*, 2: 845-868. Lewis Historical Co.. New York. 1952.

Phillips, Mrs. T. G., *Mahaska County's First School*, Annals (3), 3: 213-219, Oct., 1897.

Pickard, Josiah L., *Pioneer Schools of the Northwest*, Historical Record, 14: 227-236, Jan., 1898.

Plaehn, Erma B., *Taxes Underwrite Education*, Palimpsest, 27: 86-96, March, 1946.

Seashore, Carl E., *The District School*, Palimpsest, 23: 99-110, March, 1942.

Street, John Purcell, *Iowa Department of Public Instruction*, Annals (3), 30: 397-452, Oct., 1950.

Swisher, Jacob A., *A Century of School Legislation in Iowa*, Iowa Journal, 44: 174-204, April, 1946.

Swisher, Jacob A., *Grant's Des Moines Speech*, Palimpsest, 6: 409-421, Dec., 1925.

Swisher, Jacob A., *Iowa Schools in 1846*, Palimpsest, 27: 65-74, March, 1946.

Swisher, Jacob A., *Public School Beginnings*, Palimpsest, 20: 281-294, Sept., 1939.

Swisher, Jacob A., *The Rise of Education*, Palimpsest, 16: 137-166, May, 1935.

Teakle, Thomas, *The Defalcation of Superintendent James D. Eads*, Iowa Journal, 12: 205-244, April, 1914.

Tjernagel, N., *The Sheldall School*, Palimpsest, 12: 359-369, Sept., 1931.

Younger, Edward, *The Education of John A. Kasson*, Iowa Journal, 49: 289-310, Oct., 1951.

Material may also be found in the official reports of the State Superintendent of Public Instruction, and in county histories.

Courses of Study

Aurner, Clarence R., *Courses of Study*, Palimpsest, 11: 446-461, Oct., 1930.

Aurner, Clarence R., *Historical Survey of Civic Instruction and Training for Citizenship in Iowa*, Iowa Journal, 17: 135-222, April, 1919.

Aurner, Clarence R., *History of Education in Iowa*, 1: 343-364; 2: 274-288; 3: 279-380. SHSI. 1914, 1915.

Chase, Charles P., *A Half Century of Engineering*, Palimpsest, 28: 310-320, Oct., 1947.

Cooper, Frank B., *Current Movements in Elementary Education*, Midland Monthly, 5: 67-75, Jan., 1896.

Donovan, Josephine, *School Books of Sarah Gillespie*, Palimpsest, 28: 113-121, April, 1947.

Gallaher, Ruth A., *From Digits to Centennials*, Palimpsest, 27: 30-32, Jan., 1946.

James, Edmund J., *State History in the Public High Schools*, Iowa Journal 1: 153-164, April, 1903.

Klingaman, O. E., *Text-book Legislation in Iowa*, Iowa Journal, 13: 53-113, Jan., 1915.

Higher Education

Abernethy, Alonzo, *History of Iowa Baptist Schools*. Alonzo Abernethy, Osage, Iowa. 1907.

Aurner, Clarence R., *The Founding of Iowa College*, Palimpsest, 25: 65-76, March, 1944.

Aurner, Clarence R., *History of Education in Iowa*, 3, 4. SHSI. 1915, 1916.

Aurner, Clarence R., *Many Foundations*, Palimpsest, 11: 417-431, Oct., 1930.

Aurner, Clarence R., *Mechanics' Institutions*, Iowa Journal, 19: 389-413, July, 1921.

Clark, Dan E., *John A. Nash and the Early History of Des Moines College*, Iowa Journal, 13: 392-415, July, 1915.

Clayton, Ben F., *The "Athens" of Iowa Methodism* [Simpson], Midland Monthly, 4: 80-87, July, 1895.

Cruikshank, C. W., *Denmark Academy as I Knew It*, Iowa Journal, 38: 182-202, April, 1940.

Ensign, Forest C., *The Era of Private Academies*, Palimpsest, 27: 75-85, March, 1946.

Farquhar, Catharine Grace Barbour, *Tabor and Tabor College*, Iowa Journal, 41: 337-393, Oct., 1943.

Ferguson, William R., *Life of Lenox College*, Palimpsest, 28: 257-288, Sept., 1947.

Flude, Alfred L., *A Typical Western College* [Lenox], Midland Monthly, 2: 93-98, Aug., 1894.

Galer, R. S., *The Old Mill* [Howe's Academy], Palimpsest, 12: 381-401, Oct., 1931.

Grahame, Pauline P., *The Normal Academy of Music*, Palimpsest, 10: 328-340, Sept., 1929.

Hoffmann, M. M., *St. Raphael's Seminary*, Palimpsest, 20: 196-206, June, 1939.

Kerr, Robert Y., *The Wittemberg Manual Labor College*, Iowa Journal, 24: 290-304, April, 1926.

Ludwig, Mary Culbertson, *Take a Letter*, Palimpsest, 29: 87-96, March, 1948.

Macbride, Thomas H., *The College of the Pioneer*, Palimpsest, 16: 174-188, June, 1935.

Millsap, Kenneth F., *Parsons College*, Palimpsest, 31: 281-328, Aug., 1950.

Parker, Leonard F., *Higher Education in Iowa*. Government Printing Office, Washington. 1893.

Perry, Theodore B., *The Iowa Board of Education*, Annals (3), 3: 200-207, Oct., 1897.

Petersen, William J., *The Story of Iowa*, 2: 869-902. Lewis Historical Co., New York. 1952.

Quinton, Mrs. Harlan B., *Early Denmark and Denmark Academy*, Annals (3), 7: 1-15, April, 1905.

Starbuck, Winifred, *The Scattergood Seminary*, Palimpsest, 9: 256-262, July, 1928.

Tweito, Thomas E., *A College in a Cornfield* [Morningside], Palimpsest. 25: 340-352, Nov., 1944.

White, Ed. S., *Elk Horn College*, Midland Monthly, 2: 461-462, Dec., 1894.

Wilson, Ben H., *Iowa Wesleyan College*, Palimpsest, 11: 432-445, Oct., 1930.

Wright, D. Sands, *Whittier College Days*, Palimpsest, 10: 421-431, Dec., 1929.

STATE UNIVERSITY OF IOWA

Aurner, Clarence R., *History of Education in Iowa*, 4, 3-190. SHSI. 1916.

Barnhart, Cornelia Mallett, *Old Gold*, Palimpsest, 28: 144-149, May, 1947.

Bates, Katherine V., *Old South Hall*, Palimpsest, 29: 97-110, April, 1948.

Cowperthwaite, Lowery LeRoy, *Forensics at the State University 1860-1924*, Iowa Journal, 46: 266-295, July, 1948.

Dill, Homer R., *The University Museum of Natural History*, Palimpsest, 33: 33-64, Feb., 1952.

For Harrison and Reid, Palimpsest, 13: 239-258, June, 1932.

Haefner, Marie, *A President for the University*, Palimpsest, 15: 129-138, April, 1934.

Irish, John P., *The Origin of the Law College of the State University of Iowa*, Iowa Journal, 8: 553-557, Oct., 1910.

Irish, John P., *Some Episodes in the History of the Founding of the Medical College of the State University of Iowa*, Iowa Journal, 18: 125-129, Jan., 1920.

Macbride, Thomas Huston, Palimpsest, 15: 161-190, May, 1934.

Patrick, George T. W., *Founding the Psychological Laboratory at the State University of Iowa*, Iowa Journal, 30: 404-416, July, 1932.

Petersen, William J., *The Story of Iowa*, 2: 903-913. Lewis Historical Co., New York. 1952.

Pickard, Josiah L., *Historical Sketch of the State University of Iowa*, Annals (3), 4: 1-66, April, 1899.

Rich, Ellen M., *State University of Iowa and the Civil War*, Historical Record, 15: 395-408, Jan., 1899.

Rockwood, Alan C., *A History of the Military Department of the State University of Iowa*, Iowa Journal, 21: 183-312, April, 1923.

Rohbach, James A., *Alumni of the State University of Iowa in Public Life*, Historical Record, 11: 259-281, April, 1895.

State University of Iowa, The, Midland Monthly, 1: 177-186, Feb., 1894.

Swisher, Jacob A., *Charles Ashmead Schaeffer*, Palimpsest, 28: 49-62, Feb., 1947.

Swisher, Jacob A., *The Cradle of the University*, Palimpsest, 28: 129-143, May, 1947.

Swisher, Jacob A., *Three Deans and a College*, Palimpsest, 30: 65-71, March, 1949.

Thornton, Harrison John, *Coeducation at the State University of Iowa*, Iowa Journal, 45: 380-412, Oct., 1947.

Thornton, Harrison John, *Locating the State University of Iowa*, Iowa Journal, 47: 50-62, Jan., 1949.

Thornton, Harrison John, *A State University is Born*, Palimpsest, 28: 33-48, Feb., 1947.

Thornton, Harrison John, *The State University of Iowa and the Civil War*, Annals (3), 30: 198-209, Jan., 1950.

IOWA STATE COLLEGE

Aurner, Clarence R., *History of Education in Iowa*, 4: 193-311. SHSI. 1916.

Burke, Tom, *Student Life at Ames*, Midland Monthly, 1: 269-283, March, 1894.

Moore, W. S., *Agriculture and the Mechanic Arts*, Midland Monthly, 6: 241-256, Sept., 1896.

Morgan, Barton A., *A History of the Extension Service of Iowa State College*. Iowa State College Press, Ames. 1934.

Mott, David C., *William Duane Wilson*, Annals (3), 20: 361-374, July, 1936.

Petersen, William J., *J. Brownlee Davidson*, Palimpsest, 31: 77-78, March, 1950.

Petersen, William J., *The Story of Iowa*, 2: 907-909. Lewis Historical Co., New York. 1952.

Ross, Earle D., *Democracy's College*. Iowa State College Press, Ames. 1942.

IOWA STATE TEACHERS COLLEGE

Aurner, Clarence R., *History of Education in Iowa*, 4: 315-381. SHSI. 1916.

Hearst, Gladys Whitley, *The WAVES at Cedar Falls*, Palimpsest, 28: 367-380, Dec., 1947.

Riggs, Sara M., *Iowa State Normal School*, Midland Monthly, 4:524-532, Dec., 1895.

Wright, D. Sands, *Iowa State Normal School*, Palimpsest, 13: 1-35, Jan., 1932.

Cornell College

Cornell College: Fiftieth Anniversary 1853-1903. Cornell College, Mount Vernon. 1904.

Crary, Bessie J., *Cornell College, Mount Vernon, Iowa*, Midland Monthly, 9: 129-144, February, 1898.

Crawford, Bartholow V., *The Cornell Music Festival*, Palimpsest, 11: 107-112, March, 1930.

Grahame, Pauline P., *Elder Bowman*, Palimpsest, 17: 37-48, Feb., 1936.

Tull, Clyde, and Anya Plummer, *Stories from the Husk*. English Club of Cornell College, Mount Vernon, Iowa. 1940.

Williams, Ora, *College Student and Soldier Boy*, Annals (3), 26: 45-54, July, 1944.

Drake University

Blanchard, Charles, *Building for the Centuries*. Drake University, Des Moines. 1931.

Carpenter, Mary A., *Drake University*, Midland Monthly, 9: 353-368, April, 1898.

Herriott, Frank I., *Alfred John Pearson, An Appreciation, Professor of German Language and Literature, 1907-1939*, Annals (3), 22: 515-542, Jan., 1941.

Herriott, Frank I., *Norman Dunshee: Professor of Ancient Languages, 1881-1890*, Annals (3), 20: 163-206, 253-296, Jan., April, 1936.

Herriott, Frank I., *Roland Ellsworth Conklin: Professor of Botany and Geology, 1907-1929*, Annals (3), 21: 403-439, Oct., 1938.

Herriott, Frank I., *William Stebbins Barnard: Professor of Biology, 1886-1887*, Annals (3), 20: 323-359, July, 1936.

Wilson, Ben H., *Daniel Walter Morehouse*, Palimpsest, 23: 337-369, Nov., 1942.

Grinnell College

Hill, James L., *Iowa College in the War*, Historical Record, 15: 408-419, Jan., 1899.

McCowan, Hervy S., *Iowa College, Grinnell*, Midland Monthly, 1: 492-501, May, 1894.

Mahan, Bruce E., *The First Iowa Field Day*, Palimpsest, 4: 137-150, May, 1923.

Morris, Helen B., and Emeline B. Bartlett, *The Social Life of a Girl in Iowa College*, Midland Monthly, 9: 449-456, May, 1898.

Parker, Leonard F., *The Founders of Iowa College*, Historical Record, 14: 360-375, Oct., 1898.

Payne, Charles E., *Josiah Bushnell Grinnell*. SHSI. 1938.
Swisher, Jacob A., *Leonard Fletcher Parker*, 78-88, 154-176. SHSI. 1927.

SOME EDUCATIONAL LEADERS OF IOWA

Aurner, Clarence R., *Some Early Educational Leaders in Iowa*, Iowa Journal, 22: 532-568, Oct., 1924.

Barnhart, Cornelia Mallett, *Phoebe W. Sudlow*, Palimpsest, 28: 25-32, Jan., 1947.

Berryhill, Virginia J., *Amos Noyes Currier*, Annals (3), 10: 90-118, July, 1911.

Clark, Dan E., *John A. Nash and the Early History of Des Moines College*, Iowa Journal, 13: 392-415, July, 1915.

Clarkson, Anna H., *A Beautiful Life—A Biographical Sketch* (Mrs. Druscilla Allen Stoddard), Annals (3), 11: 188-199, July-Oct., 1913.

Dean, Amos H., *Amos Dean*, Historical Record, 11: 241-257, April, 1895.

Galer, Roger S., *Seward C. Howe An Individualist in Education*, Iowa Journal, 41: 69-84, Jan., 1943.

Haefner, Marie, *An American Lady* [Kate Harrington], Palimpsest, 12: 169-178, May, 1931.

Herriott, Frank I., *Alfred John Pearson, An Appreciation, Professor of German Language and Literature, Drake University, 1907-1939*, Annals (3), 22: 515-542, Jan., 1941.

Herriott, Frank I., *Norman Dunshee: Professor of Ancient Languages, Drake University, 1881-1890*, Annals (3), 20: 163-206, 253-296, Jan., April, 1936.

Herriott, Frank I., *William Stebbins Barnard: Professor of Biology, Drake University, 1886-1887*, Annals (3), 20: 323-359, July, 1936.

Herriott, Frank I., *Roland Ellsworth Conklin: Professor of Botany and Geology, Drake University, 1907-1929*, Annals (3), 21: 403-439, Oct., 1938.

Hilmer, Gertrude, *An Apostle of Free Education*, Palimpsest, 29: 49-63, Feb., 1948.

Hurlburt, Rollo F., *William Fletcher King*, Annals (3), 9: 484-492, July-Oct., 1910.

Loos, Isaac A., *William Miller Beardshear*, Historical Record, 18: 553-586, Oct., 1902.

Macbride, Thomas Huston, Palimpsest, 15: 161-192, May, 1934.

Parvin, Theodore S., *Thomas Hart Benton, Jr.*, Historical Record, 16: 1-14, Jan., 1900.

Springer, John, *Charles Ashmead Schaeffer*, Historical Record, 15: 433-448, April, 1899.

Swisher, Jacob A., *Charles Ashmead Schaeffer*, Palimpsest, 28: 49-62, Feb., 1947.

Watson, Samuel N., *Silas Totten*, Historical Record, 11: 337-341, Oct., 1895.

Wilson, Ben H., *Daniel Walter Morehouse*, Palimpsest, 23: 337-369, Nov., 1942.

Wilson, James F., *Christian W. Slagle,* Historical Record, 3: 529-543, Oct., 1887.

Wright, D. Sands, *James Cleland Gilchrist,* Palimpsest, 13: 6-16, Jan., 1932.

Wright, D. Sands, *Moses Willard Bartlett,* Palimpsest, 13: 25-35, Jan., 1932.

LIBRARIES

Brigham, Johnson, *Pioneer History of the Territorial and State Library of Iowa,* Annals (3), 10: 481-538, 590-628, Oct., 1912, Jan., 1913.

Dahlberg, Charles L., *Biography of Hon. Charles John Alfred Ericson,* Annals (3), 11: 16-31, April, 1913.

Gingerich, Melvin, *The Henry County Institute of Science,* Palimpsest, 22: 33-64, Feb., 1941.

Iowa Masonic Library, Historical Record, 13: 134-141, July, 1897.

McGuire, Letha P., *A Study of the Public Library Movement in Iowa,* Iowa Journal, 35: 22-72, Jan., 1937.

Petersen, William J., *The Story of Iowa,* 2: 914-922. Lewis Historical Co., New York. 1952.

Stevenson, S. K., *School Libraries,* Midland Monthly, 6: 130-135, Aug., 1896.

Wright, Luella M., *Iowa's Oldest Library,* Iowa Journal, 38: 408-428, Oct., 1940.

Wright, Luella M., *Johnson Brigham—Librarian,* Palimpsest, 33: 225-256, Aug., 1952.

LECTURERS IN IOWA

Braden, Waldo W., *Iowa Reaction to Wendell Phillips, 1867,* Iowa Journal, 50: 35-46, Jan., 1952.

Briggs, John E., *When Barnum Came to Iowa,* Palimpsest, 8: 407-413, Dec., 1927.

Hoeltje, Hubert H., *Emerson at Davenport,* Palimpsest, 7: 265-276, Sept., 1926.

Hoeltje, Hubert H., *"Nincompoopiana"* [Oscar Wilde], Palimpsest, 18: 177-212, June, 1937.

Hoeltje, Hubert H., *Notes on the History of Lecturing in Iowa 1855-1885,* Iowa Journal, 25: 62-131, Jan., 1927.

Hoeltje, Hubert H., *Ralph Waldo Emerson in Iowa,* Iowa Journal, 25: 236-276, April, 1927.

Hoeltje, Hubert H., *Some Iowa Lectures and Conversations of Amos Bronson Alcott,* Iowa Journal, 29: 375-401, July, 1931.

Lorch, Fred W., *Lecture Trips and Visits of Mark Twain in Iowa,* Iowa Journal, 27: 507-547, Oct., 1929.

Lorch, Fred F., *Mark Twain in Iowa,* Iowa Journal, 27: 408-456, July, 1929.

Lorch, Fred W., *A Mark Twain Letter,* Iowa Journal, 28: 268-276, April, 1930.

Schmidt, G. Perle, *A Magic Lantern Lecture,* Palimpsest, 26: 110-118, April, 1945.

Wilson, Ben H., *Ian Maclaren,* Palimpsest, 12: 273-286, July, 1931.
Wright, Luella M., *Culture Through Lectures,* Iowa Journal, 38: 115-162, April, 1940.

SCIENCE

Clarke, J. Fred., *Reminiscences of the Agassiz Association in Iowa with Special Reference to the Fairfield Chapter,* Iowa Journal, 39: 286-315, July, 1941.

Crosby, James O., *Scientific Studies of Dr. Asa Horr,* Annals (3), 12: 161-164, Oct., 1915.

Gingerich, Melvin, *The Henry County Institute of Science,* Palimpsest, 22: 33-64, Feb., 1941.

Hall, Reeves, *Artic Exploration,* Palimpsest, 25: 33-49, Feb., 1944.

Keyes, Charles Rollin, *An Epoch in the History of American Science,* Annals (3), 2: 345-364, April, 1896.

Keyes, Charles Rollin, *An Iowa Scientist and His Work,* Annals (3), 4: 383-392, April, 1900.

Keyes, Charles Rollin, *Scientific Achievements of Frank Springer,* Annals (3), 16: 505-515, Jan., 1929.

Reed, Charles D., *George Washington Carver, Mystic Scientist,* Annals (3), 24: Part 1, 248-253, Jan., 1943.

Reed, Charles D., *A Half Century of Service* (Tribute to Life of David E. Hadden), Annals (3), 25: 229-230, Jan., 1944.

Swisher, Jacob A., *The Iowa Academy of Science,* Iowa Journal, 29: 315-374, July, 1931.

Swisher, Jacob A., *A Scientific Tour,* Palimpsest, 14: 396-403, Nov., 1933.

Taylor, Wilson L., *Charles Cleveland Nutting,* Palimpsest, 24: 269-300, Sept., 1943.

Teeters, Wilber J., *Science Fights Crime,* Palimpsest, 30: 79-92, March, 1949.

White, Charles A., *Biographical Memoir of Charles Christopher Parry,* Annals (3), 7: 413-430, July, 1906.

Wilson, Ben H., *Daniel Walter Morehouse,* Palimpsest, 23: 337-369, Nov., 1942.

Wilson, Ben H., *David E. Hadden,* Palimpsest, 25: 256-288, Sept., 1944.

Wylie, Charles C., *Gustavus Detlef Hinrichs,* Palimpsest, 11: 193-201, May, 1930.

Wylie, Robert B., *The Scholar* (T. H. Macbride), Palimpsest, 15: 173-182, May, 1934.

SOCIETIES FOR THE PROMOTION OF LEARNING

Aurner, Clarence R., *History of Education in Iowa,* 2: 189-252. SHSI. 1914.

Baconian Club of Iowa City, The, Iowa Journal, 9: 57-113, Jan., 1911.

Braden, Waldo W., *College Oratory in the Nineties,* Palimpsest, 28: 343-349, Nov., 1947.

Cowperthwaite, Lowery LeRoy, *Forensics at the State University 1860-1924,* Iowa Journal, 46: 266-295, July, 1948.

Gingerich, Melvin, *The Henry County Institute of Science*, Palimpsest, 22: 33-64, Feb., 1941.

For Harrison and Reid (Zetagathian Literary Society), Palimpsest, 13: 239-258, June, 1932.

Horack, Frank E., *A Brief History of the Political Science Club 1896-1906*, Iowa Journal, 5: 213-233, April, 1907.

Iowa Congress of Parents and Teachers, Palimpsest, 31: 425-464, Nov., 1950.

Lovell, Miriam Fay, *The Monticello Friday Club*, Palimpsest, 24: 59-70, Feb., 1943.

Lyon, Bessie L., *The Webster City Lyceum*, Palimpsest, 15: 267-274, Aug., 1934.

Swisher, Jacob A., *The Iowa Academy of Science*, Palimpsest, 11: 202-213, May, 1930.

Swisher, Jacob A., *The Iowa Academy of Science*, Iowa Journal, 29: 315-374, July, 1931.

Religion in Iowa

RELIGION AND MORALITY

Barnhart, Cornelia Mallett, *Church Foundations in Iowa*, Palimpsest, 27: 97-115, April, 1946.

Collins, Hubert E., *The Story of Mahlon Day Collins*, Iowa Journal, 28: 55-131, Jan., 1930.

Gallaher, Ruth A., *Religion and Morality*, Palimpsest, 8: 28-33, Jan., 1927.

Gallaher, Ruth A., *Religion and Morality*, Palimpsest, 32: 28-33, Jan., 1951.

Harvey, R. E., *Faith and Works in the Black Hawk Purchase*, Annals (3), 21: 241-282, April, 1938.

Herriott, Frank I., *Regulation of Trade and Morals by Iowa Town Councils Prior to 1858*, Annals (3), 5: 126-134, July, 1901.

Macbride, Thomas H., *In Cabins and Sod-Houses*, 21-33, 105-120, 171-179. SHSI. 1928.

McCarty, Dwight G., *Early Social and Religious Experiments in Iowa*. SHSI. 1902. Reprinted from the Historical Record, 18: 407-437, Jan., 1902.

Petersen, William J., *Religion and Morality*, Palimpsest, 19: 215-229, June, 1938.

Petersen, William J., *The Story of Iowa*, 2: 661-755. Lewis Historical Co., New York. 1952.

Richman, Irving B., *Ioway to Iowa*, 285-314. SHSI. 1931.

Two Burlington Churches Occupied, Annals (3), 29: 473-476, Oct., 1948.

PROTESTANT CHURCHES — MISCELLANEOUS

Briggs, John E., *Iowa Old and New*, 421-456. University Publishing Co., Lincoln, Nebr. 1939.

Co-operative Christianity, Historical Record, 5: 212-222, Jan., 1889.

Duffield, George C., *Frontier Church Going—1837*, Annals (3), 6: 266-275, Jan., 1904.

Early Clergy of Iowa, The, Iowa Historical Lectures, 1894, 100-135. SHSI.

Gallaher, Ruth A., *Religion and Morality,* Palimpsest, 8: 28-33, Jan., 1927.

Goodykoontz, Colin B., *Home Missions on the American Frontier.* Caxton Printers, Caldwell, Idaho. 1939.

Harvey, R. E., *Faith and Works in the Black Hawk Purchase,* Annals (3), 21: 241-282, April, 1938.

Harvey, R. E., *The Local Preacher,* Annals (3), 22: 54-63, July, 1939.

Hawley, Charles A., *A Communistic Swedenborgian Colony in Iowa,* Iowa Journal, 33: 3-26, Jan., 1935.

Hawley, Charles A., *Excelsior,* Palimpsest, 16: 189-198, June, 1935.

Judd, Francis E., *Establishment of the Diocese of Iowa, Protestant Episcopal Church of America,* Annals (3), 11: 291-303, Jan., 1914.

Kuhns, Frederick I., *The Evangelical and Reformed Church in Iowa,* Palimpsest, 33: 161-192, June, 1952.

Meredith, Mabel M., *Early Iowa Camp-Meetings,* Palimpsest, 8: 164-168, May, 1927.

Mohler, John E., *The Dunkers in Iowa,* Annals (3), 7: 270-282, Jan., 1906.

Ogburn, Cal., *The Pioneer Religious Revival,* Annals (3), 15: 483-506, Jan., 1927.

Petersen, William J., *Religion and Morality,* Palimpsest, 19: 215-229, June, 1938.

Snyder, Charles E., *Unitarianism in Iowa,* Palimpsest, 30: 345-376, Nov., 1949.

Tucker, Elva L., *The History of the Universalist Church in Iowa: 1843-1943.* M.A. Thesis, State University of Iowa, 1944.

THE BAPTIST CHURCH

Abernethy, Alonzo, *History of Iowa Baptist Schools,* Alonzo Abernethy, Osage, Iowa. 1907.

Ahlstrom, L. J., *Eighty Years of Swedish Baptist Work in Iowa: 1853-1933.* Swedish Baptist Conference of Iowa, Des Moines. 1933.

Gallaher, Ruth A., *An Adventure in Faith,* Palimpsest, 13: 93-105, March, 1932.

Haefner, Marie, *Called to Iowa,* Palimpsest, 15: 193-206, June, 1934.

Mitchell, G. P., *A Century of Iowa Baptist History: 1834-1934.* Baptist Record, Pella, Iowa. 1934.

Mitchell, S. H., *Historical Sketches of Iowa Baptists.* Burdette Company, Burlington, Iowa. 1886.

Petersen, William J., *The Story of Iowa,* 2: 689-696. Lewis Historical Co., New York. 1952.

THE CONGREGATIONAL CHURCH

Aurner, Clarence R., *The Founding of Iowa College,* Palimpsest, 25: 65-77, March, 1944.

Christensen, Thomas P., *Denmark—An Early Stronghold of Congregational-ism,* Iowa Journal, 24: 108-143, Jan., 1926.

Cruikshank, C. W., *Denmark Academy as I Knew It,* Iowa Journal, 38: 182-202, April, 1940.

Hawley, Charles A., *Beginnings of Congregationalism in Iowa,* Palimpsest, 18: 1-30, Jan., 1937.

Hawley, Charles A., *Some Aspects of Congregationalism in Relation to the Early Cultural Development of Iowa,* Iowa Journal, 35: 181-205, April, 1937.

Heffner, Joseph S., *History of the Congregational Church of Iowa City,* Iowa Journal, 15: 70-112, Jan., 1917.

Holbrook, John C., *History of the Congregational Church of Dubuque,* Annals (1), 2: 312-320, 362-365, July, Oct., 1864.

Johnson, P. Adelstein, *The First Century of Congregationalism in Iowa, 1840-1940.* Congregational Christian Conference of Iowa, Grinnell, Iowa. 1945.

Jordan, Philip D., *Forty Days with the Christian Commission: A Diary by William Salter,* Iowa Journal, 33: 123-154, April, 1935.

Jordan, Philip D., and I. H. Pierce, *Ozro French,* Palimpsest, 20: 1-30, Jan., 1939.

Jordan, Philip D., *William Salter and the Slavery Controversy,* Iowa Journal, 33: 99-122, April, 1935.

Jordan, Philip D., *William Salter: Western Torchbearer.* Mississippi Valley Press, Oxford, Ohio. 1939.

Kuhns, Frederick I., *Congregational Christians in Iowa,* Palimpsest, 32: 185-216, May, 1951.

Magoun, George F., *First Congregational Church of Lyons, Iowa,* Annals (1), 3: 544-558, Oct., 1865.

Magoun, George F., *Asa Turner: A Home Missionary Patriarch and His Times.* Congregational Sunday School and Publishing Society, Boston. 1889.

Petersen, William J., *The Story of Iowa,* 2: 679-689. Lewis Historical Co., New York. 1952.

Quinton, Mrs. H. B., *Early Denmark and Denmark Academy,* Annals (3), 7: 1-15, April, 1905.

Reed, Julius A., *Reminiscences of Early Congregationalism in Iowa.* Grinnell, Iowa. 1885.

Richman, Irving B., *Congregational Life in Muscatine, 1843-1893,* Iowa Journal, 21: 347-372, July, 1923.

THE LUTHERAN CHURCH

Christensen, Thomas P., *Frederik Lange Grundtvig,* Annals (3), 25: 105-112, Oct., 1943.

Deindörfer, Johannes, *Geschichte der Evangel.-Luth. Synode von Iowa und Anderen Staaten.* Wartburg Publishing House, Chicago. 1897.

Flentje, Henry, A. B. Leamer, N. G. Peterson, and J. A. Anderson, *Lutherans in Iowa,* Annals (3), 11: 585-593, Jan., 1915.

McIntosh, Lois A., *Biography of a Church*, Palimpsest, 29: 129-144, May, 1948.

Petersen, William J., *The Story of Iowa*, 2: 718-724. Lewis Historical Co., New York. 1952.

White, Ed. S., *Elk Horn College*, Midland Monthly, 2: 461-462, Dec., 1894.

Wick, B. L., *Early Cedar Rapids Swedish Churches*, Annals (3), 29: 468-472, Oct., 1948.

Wuerffel, L. C., *The Lutheran Church—Missouri Synod*, Palimpsest, 29: 321-352, Nov., 1948.

THE METHODIST CHURCH

Die Nordwest Deutsche Konferenz der Bischöfflichen Methodistenkirche. Charles City, Iowa. 1913. Prepared by a committee composed of E. W. Henke, W. H. Rolfing, Friedrich Schaub, L. J. Brenner, J. F. Hartke.

Gallaher, Ruth A., *The First Church in Iowa*, Palimpsest, 7: 1-10, Jan., 1926.

Gallaher, Ruth A., *The Methodist Episcopal Church of Iowa City*, Iowa Journal, 37: 379-422, Oct., 1939.

Gallaher, Ruth A., *Methodists in Conference*, Palimpsest, 25: 225-233, Aug., 1944.

Gallaher, Ruth A., *The Methodists in Iowa*, Palimpsest, 32: 57-120, Feb., 1951.

Grahame, Pauline P., *Elder Bowman*, Palimpsest, 17: 37-48, Feb., 1936.

Harvey, R. E., *Broadened Layman Activity in M. E. Church*, Annals (3), 29: 197-240, Jan., 1948.

Harvey, R. E., *Des Moines M. E. Conference Growth*, Annals (3), 25: 282-312, April, 1944.

Harvey, R. E., *Des Moines Conference Reduces Area*, Annals (3), 28: 287-329, April, 1947.

Harvey, R. E., *Hail and Farewell! The Methodist Protestant Church in Iowa*, Annals (3), 24: 59-81, July, 1942.

Harvey, R. E., *Hail and Farewell! The Methodist Protestant Church in Iowa* (concluded), Annals (3), 24: 168-189, Oct., 1942.

Harvey, R. E., *Imperial Expansion of M. E. Church*, Annals (3), 27: 119-150, Oct., 1945.

Harvey, R. E., *Reopening a Closed Chapter* (Historical Sketch of the Des Moines Conference of the M. E. Church, 1832-1860), Annals (3), 25: 192-228, Jan., 1944.

Harvey, R. E., *In Memoriam: Rev. John H. Ruble*, Annals (3), 20: 297-303, April, 1936.

Harvey, R. E., *War Years of Des Moines M. E. Conference*, Annals (3), 27: 44-61, July, 1945.

Lunt, Belle Waldrip, *Isaac Waldrip, Circuit Rider*, Annals (3), 27: 220-235, Jan., 1946.

Mitchell, Bennett, *History of the Northwest Iowa Conference: 1872-1903*. Perkins Bros., Sioux City. 1904.

Petersen, William J., *The Story of Iowa*, 2: 668-679. Lewis Historical Co., New York. 1952.

Proceedings of M. E. Conference, *Portrait of an Iowa Bishop—Unveiling and Presentation to the State*, Annals (3), 77-89, Oct., 1944.

Richards, W. Avery, *Early Methodism in Northwest Iowa*, Historical Record, 11: 296-308, July, 1895.

Schmidt, G. Perle, *Mount Hope Church*, Palimpsest, 12: 454-462, Dec., 1931.

Swisher, Jacob A., *Old Zion Church*, Palimpsest, 13: 274-284, July, 1932.

Taylor, Landon, *Pioneer Ministry*, Palimpsest, 25: 1-32, Jan., 1944.

Tweito, Thomas E., *A College in a Cornfield* [Morningside], Palimpsest, 25: 340-352, Nov., 1944.

Waring, Edmund H., *History of the Iowa Annual Conference of the Methodist Episcopal Church.*

Waring, Edmund H., *Old Zion Church, Burlington, Iowa*, Annals (3), 9: 524-534, July-Oct., 1910.

The Presbyterian Church

Belden, E. L., *History of the First Presbyterian Church of Muscatine, Iowa*, Annals (1), 2: 376-382, Oct., 1864.

Hinkhouse, J. F., *One Hundred Years of the Iowa Presbyterian Church.* Laurance Press Company, Cedar Rapids. 1932.

Hubbard, Joseph W., *The Presbyterian Church in Iowa: 1837-1900.* Superior Press, Cedar Rapids. 1907.

Kuhns, Frederick I., *New Light on the Plan of Union*, Journal of the Presbyterian Historical Society, 26: 19-43, March, 1948.

Kuhns, Frederick I., *The Presbyterians in Iowa*, Palimpsest, 33: 97-128, April, 1952.

Petersen, William J., *The Story of Iowa*, 2: 696-707. Lewis Historical Co., New York. 1952.

Van der Zee, Jacob, *History of Presbyterianism in Iowa City.* Iowa Journal, 13: 529-580, Oct., 1915.

Van der Zee, Jacob, *One Hundred Years of Presbyterianism in Iowa City, Iowa, 1840-1940.* Iowa City Presbyterian Church, Iowa City. 1941.

Some Religious Leaders Among the Protestants

Cheney, J. W., *Rev. Daniel Lane and His Keosauqua Academy*, Annals (3), 12: 283-306, April, 1920.

Clark, Sam M., *Rev. Samuel Clarke*, Annals (3), 1: 454-466, July, 1894.

Douglass, Truman O., *James Edgar Snowden*, Annals (3), 16: 131-135, Oct., 1927.

Gallaher, Ruth A., *Hummer's Bell*, Palimpsest, 3: 155-164, May, 1922.

Grahame, Pauline P., *Elder Bowman*, Palimpsest, 17: 37-48, Feb., 1936.

Haynes, Fred E., *Wilson Seeley Lewis*, Palimpsest, 11: 334-342, Aug., 1930.

Hill, James L., *Dr. Julius A. Reed, A State Builder*, Annals (3), 13: 263-278, April, 1922.

Irish, Chas. W., *Some Pioneer Preachers of Iowa*, Historical Record, 10: 121-127, July, 1894, 12: 553-564, Oct., 1896.

Lloyd, Frederick, *Samuel Storrs Howe,* Historical Record, 12: 515-523, July, 1896.

Lloyd, Frederick, *Samuel Storrs Howe,* Historical Record, 12: 515-523, July, 1896.

Magoun, George F., *An Iowa Missionary Patriarch* (Asa Turner), Annals (3), 3: 53-62, April, 1897.

Parvin, Theodore S., *Rev. Launcelot Graham Bell,* Historical Record, 9: 433-446, April, 1893.

Robeson, George F., *Henry Clay Dean,* Palimpsest, 5: 321-333, Sept., 1924.

Robeson, George F., *John Johns of Webster County,* Palimpsest, 5: 424-430, Nov., 1924.

Salter, William, *Journal of a Missionary in Jackson County, Iowa Territory, 1843-46,* Annals (3), 7: 592-607, Jan., 1907.

Swisher, Jacob A., *Billy Sunday,* Palimpsest, 11: 343-354, Aug., 1930.

THE IOWA BAND

Adams, Ephraim, *The Iowa Band.* Pilgrim Press, Boston. No date.

Adams, Ephraim, *Alden Burrill Robbins,* 51-73. Pilgrim Press, Boston. 1911.

Aurner, Clarence R., *The Founding of Iowa College,* Palimpsest, 25: 65-77, March, 1944.

Douglass, Truman O., *The Pilgrims of Iowa,* 51-73. Pilgrim Press, Boston. 1911.

Gallaher, Ruth A., *The Iowa Band,* Palimpsest, 11: 355-366, Aug., 1930.

Jordan, Philip D., *The Discovery of William Salter's Almanac-Diary,* Annals (3), 17: 466-469, Oct., 1930.

Jordan, Philip D., *William Salter—Philomathian,* Annals (3), 18: 295-312, April, 1932.

Jordan, Philip D., *William Salter's Letters to Mary Ann Mackintire, 1845-1846,* Annals (3), 19: 243-266, 363-383, 449-469, April, July, Oct., 1934.

Jordan, Philip D., *William Salter's Letters to Mary Ann Mackintire, 1845-1846,* Annals (3), 24: Part 2, 103-185, Jan., 1943.

Jordan, Philip D., *William Salter's "My Ministry in Iowa: 1843-1846",* Annals (3), 19: 539-553, 592-613, Jan., April, 1935; 20: 26-49, July, 1935.

Jordan, Philip D., *William Salter's "My Ministry in Iowa 1843-1846",* Annals (3), 24: Part 2, 1-102, Jan., 1943.

Magoun, George F., *The "Iowa Band" of 1843,* Annals (3), 1: 525-531, Oct., 1894.

THE LITTLE BROWN CHURCH

Brown, H. Clark, *Bradford—A Prairie Village,* Palimpsest, 2: 65-71, March, 1921.

Laird, Charlton G., *The Little Brown Church in the Vale,* Palimpsest, 2: 72-79, March, 1921.

Powers, Isabella, "*The Little Brown Church in the Vale*": *Its Author and Its Inspiration,* Annals (3), 12: 101-116, July, 1915.

THE ROMAN CATHOLIC CHURCH

Black, Jean Phyllis, *Mazzuchelli's Memorie,* Palimpsest, 25: 358-366, Dec., 1944.
Colton, Kenneth E., *Father Mazzuchelli's Iowa Mission,* Annals (3), 21: 297-315, April, 1938.
Early Clergy of Iowa, The, Iowa Historical Lectures, 1894, 94-99. SHSI.
Hoffmann, M. M., *The Abbe Pelamourgues,* Palimpsest, 20: 105-113, April, 1939.
Hoffmann, M. M., *Centennial History of the Archdiocese of Dubuque.* Columbia College Press, Dubuque. 1938.
Hoffmann, M. M., *The First Bishop of Iowa,* Palimpsest, 11: 321-333, Aug., 1930.
Hoffmann, M. M., *St. Raphael's Seminary,* Palimpsest, 20: 196-206, June, 1939.
An Iowa Pioneer (Mazzuchelli), Annals (3), 6: 282-288, Jan., 1904.
Kempker, John F., *Catholic Missionaries in the Early and in the Territorial Days of Iowa,* Annals (3), 10: 54-62, April, 1911.
Kempker, John F., *The First Priests in Iowa,* Historical Record, 4: 17-20, Jan., 1888.
Kempker, John F., *Very Rev. J. A. M. Pelamourgues, V. G.,* Annals (3), 6: 115-121, July, 1903.
Lenehan, B. C., *Rt. Rev. Mathias Loras, D. D., First Bishop of Dubuque,* Annals (3), 3: 577-600, Jan., 1899.
Magaret, Helene, *Father De Smet, Pioneer Priest of the Rockies.* Farrar & Rinehart, New York. 1940.
Magaret, Helene, *Father Pierre Jean De Smet,* Palimpsest, 20: 177-190, June, 1939.
Mullin, Frank A., *Father De Smet and the Pottawattamie Indian Mission,* Iowa Journal, 23: 192-216, April, 1925.
Parish, John C., *Father Mazzuchelli,* Palimpsest, 1: 101-110, Oct., 1920.
Petersen, William J., *The Story of Iowa,* 2: 663-668. Lewis Historical Co., New York. 1952.

THE TRAPPIST ABBEY OF NEW MELLERAY

Mahan, Bruce E., *New Melleray,* Palimpsest, 3: 265-309, Sept., 1922.
Perkins, W. R., *History of the Trappist Abbey of New Melleray in Dubuque County, Iowa.* State University of Iowa, Iowa City. 1892.

AMANA

Horack, Bertha M., *Amana Colony,* Midland Monthly, 6: 27-36, July, 1896.
Johnson, Ava, *Communism in Early Days,* Annals (3), 30: 73-75, July, 1949.

Noe, Charles F., A Brief History of the Amana Society, 1714-1900, Iowa
    Journal, 2: 162-187, April, 1904.
Perkins, W. R., and Barthinius L. Wick, History of the Amana Society or
    Community of True Inspiration. State University of Iowa, Iowa City.
    1891.
Shambaugh, Bertha M. H., Amana, Palimpsest, 2: 193-228, July, 1921.
Shambaugh, Bertha M. H., Amana: The Community of True Inspiration.
    SHSI. 1908.
Shambaugh, Bertha M. H., Amana—In Transition, Palimpsest, 17: 149-184,
    May, 1936.
Shambaugh, Bertha M. H., Amana That Was and Amana That Is. SHSI.
    1932.
Shambaugh, Bertha M. H., Amana That Was and Amana That Is, Palimpsest,
    31: 215-248, June, 1950.
Shambaugh, Bertha M. H., Some of the Economic and Industrial Phases of
    the Amana Society or the Community of True Inspiration, Ninth Bi-
    ennial Report of the Iowa Bureau of Labor Statistics, 1899-1900, 498-
    512.
Wick, Barthinius L., Christian Communism in the Mississippi Valley, Mid-
    land Monthly, 6: 337-341, Oct., 1896.

AMISH MENNONITES AND THE CHURCH OF THE BRETHREN

Gingerich, Melvin, Custom Built Coffins, Palimpsest, 24: 384-388, Dec., 1943.
Gingerich, Melvin, The Mennonites in Iowa. SHSI. 1949.
Gingerich, Melvin, Mennonites in Mount Pleasant, Palimpsest, 23: 373-380,
    Dec., 1942.
Ivie, Flora K., The Quest of Peace, Annals (3), 20: 243-252, April, 1936.
Kirkpatrick, Ellis L., The English River Congregation of the Church of the
    Brethren, Iowa Monograph Series, No. 2. SHSI. 1930.
Rodabaugh, Willis P., and A. H. Brower, A History of the Church of the
    Brethren in Southern Iowa. Brethren Publishing House, Elgin, Ill. 1924.
Smith, C. Henry, The Mennonites. Mennonite Book Concern, Berne, Ind.
    1920.
Swartzendruber, J. F., An Amish Migration, Palimpsest, 17: 342-357, Oct.,
    1936.
Wick, Barthinius L., The Amish Mennonites: A Sketch of Their Origin, and
    of Their Settlement in Iowa. SHSI. 1894.

THE MORMONS

Aumann, Francis R., A Minor Prophet in Iowa, Palimpsest, 8: 253-260, July,
    1927.
Bloomer, David C., The Mormons in Iowa, Annals (3), 2: 586-602, Jan.,
    1897.
First Mormon Handcart Trip Across Iowa, Annals (3), 20: 444-449, Oct.,
    1936.

Gallaher, Ruth A., *The Handcart Expeditions*, Palimpsest, 3: 214-226, July, 1922.

Harvey, R. E., *Mormon Trek Across Iowa*, Annals (3), 28: 36-60, July, 1946.

Kane, Thomas L., *The Mormons*. King & Baird, Philadelphia. 1850.

Lesan, Harry, *Anti-Polygamy Mormonism*, Midland Monthly, 8: 300-335, Oct., 1897.

Linn, William A., *The Story of the Mormons* Macmillan, New York. 1902.

Little, James A., *From Kirtland to Salt Lake City*. James A. Little, Salt Lake City. 1890.

Marks, Constant R., *Monona County, Iowa, Mormons*, Annals (3), 7: 321-346, April, 1906.

Nibley, Preston, *Exodus to Greatness: The Story of the Mormon Migration*. Deseret News Press, Salt Lake City. 1947.

Petersen, William J., *Mormons on the March*, Palimpsest, 27: 142-157, May, 1946.

Petersen, William J., *The Story of Iowa*, 1: 600-601; 2: 740-743. Lewis Historical Co., New York. 1952.

Schmidt, Louis B., *The Miller-Thompson Election Contest*, Iowa Journal, 12: 34-127, Jan., 1914.

Sketches of the Mormon Era in Hancock County, Illinois, Annals (3), 12: 561-586, April, 1921.

Stenhouse, T. B. H., *The Rocky Mountain Saints*. Appleton, New York. 1873.

Swisher, Jacob A., *Hopeville*, Palimpsest, 26: 303-315, Oct., 1945.

Van der Zee, Jacob, *The Mormon Trails in Iowa*, Iowa Journal, 12: 3-16, Jan., 1914.

Van der Zee, Jacob, *Episodes in the Early History of the Western Iowa Country*, Iowa Journal, 11: 323-363, July, 1913.

Wyman, Helen B., *Potter Christ*, Palimpsest, 14: 334-346, Sept., 1933.

Wyman, Walker D., *Council Bluffs and the Westward Movement*, Iowa Journal, 47: 99-118, April, 1949.

The Quakers

An Iowa Community [Quaker], Palimpsest, 9: 221-284, July, 1928.

Briggs, John E., *The Lay of the Land*, Palimpsest, 9: 221-227, July, 1928.

Brown, Mabel, *Dusky Lading*, Palimpsest, 9: 242-248, July, 1928.

Cammack, Eleanore, *From Indiana to Iowa*, Annals (3), 29: 400-405, July, 1948.

Gallaher, Ruth A., *The Inner Light*, Palimpsest, 9: 233-241, July, 1928.

Garretson, O. A., *Travelling on the Underground Railroad in Iowa*, Iowa Journal, 22: 418-453, July, 1924.

Hawley, Charles A., *Salem*, Palimpsest, 16: 337-369, Nov., 1935.

Hoover, Herbert, *Boyhood in Iowa*, Palimpsest, 9: 269-276, July, 1928.

Horack, Katharine, *In Quest of a Prairie Home*, Palimpsest, 5: 249-257, July, 1924.

Jones, Louis T., *The Coming of the Quakers*, Palimpsest, 9: 228-232, July, 1928.

Jones, Louis T., *The Quakers of Iowa.* SHSI. 1914.

Jones, Louis T., *The Quakers of Iowa in 1850,* Iowa Journal, 12: 262-286, 394-439, April, July, 1914.

Mott, David C., *The Quakers in Iowa,* Annals (3), 4: 263-276, Jan., 1900.

Petersen, William J., *The Story of Iowa,* 2:727-731. Lewis Historical Co., New York. 1952.

Richman, Irving B., *John Brown's Band,* Palimpsest, 9: 249-255, July, 1928.

Starbuck, Winifred, *The Scattergood Seminary,* Palimpsest, 9: 256-262, July, 1928.

Swisher, Jacob A., *Beginnings of Salem,* Palimpsest, 21: 140-150, May, 1940.

Swisher, Jacob A., *Bert Hoover,* Palimpsest, 9: 263-268, July, 1928.

Wright, D. Sands, *Whittier College Days,* Palimpsest, 10: 421-431, Dec., 1929.

THE JEWS

Glazer, Rabbi Simon, *The Jews of Iowa.* Koch Brothers Printing Co., Des Moines. 1904.

Wolfe, Jack, *A Century with Iowa Jewry.* Iowa Printing & Supply Co., Des Moines. 1941.

Cultural Activities

MUSIC

Ashton, J. W., *Old Songs for New,* Palimpsest, 15: 389-405, Dec., 1934.

Barnhart, Cornelia Mallett, *Old Gold,* Palimpsest, 28: 144-149, May, 1947.

Bidwell, Marshall, *Famous American War Songs,* Annals (3), 25: 174-184, Jan., 1944.

Bowers, L. C., *Iowa the Beautiful,* Annals (3), 29: 598, April, 1949.

Child, Bert B., *Civil War Musicians,* Annals (3), 25: 122-128, Oct., 1943.

Colson, Ethel M., *Four Famous Iowa Girls in Chicago,* Midland Monthly, 8: 107-110, Aug., 1897.

Cone, Carl B., *Ole Bull and the Fire,* Palimpsest, 24: 154-160, May, 1943.

Crawford, Bartholow V., *The Cornell Music Festival,* Palimpsest, 11: 107-112, March, 1930.

Doak, Frances, *The High School Festival,* Palimpsest, 11: 119-126, March, 1930.

Evans, Ramona, *Dvorak at Spillville,* Palimpsest, 11: 113-118, March, 1930.

Grahame, Pauline P., *The Normal Academy of Music,* Palimpsest, 10: 328-340, Sept., 1929.

Grahame, Pauline P., *Some Songs of Long Ago,* Palimpsest, 10: 93-108, March, 1929.

Hempel, Kathleen, *Ballad of Hardin Town,* Annals (3), 31: 62-63, July, 1951.

Iowa Federation of Music Clubs, *Musical Iowana 1838-1938.* Success Composition and Printing Co., Des Moines. 1938.

Jepsen, Laura, *Hope Glenn,* Palimpsest, 15: 1-9, Jan., 1934.

Jordan, Philip D., *The Hutchinson Singers,* Palimpsest, 18: 145-159, May, 1937.

Schmidt, G. Perle, *The Federated Music Clubs,* Palimpsest, 11: 97-106, March, 1930.

Smith, Lura Brown, *Claude Matteson Saner, The Phenomenal Boy Soprano,* Midland Monthly, 6: 449-451, Nov., 1896.

Stevens, Ruth W., *Musical Ottumwa,* Palimpsest, 28: 172-183, June, 1947.

Urban, Sylvanus, *A Midland Musical Center,* Midland Monthly, 10: 257-271, Sept., 1898.

Wilson, Ben H., *Grand Concert,* Palimpsest, 17: 361-372, Nov., 1936.

Wilson, Ben H., *The Iowa Eisteddfod,* Palimpsest, 22: 357-373, Dec., 1941.

ART

Baker, Isadore, *Vinnie Ream Hoxie,* Midland Monthly, 8: 405-410, Nov., 1897.

Gallaher, Ruth A., *J. N. Ding,* Palimpsest, 11: 499-514, Nov., 1930.

Haefner, Marie, *From Plastic Clay,* Palimpsest, 11: 473-482, Nov., 1930.

Hamlin, Gladys E., *Mural Painting in Iowa,* Iowa Journal, 37: 227-307, July, 1939.

Kern, Jean B., *Art Centers in Iowa,* Palimpsest, 30: 1-32, Jan., 1949.

Ness, Zenobia B., and Louise Orwig, *Iowa Artists of the First Hundred Years.* Wallace-Homestead Co., Des Moines. 1939.

Pelzer, Mildred W., *George H. Yewell,* Palimpsest, 11: 483-499, Nov., 1930.

Rischmueller, Marian Carroll, *McGregor Sand Artist,* Palimpsest, 26: 129-147, May, 1945.

Williams, Ora, *Willbur A. Reaser, Portrait Artist,* Annals (3), 24: Part 1, 245-247, Jan., 1943.

LITERARY IOWA

Brigham, Johnson, *A Book of Iowa Authors by Iowa Authors.* Iowa State Teachers Association, Des Moines. 1930. Also in Midland Schools, 1926-1928.

Buxbaum, Katherine, *A Rural Literary Society,* Palimpsest, 21: 23-30, Jan., 1940.

Crawford, Bartholow V., *Susan Glaspell,* Palimpsest, 11: 517-521, Dec., 1930.

Frederick, John T., *The Writer's Iowa,* Palimpsest, 11, 57-60, Feb., 1930.

Frederick, John T., *The Younger School,* Palimpsest, 11: 78-86, Feb., 1930

Gallaher, Ruth A., *A Helpmeet for the President,* Palimpsest, 28: 63-64, Feb., 1947.

Gallaher, Ruth A., *Maverick Poem,* Palimpsest, 29: 193-203, July, 1948.

Gallaher, Ruth A., *Phil Stong's Hawkeyes,* Palimpsest, 21: 297-308, Oct., 1940.

Gallaher, Ruth A., *S. H. M. Byers,* Palimpsest, 13: 429-469, Nov., 1932.

Grahame, Pauline P., *A Novelist of the Unsung*, Palimpsest, 11: 67-77, Feb., 1930.

Haefner, Marie, *An American Lady* [Kate Harrington], Palimpsest, 12: 169-178, May, 1931.

Haefner, Marie, *Yankee Magic*, Palimpsest, 21: 45-53, Feb., 1940.

Hartley, Lois T., *The Midland*, Iowa Journal, 47: 325-344, Oct., 1949.

Hawley, Charles A., *Jennie Shrader*, Palimpsest, 18: 285-298, Sept., 1937.

Hempel, Kathleen, *Ballad of Hardin Town*, Annals (3), 31: 62-63, July, 1951.

Hoeltje, Hubert H., *Iowa Literary Magazines*, Palimpsest, 11: 87-94, Feb., 1930.

Iowa Authors and Artists, *Prairie Gold*. Reilly & Britton, Chicago. 1917.

Iowa Dime Novels, Palimpsest, 30: 169-208, June, 1949.

Iowa Poets: An Anthology of 69 Contemporaries. Henry Harrison, New York. 1935.

Lorch, Fred W., *Orion Clemens*, Palimpsest, 10: 353-386, Oct., 1929.

Luke, Lou Mallory, *Who's Who Among Prairie Poets*. E. L. Kuhne, Des Moines. 1938.

McNally, Sherman J., *"Bob" Burdette — Humorist*, Palimpsest, 4: 173-192, June, 1923.

Marple, Alice, *Iowa Authors and Their Works*. Historical Department, Des Moines. 1918. Also in Annals (3), 11: 520-543, 600-620, Oct., 1914, Jan., 1915, 12: 45-60, 122-140, 214-228, April, July, Oct., 1915.

Mott, Frank L., *Exponents of the Pioneers*, Palimpsest, 11: 61-66, Feb., 1930.

Mott, Frank L., *Literature of Pioneer Life in Iowa*. SHSI. 1923.

Petersen, William J., *Bertha M. H. Shambaugh*, Palimpsest, 31: 213-214, June, 1950.

Petersen, William J., *Harriet Connor Brown*, Palimpsest, 30: 135-136, April, 1949.

Petersen, William J., *J. Brownlee Davidson*, Palimpsest, 31: 77-78, March, 1950.

Petersen, William J., *Louis Bernard Schmidt*, Palimpsest, 31: 163-164, April, 1950.

Reid, Mary J., *Octave Thanet at Home*, Midland Monthly, 3: 36-42, Jan., 1895.

Reid, Mary J., *The Theories of Octave Thanet and Other Western Realists*, Midland Monthly, 9: 99-108, Feb., 1898.

Rogers, Frances L., *An Old Autograph Album*, Palimpsest, 28: 247-256, Aug., 1947.

Sloan, Sam B., *Misrepresentative Fiction*, Palimpsest, 12: 41-56, Feb., 1931.

Tull, Clyde, and Anya Plummer, *Stories from the Husk*. English Club of Cornell College, Mount Vernon. 1940.

Tweito, Thomas E., *Pioneer Mental Pabulum*, Palimpsest, 21: 1-5, Jan., 1940.

Waters, Geneva, *Friend of the Farm Wife* [Herbert Quick], Palimpsest, 22: 79-88, March, 1941.

Weaver, James B., *James Depew Edmundson*, Palimpsest, 14: 1-38, Jan., 1933.

Wright, Luella M., *A Century of Verse*, Palimpsest, 27: 217-224, July, 1946.

Wright, Luella M., *Johnson Brigham—Librarian*, Palimpsest, 33: 225-256, Aug., 1950.

Wright, Luella M., *Journalistic Literature*, Palimpsest, 19: 503-514, Dec., 1938.

Wright, Luella M., *Leonard Brown—Poet and Populist*, Iowa Journal, 46: 227-265, July, 1948.

Wright, Luella M., *The Midland Monthly*, Iowa Journal, 45: 3-61, Jan., 1947.

Wright, Luella M., *Robert Lucas in Verse*, Palimpsest, 25: 234-248, Aug., 1944.

Wright, Luella M., *Verse in the Newspapers*, Palimpsest, 19: 173-184, May, 1938.

Wright, Luella M., *Views and Reviews of Iowa*, Palimpsest, 27: 240-253, Aug., 1946.

WHITTIER AND IOWA

Hawley, Charles A., *Correspondence Between John Greenleaf Whittier and Iowa*, Iowa Journal, 35: 115-141, April, 1937.

Hawley, Charles A., *Whittier and Iowa*, Iowa Journal, 34: 115-143, April, 1936.

Wright, D Sands, *Whittier College Days*, Palimpsest, 10: 421-431, Dec., 1929.

FOLKLORE AND ODD TALES

Carlson, Gretchen, *The Hobo Convention*, Palimpsest, 12: 257-272, July, 1931.

Foster, T. Henry, *Collecting Dime Novels*, Palimpsest, 30: 169-172, June, 1949.

Gallaher, Ruth A., *The Cardiff Giant*, Palimpsest, 2: 269-281, Sept., 1921.

Gallaher, Ruth A., *Hummer's Bell*, Palimpsest, 3: 155-164, May, 1922.

Grahame, Russell C., *Jumbo*, Palimpsest, 9: 109-118, March, 1928.

Mahan, Bruce E., *Siam Gold*, Palimpsest, 8: 233-252, July, 1927.

Mott, Frank Luther, *The Beadles and Their Novels*, Palimpsest, 30: 173-189, June, 1949.

Mott, Vera I., *Pioneer Iowa in Beadle Fiction*, Palimpsest, 30: 190-208, June, 1949.

Stout, Earl J., *Folklore from Iowa*. American Folk-lore Society, New York. 1936.

Wilson, Ben H., *Grand Concert*, Palimpsest, 17: 361-372, Nov., 1936.

LITERATURE WITH AN IOWA BACKGROUND

Aldrich, Bess Streeter
 The Cutters, Appleton, New York. 1926.
 A Lantern in Her Hand. Appleton, New York. 1928.
 Miss Bishop. Appleton-Century, New York. 1933.
 The Man Who Caught the Weather and Other Stories. D. Appleton-
  Century, New York. 1936.
 Song of Years. Appleton-Century, New York. 1939.
Brigham, Johnson, *The Sinclairs of Old Fort Des Moines.* Hertzberg Bindery,
 Des Moines. 1927.
Brown, Bernice, *The Shining Road.* Putnam's Sons, New York. 1923.
Brown, Harriet C., *Grandmother Brown's Hundred Years, 1827-1927.* Little,
 Brown, Boston. 1929.
Butler, Ellis Parker
 Dominie Dean. Fleming H. Revell, New York. 1917.
Corey, Paul
 Acres of Antaeus. 1946.
 County Seat. Bobbs-Merrill, Indianapolis. 1941.
 Corngold Farm. 1948.
 The Road Returns. Bobbs-Merrill, Indianapolis. 1941.
 Red Tractor. 1944.
 Three Miles Square. Bobbs-Merrill, Indianapolis. 1939.
Donovan, Josephine B., *Black Soil.* Stratford Co., Boston. 1930.
Downing, J. Hyatt
 Anthony Trant. Putnam's Sons, New York. 1941.
 Sioux City. Putnam's Sons, New York. 1940.
 The Harvest is Late. Morrow. New York. 1944.
Duncan, Thomas
 Gus The Great. Lippincott, New York. 1947.
 O, Chautauqua. Coward-McCann, New York. 1935.
 We Pluck This Flower. Coward-McCann, New York. 1937.
Dye, Eva E., *The Conquest: The True Story of Lewis and Clark.* McClurg,
 Chicago. 1902.
Engle, Paul, *Always the Land.* Random House, New York. 1941.
Erickson, Howard, *Son of Earth.* Dial Press, New York. 1933.
Feikema, Feike [Manfred, Frederick Feikema]
 This is the Year, Doubleday, Garden City, N. Y. 1947.
 The Chokecherry Tree. Doubleday, Garden City, N. Y. 1948.
Fleming, A. M., *Iowa Pioneers.* Meadow Publishing Co., Boston. 1933.
Ford, Elisabeth, *No Hour of History.* Ives Washburn, New York. 1940.
Frederick, John T.
 The Farm in Iowa Fiction, Palimpsest, 32: 121-152, March, 1951.
 Stories from The Midland. Knopf. New York. 1924.
 Out of the Midwest. Whittlesey House, New York. 1944.
 Druida. Knopf, New York. 1923.

Garland, Hamlin
    Back-Trailers from the Middle Border. Macmillan, New York. 1928.
    Boy Life on the Prairie, Macmillan, New York. 1899.
    A Daughter of the Middle Border. Macmillan, New York. 1922.
    Main Traveled Roads. Arena Publishing Co., Boston. 1891.
    Other Main Traveled Roads. Harper & Bros., New York. 1910.
    Prairie Folks. F. J. Schulte, Chicago. 1893.
    A Son of the Middle Border. Macmillan, New York. 1922.
    Trailmakers of the Middle Border. Macmillan, New York. 1926.

Glaspell, Susan
    The Glory of the Conquered. Burt, New York. 1909.
    The Visioning. Stokes, New York. 1911.

Herbst, Josephine, *Nothing is Sacred.* Coward-McCann, New York. 1928.

Hueston, Ethel
    Preacher's Wife. Bobbs-Merrill, Indianapolis. 1941.
    Prudence of the Parsonage. Grosset & Dunlap, New York. 1915.
    Prudence Says So. Grosset & Dunlap, New York. 1916.

Jackson, Dan, *Archer Pilgrim.* Dodd, Mead, New York. 1942.

Jerger, Joseph A., *Doctor—Here's Your Hat.* Prentiss-Hall, New York. 1939.

Kantor, MacKinlay
    Happy Land, Coward-McCann, New York. 1942.
    Valedictory. Coward-McCann, New York. 1939.

Medary, Marjorie, *Prairie Anchorage.* Longmans, Green, New York. 1933.

Meigs, Cornelia, *As the Crow Flies.* Macmillan, New York. 1927.

Mott, Vera I., *Pioneer Iowa in Beadle Fiction,* Palimpsest, 30: 190-208, June, 1949.

Moulton, Charles W., *On a Western Campus.* Author, Buffalo. 1897.

Muilenburg, Walter J., *Prairie.* Viking Press, New York. 1925.

Quick, Herbert
    Aladdin & Co. Henry Holt, New York. 1904.
    The Brown Mouse. Bobbs-Merrill, Indianapolis. 1915.
    The Fairview Idea. Bobbs-Merrill, Indianapolis. 1919.
    The Hawkeye. Bobbs-Merrill, Indianapolis. 1923.
    The Invisible Woman. Bobbs-Merrill, Indianapolis. 1924.
    One Man's Life (Autobiography), Bobbs-Merrill, Indianapolis. 1925.
    Vandemark's Folly. Bobbs-Merrill, Indianapolis. 1924.

Russell, Charles E., *A-Rafting on the Mississip'.* Century, New York. 1928.

Saltzman, Eleanor, *Ever Tomorrow.* Coward-McCann, New York. 1936.

Sergel, Roger L., *Arlie Gelston.* Huebsch, New York. 1923.

Sigmund, J. G., *Wapsipinicon Tales,* Prairie Publishing Co., Cedar Rapids. 1927.

Spence, Hartzell
    Get Thee Behind Me. McGraw-Hill, New York. 1942.
    One Foot in Heaven. McGraw-Hill, New York. 1940.

Stegner, Walter, *Remembering Laughter.* Little, Brown, Boston. 1937.

Stong, Philip D.
> *Buckskin Breeches.* Farrar & Rinehart, New York. 1937.
> *Career.* Harcourt, Brace, New York. 1936.
> *If School Keeps.* Stokes, New York. 1940.
> *Ivanhoe Keeler.* Farrar & Rinehart, New York. 1939.
> *The Long Lane.* Farrar & Rinehart, New York. 1939.
> *One Destiny.* Reynal & Hitchcock Inc., New York. 1942.
> *The Princess.* Farrar & Rinehart, New York. 1941.
> *State Fair.* Century, New York. 1932.
> *Stranger's Return.* Harcourt, Brace, New York. 1930.
> *Village Tale.* Harcourt, Brace, New York. 1934.

Suckow, Ruth
> *The Bonney Family.* Knopf, New York. 1928.
> *Children and Older People.* Knopf, New York. 1931.
> *Cora.* Knopf, New York. 1929.
> *Country People.* Knopf, New York. 1924.
> *The Folks.* Farrar & Rinehart, New York. 1934.
> *Iowa Interiors.* Knopf, New York. 1926.
> *The Kramer Girls.* Knopf, New York. 1930.
> *New Hope.* Farrar & Rinehart, New York. 1942.
> *The Odyssey of a Nice Girl.* Knopf, New York. 1925.
> *Some Others and Myself.* Rinehart & Co., New York. 1952.

Thanet, Octave (Alice French), *Stories of a Western Town.* Scribners, New York. 1897.

Van Etten, Winifred, *I Am the Fox.* Little, Brown, Boston. 1936.

Van Vechten, Carl, *The Tatooed Countess.* Knopf, New York. 1924.

Willson, Meredith, *There I Stood With My Piccolo.* Doubleday, Garden City, N. Y. 1948.

Wilson, Margaret
> *The Able McLaughlins.* Harper & Brothers, New York. 1923.
> *The Law and the McLaughlins.* Cassell, London. 1936.

Wright, Luella M., *Fiction as History*, Palimpsest, 28: 97-112, April, 1947.

Yoseloff, Martin
> *The Family Members.* E. P. Dutton & Co., New York. 1948.
> *No Greener Meadows.* Ackerman, N. Y. 1946.

CLUBS AND CULTURAL ORGANIZATIONS

Beall, Walter H., *A Study Club for Men*, Palimpsest, 23: 73-84, March, 1942.

Braden, Waldo W., *The YMA of Mount Pleasant*, Palimpsest, 29: 76-86, March, 1948.

Cone, Carl Bruce, *The Iowa Firemen's Association*, Iowa Journal, 42: 227-265, July, 1944.

Durley, Ella H., *Club Federation in Iowa*, Midland Monthly, 3: 581-589, June, 1895.

Jack, Frances E., *P. E. O. Beginnings*, Palimpsest, 23: 85-98, March, 1942.

Johnson, Hildegard Binder, *List of Lectures and Debates Given Before the Davenport Turngemeinde*, Iowa Journal, 44: 54-60, Jan., 1946.

Lovell, Miriam Fay, *The Monticello Friday Club*, Palimpsest, 24: 59-70. Feb., 1943.

Smith, Frederic C., *The Keokuk Lantern Club*, Palimpsest, 27: 116-125, April, 1946.

Swisher, Jacob A., *The Community Clubs*, Palimpsest, 9: 277-281, July, 1928.

Swisher, Jacob A., *Good Templars in Iowa*, Iowa Journal, 45: 235-260, July, 1947.

Thornton, Harrison John, *Birth of the Grand Lodge*, Palimpsest, 25: 173-178, June, 1944.

Thornton, Harrison John, *A Century of Iowa Masonry*, Palimpsest, 25: 210-224, July, 1944.

Thornton, Harrison John, *Origins of Iowa Masonry*, Palimpsest, 25: 161-172, June, 1944.

Towner, Harriet C., *The Second Biennial Meeting of the Iowa Federation of Women's Clubs*, Midland Monthly, 7: 548-557, June, 1897.

The World's "Last Best Hope" (Constitution Day Observance), Annals (3), 25: 228, Jan., 1944.

Wright, Luella M., *The Cedar Falls Parlor Reading Circle*, Iowa Journal, 34: 339-374, Oct., 1936.

Wright, Luella M., *The Mind and the Soil*, Palimpsest, 17: 373-394, Nov., 1936.

Amusements and Recreation

AMUSEMENTS AND GAMES

Bennett, H. Arnold, *The Great Snake Hunt*, Palimpsest, 9: 334-337, Sept., 1928.

Braden, Waldo W., *College Oratory in the Nineties*, Palimpsest, 28: 343-349, Nov., 1947.

Cone, Carl B., *Champion Fire Teams*, Palimpsest, 23: 273-281, Sept., 1942.

Evans, Ramona, *Fashions in the Fifties*, Palimpsest, 10: 16-29, Jan., 1929.

Felton, Oliver J., *Pioneer Life in Jones County*, Iowa Journal, 29: 233-281, April, 1931.

Grahame, Pauline P., *The First Day of the Twentieth Century*, Palimpsest, 10: 1-15, Jan., 1929.

Hall, Reeves, *First Iowa Husking Meets*, Palimpsest, 24: 333-347, Nov., 1943.

Kaloupek, Walter E., *The Plight of Fiddlin' Jim*, Palimpsest, 20: 310-312, Sept., 1939.

Mahan, Bruce E., *Frontier Fun*, Palimpsest, 8: 38-42, Jan., 1927.

Mahan, Bruce E., *Frontier Fun*, Palimpsest, 32: 38-42, Jan., 1951.

Mahan, Bruce E., *The Old Square Dances*, Palimpsest, 10: 82-90, Feb., 1929.

Mahan, Bruce E., and Pauline P. Grahame, *Play-Party Games*, Palimpsest, 10: 33-67, Feb., 1929.

Mahan, Bruce E., and Pauline P. Grahame, *School-Day Games*, Palimpsest, 10: 68-81, Feb., 1929.

Petersen, William J., *Homespun Amusements*, Palimpsest, 19: 485-494, Dec., 1938.

Petersen, William J., *Legal Holidays in Iowa*, Iowa Journal, 43: 3-68, Jan., 1945.

Petersen, William J., *Legal Holidays in Iowa*, Iowa Journal, 43: 113-191, April, 1945.

Rischmueller, Marian Carroll, *The Ringlings of McGregor*, Palimpsest, 25: 179-192, June, 1944.

Swisher, Jacob A., *The Community Clubs*, Palimpsest, 9: 277-281, July, 1928.

Wagner, Dorothy, *The Varsity Whirl*, Palimpsest, 10: 109-126, March, 1929.

THEATER AND STAGE

Briggs, John E., *When Barnum Came to Iowa*, Palimpsest, 8: 407-413, Dec., 1927.

Ekdale, Edith Harper, *The Grand Opera House*, Palimpsest, 28: 184-192, June, 1947.

Grahame, Pauline P., *La Follette Wins*, Palimpsest, 12: 179-188, May, 1931.

Hill, Raymond S., *The Princess Theater of Des Moines*, Iowa Journal, 49: 1-22, Jan., 1951.

Kelm, William E., *The People's Theater*, Palimpsest, 9: 89-105, March, 1928.

Kintzle, Clarence A., *The Julien Theater*, Palimpsest, 15: 139-158, April, 1934.

Mahan, Bruce E., *At the Opera House*, Palimpsest, 5: 408-423, Nov., 1924.

Mahan, Bruce E., *The Iowa Thespians*, Palimpsest, 4: 14-24, Jan., 1923.

Mahan, Bruce E., *Pleasant Hill Dramatics*, Palimpsest, 4: 25-29, Jan., 1923

Mott, David C., *The Pivotal Convention of 1883*, Annals (3), 26: 254-260, April, 1945.

New York Spirit of the Times, *A Theatre Scene—Indian Gallantry*, Annals (3), 27: 70-72, July, 1945.

Payne, W. O., *Moore's Opera House*, Annals (3), 17: 163-167, Jan., 1930.

Schick, Joseph A., *The American Theater*, Palimpsest, 31: 8-23, Jan., 1950.

Schick, Joseph A., *Drama on the Iowa Frontier*, Palimpsest, 31: 1-7, Jan., 1950.

Schick, Joseph S., *The Early Theater in Eastern Iowa*. University of Chicago Press, Chicago. 1939.

Schick, Joseph S., *The German Theater*, Palimpsest, 31: 24-44, Jan., 1950.

CHAUTAUQUA

Duncan, Thomas W., *O, Chautauqua*. Coward-McCann, New York. 1935.

Gingerich, Melvin, *The Washington Chautauqua*, Palimpsest, 26: 370-376, Dec., 1945.

Schick, Joseph S., *The Early Theater in Eastern Iowa*. University of Chicago Press, Chicago. 1939.

Sweet, Oney Fred, *Through Iowa on Chautauqua*, Iowa Journal, 39: 115-147, April, 1941.

Thornton, Harrison John, *Chautauqua in Iowa*, Iowa Journal, 50: 97-122, April, 1952.

STATE PARKS

Byers, S. H. M., *Resting at Okoboji*, Midland Monthly, 3: 438-443, May, 1895.

Calvin, Samuel, *The Devil's Backbone*, Midland Monthly, 6: 20-26, July, 1896.

Calvin, Samuel, *The Switzerland of Iowa*, Midland Monthly, 3: 403-414, May, 1895.

Christensen, Thomas P., *The State Parks of Iowa*, Iowa Journal, 26: 331-414, July, 1928.

Cole, Oc. C., *Views on the Volga*, Midland Monthly, 6: 128-130, Aug., 1896.

Glass, Remley J., *Conservation of Recreational Area*, Annals (3), 28: 149-157, Oct., 1946.

Harlan, Edgar R., *Who Owns the Lakes, Anyway?*, Annals (3), 16: 98-106, Oct., 1927.

Iowa: A Guide to the Hawkeye State, 3-25. Viking Press, New York. 1938.

Keyes, Charles Reuben, *Minott's Rock Shelter*, Palimpsest, 24: 1-40, Jan., 1943.

McLaughlin, Wm. M., *Pioneer Park and Its Pioneer*, Annals (3), 30: 453-457, Oct., 1950.

Pammel, Louis H., *The Arbor Day, Park and Conservation Movements in Iowa*, Annals (3), 17: 83-104, Oct., 1929, 198-232, 270-313, Jan., April, 1930.

Swisher, Jacob A., *Iowa State Parks*, Palimpsest, 12: 201-253, June, 1931.

See also the various publications of the State Conservation Commission.

STATE AND LOCAL FAIRS

Beinhauer, Myrtle, *The County, District, and State Agricultural Societies of Iowa*, Annals (3), 20: 50-69, July, 1935.

Briggs, John E., *The Sioux City Corn Palaces*, Palimpsest, 3: 313-326, Oct., 1922.

Kreiner, Carl B., *The Ottumwa Coal Palace*, Palimpsest, 3: 336-342, Oct., 1922.

Mahan, Bruce E., *The Blue Grass Palace*, Palimpsest, 3: 327-335, Oct., 1922.

Mahan, Bruce E., *The Seventh Iowa State Fair*, Palimpsest, 7: 309-320, Oct., 1926.

Petersen, William J., *The Dairy Cattle Congress*, Palimpsest, 15: 357-386, Nov., 1934.

Pollock, Margaret, *The Clay County Fair*, Palimpsest, 31: 165-212, May, 1950.

Ross, Earle D., *The Evolution of the Agricultural Fair in the Northwest*, Iowa Journal, 24: 445-480, July, 1926.

Ross, Earle D., *The Iowa State Fair*, Palimpsest, 10: 269-316, Aug., 1929.

IOWA AT THE WORLD'S FAIRS

Mahan, Bruce E., *Iowa at the Centennial,* Palimpsest, 5: 334-338, Sept., 1924.
Mahan, Bruce E., *Iowa at the New Orleans Fair,* Palimpsest, 6: 77-94, March, 1925.
Mahan, Bruce E., *Iowa at the World's Fair,* Palimpsest, 6: 146-163, May, 1925.
Miller, Ora E., *Iowa at the World's Fair,* Midland Monthly, 1: 73-83, 255-268, Jan., March, 1894.

THE FOURTH OF JULY

Aldrich, Charles, *The Fourth at Webster City,* Palimpsest, 16: 226-230, July, 1935.
Hall, Reeves, *Rickenbacker Wins,* Palimpsest, 23: 381-394, Dec., 1942.
Mahan, Bruce E., *Fourth of July in 1860,* Palimpsest, 7: 209-212, July, 1926.
Petersen, William J., *The Birthday of the Territory,* Palimpsest, 19: 241-250, July, 1938.
Petersen, William J., *The Fourth of July,* Iowa Journal, 43: 113-131, April, 1945.
Petersen, William J., *Independence Day in 1845,* Palimpsest, 26: 193-201, July, 1945.
Petersen, William J., *The Story of Iowa,* 2:986-996. Lewis Historical Co., New York. 1952.

CHRISTMAS

Baily, Matie L., *Christmas of a Pioneer Family,* Annals (3), 31: 152-153, Oct., 1951.
Petersen, William J., *Christmas,* Iowa Journal, 43: 172-191, April, 1945.
Petersen, William J., *Christmas in Iowa,* Palimpsest, 16: 373-388, Dec., 1935.
Petersen, William J., *The Iten Christmas Display,* Palimpsest, 16: 389-396, Dec., 1935.
Petersen, William J., *The Story of Iowa,* 2: 1018-1028. Lewis Historical Co., New York. 1952.
Whitley, Cora Call, *A Pioneer Christmas Tree,* Palimpsest, 18: 381-388, Dec., 1937.

SPORTS

Anson, Adrian C., *A Ball Player's Career.* Era Publishing Co., Chicago. 1900.
Baseball! The Story of Iowa's Early Innings, Annals (3), 22: 625-654, April, 1941.
Bennett, H. Arnold, *The Great Snake Hunt,* Palimpsest, 9: 334-337, Sept., 1928.

Briggs, John E., *That 1900 Football Team*, Palimpsest, 3: 345-363, Nov., 1922.

Chisholm, R. H., *Iowa Girls' High School Athletic Union*, Palimpsest, 31: 57-64, Feb., 1950.

Chisholm, R. H., *State Tournament*, Palimpsest, 31: 65-76, Feb., 1950.

Cone, Carl B., *Baseball and Telephony*, Palimpsest, 24: 248-254, Aug., 1943.

Cone, Carl B., *Champion Fire Teams*, Palimpsest, 23: 273-282, Sept., 1942.

Eriksson, Erik M., *Baseball Beginnings*, Palimpsest, 8: 329-338, Oct., 1927.

Geary, Thomas C., *John McGraw in Iowa Baseball*, Palimpsest, 17: 310-326, Sept., 1936.

Hall, Reeves, *Rickenbacker Wins*, Palimpsest, 23: 381-394, Dec., 1942.

Harlan, James R., *The Iowa Game Book of George E. Poyneer*, Annals (3), 23: 189-211, Jan., 1942.

Iowa: A Guide to the Hawkeye State, 119-123. Viking Press, New York. 1938.

Kirby, Chester H., *The World's Series of 1891*, Palimpsest, 3: 364-373, Nov., 1922.

Mahan, Bruce E., *Baseball in 1867*, Palimpsest, 8: 177-180, May, 1927.

Mahan, Bruce E., *The First Iowa Field Day*, Palimpsest, 4: 137-150, May, 1923.

Mahan, Bruce E., *John Van Fleet Crum*, Palimpsest, 13: 217-238, June, 1932.

McMurry, Donald L., *The Pacific City Fight*, Palimpsest, 2: 182-189, June, 1921.

Musgrove, Jack W., *Market Hunting in Northern Iowa*, Annals (3), 26: 173-197, Jan., 1945.

Petersen, William J., *Beginnings of Girls' Basketball*, Palimpsest, 31: 45-56, Feb., 1950.

Petersen, William J., *Homespun Amusements*, Palimpsest, 19: 485-494, Dec., 1938.

Petersen, William J., *Lexington of the North*, Palimpsest, 13: 333-394, Sept., 1932.

Petersen, William J., *Lexington of the North*, Palimpsest, 31: 329-392, Sept., 1950.

Petersen, William J., *Sleighing Time*, Palimpsest, 26: 33-46, Feb., 1945.

Pollock, Margaret, *Bicycles, Trotters, Barbecues*, Palimpsest, 31: 177-182, May, 1950.

Regur, Dorothy W., *In the Bicycle Era*, Palimpsest, 14: 349-362, Oct., 1933.

Rinehart, G. F., *Is Cycling a Fad?*, Midland Monthly, 4: 277-282, Sept., 1895.

Smith, Frederic C., *Keokuk in Big League Baseball*, Palimpsest, 27: 204-216, July, 1946.

Swisher, Jacob A., *Adrian C. Anson*, Palimpsest, 3: 374-378, Nov., 1922.

White, Ed. S., *"Who's Crum?"*, Midland Monthly, 4: 46-47, July, 1895.

Wilcox, Francis O., *First in the Mile Relay*, Palimpsest, 13: 181-197, May, 1932.

Health in Iowa

MEDICAL PRACTICE IN IOWA

The Ague in Iowa, Annals (3), 26: 60, July, 1944.

Emhoff, Floy L., *A Pioneer Doctor of Marshall County: Elmer Yocum Lawrence*, Iowa Journal, 31: 576-588, Oct., 1933.

Fairchild, D. S., *Medicine in Iowa from Its Earliest Settlement to 1876.* Reprinted from the Journal of the Iowa State Medical Society.

Fairchild, D. S., *Physicians Who Located in Iowa in the Period Between 1850 and 1860*, Journal of the Iowa State Medical Society, April, 1922.

Fulton, Charles J., *A Wartime Doctor's Account Book, 1861-1862*, Annals (3), 14, 540-544, Jan., 1925.

Irish, John P., *Some Episodes in the History of the Founding of the Medical College of the State University*, Iowa Journal, 18: 125-129, Jan., 1920.

Keyes, Charles Rollin, *A Pioneer Medicine Man of Iowa*, Annals (3), 14: 533-539, Jan., 1925.

Petersen, William J., *Diseases and Doctors in Pioneer Iowa*, Iowa Journal, 49: 97-116, April, 1951.

Petersen, William J., *Doctors, Drugs, and Dentists*, Palimpsest, 19: 401-412, Oct., 1938.

Petersen, William J., *Doctors, Drugs, and Pioneers*, Palimpsest, 30: 93-96, March, 1949.

Petersen, William J., *The Story of Iowa*, 2: 756-799. Lewis Historical Co., New York. 1952.

Snyder, Charles E., *John Emerson, Owner of Dred Scott*, Annals (3), 21: 441-461, Oct., 1938.

Still College and Infirmary of Osteopathy, The Dr. S. S., Midland Monthly, 10: vii-xvii, advertisement, July, 1898.

Throne, Mildred, *Diary of W. H. Turner, M. D., 1863*, Iowa Journal, 48: 267-282, July, 1950.

Tjernagel, N., *Angels of the Sick Room*, Palimpsest, 23: 298-304, Sept., 1942.

Watson, William, *Early Medical Practitioners*, Iowa Historical Lectures, 1894. SHSI.

PUBLIC HEALTH

Hargrave, William M., *Municipal Administration of Public Health*, Applied History, 6: 513-556. SHSI. 1930.

McGee, N. W., *State Administration of Public Health in Iowa*, Iowa Journal, 31: 163-210, April, 1933.

Social and Economic Problems

REGULATION OF THE LIQUOR TRAFFIC

Beaman, D. C., *A Reminiscence of the Iowa Bar*, Annals (3), 10: 147, 148, July, 1911.

Clark, Dan E., *The Beginnings of Liquor Legislation in Iowa*, Iowa Journal, 5: 193-212, April, 1907.

Clark, Dan E., *The History of Liquor Legislation in Iowa 1846-1898*, Iowa Journal, 6: 55-87, 339-374, 503-608, Jan., July, Oct., 1908.

Clark, Dan E., *Recent Liquor Legislation in Iowa*, Iowa Journal, 15: 42-69, Jan., 1917.

Cosson, George, *The Cosson Laws*, Annals (3), 30: 159-174, Jan., 1950.

Gallaher, Ruth A., *Annie Turner Wittenmyer*, Iowa Journal, 29: 564-569, Oct., 1931.

Gallaher, Ruth A., *Liquor Merry-Go-Round*, Palimpsest, 14: 213-232, June, 1933.

Petersen, William J., *George C. Haddock*, Palimpsest, 14: 233-248, June, 1933.

Wines, F H., and John Koren, *The Liquor Problem in Its Legislative Aspects*. Houghton Mifflin, Boston. 1897.

TAXATION AND GOVERNMENT FINANCE

Brindley, John E., *History of Taxation in Iowa*. 2 vols. SHSI. 1911.

Brindley, John E., *History of Taxation in Iowa 1910-1920*, Iowa Journal, 19: 44-93, Jan., 1921.

Brindley, John E., *Tax Administration in Iowa*, Applied History, 1: 495-606. SHSI. 1912.

Erbe, Carl H., *Constitutional Limitations on Indebtedness in Iowa*, Iowa Journal, 22: 363-417, July, 1924.

Gallaher, Ruth A., *The Administration of Municipal Finance*, Applied History, 6: 3-142. SHSI. 1930.

Gallaher, Ruth A., *To Pay or Not to Pay*, Palimpsest, 27: 158-160, May, 1946.

Plaehn, Erma B., *Taxes Underwrite Education*, Palimpsest, 27: 86-96, March, 1946.

Pollock, Ivan L., *Administration of Taxation and Finance in the County*, Applied History, 4: 472-533. SHSI. 1925.

Pollock, Ivan L., *The Iowa Civil War Loan*, Iowa and War, No. 3, Sept., 1917. SHSI.

Pollock, Ivan L., *The Iowa War Loan of 1861*, Iowa Journal, 15: 467-502, Oct., 1917.

Pollock, Ivan L., *State Finances in Iowa During the Civil War*, Iowa Journal 16: 53-107, Jan., 1918.

Scott, David C., *Iowa State Tax Commission*, Studies in Iowa Government. No. 1, SHSI. March, 1950.

Williams, Ora, *Iowa and the Tariff*, Annals (3), 29: 47-56, July, 1947.

LABOR LEGISLATION

Briggs, John E., *History of Social Legislation in Iowa*, 240-283. SHSI. 1915.

Brookman, Donald W., *Prison Labor in Iowa*, Iowa Journal, 32: 124-165, April, 1934.

Downey, E. H., *History of Labor Legislation in Iowa*. SHSI. 1910.

Downey, E. H., *History of Work Accident Indemnity in Iowa*. SHSI. 1912.

Downey, E. H., *Work Accident Indemnity in Iowa*, Applied History, 1: 419-492. SHSI. 1912.

Pollock, Ivan L., *History of Economic Legislation in Iowa*, 251-276. SHSI. 1918.

SOCIAL WELFARE

Aurner, Clarence R., *History of Education in Iowa*, 5: Pts. I, II, V. SHSI. 1920.

Board of Control, *Bulletin of Iowa Institutions*, 39 vols. State of Iowa, Des Moines. 1899-1937. See especially Vol. II for histories of State institutions.

Briggs, John E., *History of Social Legislation in Iowa*. SHSI. 1915.

Briggs, John E., *Social Legislation in Iowa*, Applied History, 2: 497-555. SHSI. 1914.

Collins, William J., *Administration of Old-Age Assistance in Iowa 1934-1939*, Iowa Journal, 41: 3-68, Jan., 1943.

Fullbrook, Earl S., *County Welfare Work*. Applied History, 4: 363-415. SHSI. 1925.

Gallaher, Ruth A., *An Adventure in Faith*, Palimpsest, 13: 93-105, March, 1932.

Gillin, John L., *History of Poor Relief Legislation in Iowa*. SHSI. 1914.

Gillin, John L., *Poor Relief Legislation in Iowa*, Applied History, 2: 629-659. SHSI. 1914.

Haynes, Fred E., *Child Labor Legislation in Iowa*, Applied History, 2: 557-627. SHSI. 1914.

Herriott, Frank I., *Regulation of Trade and Morals by Iowa Town Councils Prior to 1858*, Annals (3), 5: 126-134, July, 1901.

Johnson, Jack T., *The Iowa Department of Social Welfare*, Iowa Journal, 39: 148-179, April, 1941.

Kinne, L. G., *The Origin, Growth and Development of the Board of Control System in Iowa*, Annals (3), 6: 321-339, April, 1904.

London, Lena, *The Adoption of Homestead Exemption in Iowa*, Iowa Journal, 48: 133-140, April, 1950.

Loos, Isaac A., *Child Labor Legislation in Iowa*, Iowa Journal, 3: 562-582, Oct., 1905.

Snyder, Charles E., *Army Camp and Orphans Home*, Annals (3), 29: 307-314, April, 1948.

CARE OF DEFECTIVES AND DELINQUENTS

Aurner, Clarence R., *History of Education in Iowa*, 5: Pts. I, II, V. SHSI. 1920.

Briggs, John E., *A Penitentiary for Iowa*, Palimpsest, 20: 400-410, Dec., 1939.

Briggs, John E., *Social Legislation in Iowa*, 169-199. SHSI. 1915.

Brookman, Donald W., *Prison Labor in Iowa*, Iowa Journal, 32: 124-165, April, 1934.

Haynes, Fred E., *County Jails in Iowa*, Iowa Journal, 44: 61-85, Jan., 1946.

Haynes, Fred E., *Friend of the Friendless*, Palimpsest, 29: 214-224, July, 1948.

Hillis, Hazel, *Securing the Juvenile Court Law for Iowa*, Annals (3), 23: 163-188, Jan., 1942.

Shea, Robert W., *History and Administration of the Iowa Bureau of Criminal Investigation*, Iowa Journal, 34: 262-311, July, 1936.

Printing and Publishing

THE PRESS OF IOWA

Aldrich, Charles, *Early Journalism in Iowa*, Historical Record, 9: 394-414, Jan., 1893.

Aldrich, Charles, *Journalism of Northwest Iowa*, Annals (3), 13: 509-528, Jan., 1923.

Aman, John A., *Views of Three Iowa Newspapers on the League of Nations 1919-1920*, Iowa Journal, 39: 227-285, July, 1941.

Barnhart, Cornelia Mallett, *The Fourth Estate in 1846*, Palimpsest, 27: 33-48, Feb., 1946.

Battell, Frederic C., *The Du Buque Visitor and Its Press*, Iowa Journal, 47: 193-214, July, 1949.

Bell, Edith M., *The Bloomington Herald*, Palimpsest, 21: 331-344, Oct., 1940.

Bowers, Luther F., *The Iowa Sun*, Palimpsest, 19: 313-322, Aug., 1938.

Briggs, John E., *The Fort Madison Patriot*, Palimpsest, 19: 98-105, March, 1938.

Clement, Ernest W., *Jesse Clement: A Yankee Westernized*, Iowa Journal, 38: 233-281, July, 1940.

Clement, Jesse, *Gleanings from the Note Book of the Itinerating Editor*, Iowa Journal, 38: 282-305, July, 1940.

Fox, James, *Crum and the Standard*, Palimpsest, 21: 318-330, Oct., 1940.

Gallaher, Ruth A., *An Editor Speaks*, Palimpsest, 26: 316-318, Oct., 1945.

Hall, W. Earl, *The Mason City Globe-Gazette*, Palimpsest, 31: 421-424, Oct., 1950.

Harrison, Hugh, *The Davenport Democrat*, Palimpsest, 31: 417-420, Oct., 1950.

Johnston, Clarence S., *The Ottumwa Courier*, Palimpsest, 31: 401-406, Oct., 1950.

Lazell, Fred J., *Some Prominent Editors*, Palimpsest, 17: 137-146, April, 1936.

Leysen, Ralph J., *The Davenport Times*, Palimpsest, 31: 407-411, Oct., 1950.

McMurtrie, Douglas C., *The Beginnings of Printing in Iowa*, Annals (3), 19: 3-22, July, 1933.

McMurtrie, Douglas C., *Directories of Iowa Newspapers, 1850-1869*, Annals (3), 20: 11-25, July, 1935.

McMurtrie, Douglas C., *The First Printing at Council Bluffs*, Annals (3), 18: 3-11, July, 1931.

McMurtrie, Douglas C., *Two Early Issues of the Council Bluffs Press*, Annals (3), 18: 83-86, Oct., 1931.

Mills, George, *The Des Moines Register*, Palimpsest, 30: 273-304, Sept., 1949.

Mott, David C., *Early Iowa Newspapers*, Annals (3), 16: 161-233, Jan., 1928.

Mullin, Frank A., *Gleanings of an Editor*, Palimpsest, 6: 250-261, July, 1925.

Neidig, A. H., *Iowa Press Association Meeting in 1875*, Annals (3), 26: 300-304, April, 1945.

Parish, John C., *An Old-Time Editorial Dialogue*, Palimpsest, 1: 47-55, Aug., 1920.

Parish, John C., *Perils of a Pioneer Editor*, Palimpsest, 2: 233-239, Aug., 1921.

Parish, John C., *Three Men and a Press*, Palimpsest, 1: 56-60, Aug., 1920.

Payne, W. O., *The Printing Industry in Iowa*, Midland Schools, 44: 48-49, 60, Oct., 1929.

Perkins, George D., *Two Lay Sermons*, Palimpsest, 5: 305-317, Aug., 1924.

Petersen, William J., *Beginnings of Journalism in Iowa*, Iowa Journal, 45: 261-289, July, 1947.

Petersen, William J., *Du Buque Visitor*, Palimpsest, 17: 117-128, April, 1936.

Petersen, William J., *Iowa Editors and the Second World War*, Iowa Journal, 40: 115-152, April, 1942.

Petersen, William J., *Newspapers—Chroniclers of History*, Palimpsest, 31: 465-467, Dec., 1950.

Petersen, William J., *Stumping Iowa in 1860*, Palimpsest, 31: 468-483, Dec., 1950.

Petersen, William J., *The Story of Iowa*, 2: 628-660. Lewis Historical Co., New York. 1952.

Pittman, Edward F., *The Newspaper Collection of the Historical, Memorial and Art Department of Iowa*, Annals (3), 17: 483-512, Jan., 1931.

Russell, Walter, *The Muscatine Journal*. Palimpsest, 31: 412-416, Oct., 1950.

Shambaugh, Bertha M. H., *Newspaper History*, Palimpsest, 1: 33-46, Aug., 1920.

Sherman, Roy V., *Pioneer Politics*, Palimpsest, 8: 47-50, Jan., 1927.

Stout, Velma C., *The First Five Years*, Palimpsest, 17: 129-136, April, 1936.

Swisher, Jacob A., *The News*, Palimpsest, 8: 43-46, Jan., 1927.

Swisher, Jacob A., *The News*, Palimpsest, 32: 43-46, Jan., 1951.

Tweito, Thomas E., *Frontier Journalism*, Palimpsest, 32: 441-456, Dec., 1951.

Wilkie, Franc B., *Biography of a Newspaper*, Palimpsest, 8: 339-352, Oct., 1927.

Wright, Luella M., *Journalistic Literature*, Palimpsest, 19: 503-514, Dec., 1938.

Wright, Luella M., *Verse in the Newspapers*, Palimpsest, 19: 173-184, May, 1938.

See also Agricultural Publications.

IOWA JOURNALISTS

Bailey, A. K., *Pioneer Editors of Northeastern Iowa*, Annals (3), 5: 117-125, July, 1901.

Cole, Cyrenus, *"Father" Clarkson*, Midland Monthly, 1: 59-73, Jan., 1894.

Colson, Ethel M., *Four Famous Iowa Girls in Chicago*, Midland Monthly, 8: 107-110, Aug., 1897.

Davis, Fred, *The Man He Was* [G. D. Perkins], Palimpsest, 5: 292-304, Aug., 1924.

Fox, James, *Crum and the Standard*, Palimpsest, 21: 318-330, Oct., 1940.

Frazee, George, *Clark Dunham, Sometime Editor of the Burlington Hawk-Eye*, Annals (3), 4: 209-218, Oct., 1899.

Heizer, E. P., *A Journalist of Purpose* [G. D. Perkins], Palimpsest, 5: 273-291, Aug., 1924.

Herriott, Frank I., *August P. Richter*, Annals (3), 17: 243-269, 357-390, April, July, 1930.

Jordan, Philip D., *James Gardiner Edwards*, Palimpsest, 19: 106-116, March, 1938.

Jordan, Philip D., *James Madison Broadwell—A Genealogical Note*, Annals (3), 19: 55-62, July, 1933.

Kelly, Henry C., *Northern Iowa—1858*, Palimpsest, 30: 42-60, Feb., 1949.

Leysen, Ralph J., *Iowa and the Lee Papers*, Palimpsest, 31: 393-400, Oct., 1950.

Mills, George, *Barlow Granger—Pioneer*, Palimpsest, 30: 275-278, Sept., 1949.

Mills, George, *Cowles and Ingham*, Palimpsest, 30: 290-294, Sept., 1949.

Mills, George, *The Fighting Clarksons*, Palimpsest, 30: 283-289, Sept., 1949.

Mills, George, *Notable Journalists*, Palimpsest, 30: 295-301, Sept., 1949.

Moeller, Leslie G., *What Makes a Master Editor?*, Palimpsest, 32: 161-174, April, 1951.

Parvin, Theodore S., *Thomas Hughes*, Historical Record, 6: 433-445, April, 1890.

Perkins, George D., *Azro Benjamin Franklin Hildreth*, Annals (3), 9: 321-336, April, 1910.

Perkins, George D., Palimpsest, 5: 273-317, Aug., 1924.

Perkins, George D., and G. Walter Barr, *Samuel Mercer Clark*, Historical Record, 17: 277-292, April, 1901.

Petersen, William J., *Roving Correspondents*, Palimpsest, 30: 61-64, Feb., 1949.

Petersen, William J., *The Story of Iowa*, 2: 628-660. Lewis Historical Co., New York. 1952.

Reid, Don, *History of the Award*, Palimpsest, 32: 153-160, April, 1951.

Richter, August P., *Clint Parkhurst*, Palimpsest, 1: 183-192, Dec., 1920.

Smith, Luther—Mahaney, Paul J., *Sketches of Master Editors*, Palimpsest, 32: 175-184, April, 1951.

Swisher, Jacob A., *Samuel Mercer Clark*, Palimpsest, 29: 111-120, April, 1948.

Tillinghast, B. F., *D. N. Richardson*, Historical Record, 15: 481-495, July, 1899.

White, Hiram F., *The Career of Samuel R. Thurston in Iowa and Oregon*, Iowa Journal, 14: 239-264, April, 1916.

Wright, Luella M., *Henry A. and George D. Perkins in the Campaign of 1860*, Iowa Journal, 42: 162-191, April, 1944.

EARLY IOWA IMPRINTS

A Check List of Iowa Imprints, 1838-1860. WPA Historical Records Survey Project, Chicago. 1940.

Moffit, Alexander, *A Checklist of Iowa Imprints 1837-1860*, Iowa Journal, 36: 3-95, Jan., 1938.

Moffit, Alexander, *Iowa Imprints Before 1861*, Iowa Journal, 36: 152-205, April, 1938.

Mott, Frank L., *Literature of Pioneer Life in Iowa*. SHSI. 1923.

Transportation and Communication

TRANSPORTATION AND COMMUNICATION — IN GENERAL

Book of Iowa, The, 177-193. State of Iowa, Des Moines. 1932.

Briggs, John E., *Iowa Old and New*, 271-300. University Publishing Co., Lincoln, Nebr. 1939.

Gallaher, Ruth A., *Wheels, Planes and Power*, Palimpsest, 27: 317-320, Oct., 1946.

Henely, Louise Miller, *Crossing the Mississippi*, Palimpsest, 26: 215-217, July, 1945.

Iowa: A Guide to the Hawkeye State, 84-90. Viking Press, New York. 1938.

Johnson, E. A., *Antique and Modern*, Annals (3), 30: 297-301, April, 1950.

Larson, Gustav E., *Notes on the Navigation of Iowa Rivers*, Iowa Journal, 39: 403-412, Oct., 1941.

Petersen, William J., *A Century of River Traffic*, Palimpsest, 27: 289-300, Oct., 1946.

Petersen, William J., *The Story of Iowa*, 1: 496-606; 2: 607-627. Lewis Historical Co., New York. 1952.

Petersen, William J., *Transportation by Land*, Palimpsest, 27: 301-316, Oct., 1946.

STEAMBOATING ON THE UPPER MISSISSIPPI

Bissell, Richard, *A Stretch on the River*. Little, Brown, Boston. 1950.

Blanchard, B. W., *The Torpedo-Boat, "Ericsson"*, Midland Monthly, 2: 85-88, Aug., 1894.

Campbell, A. B., *Up the Mississippi in 1835*, Midland Monthly, 8: 326-328, Oct., 1897.

Fugina, Frank, *Lore and Lure of the Scenic Upper Mississippi River*. Published by the author, Winona, Minn. 1945.

Gist, W. W., *Some Attractions on the Upper Mississippi*, Midland Monthly, 5: 395-400, May, 1896.

Haefner, Marie, *Argonauts of the Mississippi*, Palimpsest, 13: 473-486, Dec., 1932.

Hartsough, Mildred L., *From Canoe to Steel Barge on the Upper Mississippi*. University of Minnesota Press, Minneapolis. 1934.

Havighurst, Walter E., *The Upper Mississippi*. Farrar & Rinehart, New York. 1938.

Iowa Sun, *Fast Traveling*, Annals (3), 27: 118, Oct., 1945.

Klingaman, O. E., *Upper Mississippi in 1840*, Annals (3), 29: 176-196, Jan., 1948.

Latrobe, Charles J., *A River Trip in 1833*, Palimpsest, 2: 244-263, Aug., 1921.

Merrick, George B., *Old Times on the Upper Mississippi*. Arthur H. Clark, Cleveland. 1909.

Merrick, George B., *Joseph Reynolds and the Diamond Jo Line Steamers, 1862-1911*, Proceedings of the Mississippi Valley Historical Association, 1914-1915, 8: 217-261.

Mississippi Navigation in 1844, Annals (3), 29: 56, July, 1947.

Petersen, William J., *Captain Daniel Smith Harris*, Iowa Journal, 28: 505-542, Oct., 1930.

Petersen, William J., *Captain Joseph Throckmorton*, Palimpsest, 10: 129-144, April, 1929.

Petersen, William J., *"Diamond Jo" Reynolds*, Palimpsest, 24: 205-236, July, 1943.

Petersen, William J., *The Grand Excursion of 1854*, Palimpsest, 14: 301-314, Aug., 1933.

Petersen, William J., *Indians and the Steamboats on the Upper Mississippi*, Iowa Journal, 30: 155-181, April, 1932.

Petersen, William J., *Iowa: The Rivers of Her Valleys*, 24-205. SHSI. 1941.

Petersen, William J., *Steam Sleighs for Steamboats*, Palimpsest, 17: 1-8, Jan., 1936.

Petersen, William J., *Steamboating on the Upper Mississippi*. SHSI. 1937.

Petersen, William J., *Steamboats Dubuque*, Palimpsest, 10: 398-411, Nov., 1929.

Petersen, William J., *The Story of Iowa*, 1: 496-522. Lewis Historical Co., New York. 1952.

Petersen, William J., *Troops and Military Supplies on the Upper Mississippi River Steamboats*, Iowa Journal, 33: 260-286, July, 1935.

Petersen, William J., *The Voyage of the Virginia*, Palimpsest, 13: 297-317, Aug., 1932.

Petersen, William J., *Winter River Traffic*, Palimpsest, 25: 97-128, April, 1944.

Quick, Herbert, and Edward Quick, *Mississippi Steamboatin'*. Henry Holt, New York. 1926.

Shippee, Lester B., *Steamboating on the Upper Mississippi after the Civil War: A Mississippi Magnate*, Mississippi Valley Historical Review, 6: 470-502, March, 1920.

A *Western Demand for Internal Improvements*, Iowa Journal, 14: 265-267, April, 1916.

Wilson, Ben H., *The Des Moines Rapids Canal*, Palimpsest, 5: 117-132, April, 1924.

Wilson, Ben H., *The Ericsson*, Palimpsest, 14: 177-210, May, 1933.

Wilson, Ben H., *Over the Rapids*, Palimpsest, 4: 361-378, Nov., 1923.

RAFTING ON THE MISSISSIPPI

Blair, Walter A., *A Raft Pilot's Log*. Arthur H. Clark, Cleveland. 1930.

Meyer, Marie E., *Rafting on the Mississippi*, Palimpsest, 8: 121-131, April, 1927.

Meyer, Marie E., *River Towns*, Palimpsest, 7: 381-389, Dec., 1926.

Russell, Charles E., *A-Rafting on the Missisip'*. Century, New York. 1928.

Material on rafting may also be found in the histories of the counties along the Mississippi River and in the files of the *Burlington Post*.

STEAMBOATING ON THE MISSOURI RIVER

Chittenden, Hiram M., *History of Early Steamboat Navigation on the Missouri River*. 2 vols. Francis P. Harper, New York. 1903.

De Girardin, E., *A Trip to the Bad Lands*, Palimpsest, 8: 89-101, March, 1927.

Dye, Eva E., *The Conquest: The True Story of Lewis and Clark* (novel). McClurg, Chicago. 1912.

Freeman, Lewis R., *Trailing History Down the Big Muddy*, National Geographic, 54: 73-120, July, 1928.

Hanson, Joseph M., *The Conquest of the Missouri*. McClurg, Chicago. 1910.

Holt, Edgar A., *A Voyage of the Omaha*, Palimpsest, 6: 128-136, April, 1925.

Neihardt, John G., *The River and I*. Macmillan, New York. 1927.

Niles' National Register, *On the Frontier in 1845*, Palimpsest, 9: 199-201, June, 1928.

Petersen, William J., *Iowa: The Rivers of Her Valleys*, 206-311. SHSI. 1941.

Petersen, William J., *Ho! for the Mountains*, Palimpsest, 26: 148-160, May, 1945.

Petersen, William J., *Steamboating on the Upper Mississippi*, 81-89. SHSI. 1937.

Petersen, William J., *Up the Missouri with Atkinson*, Palimpsest, 12: 315-325, Aug., 1931.

Vestal, Stanley, *The Missouri*. Farrar & Rinehart, New York. 1945.

See also references under Fur Trade, Lewis and Clark, Council Bluffs, and Sioux City.

STEAMBOATING ON THE DES MOINES RIVER

Bloomington, Herald, *Navigation of the Des Moines*, Annals (3), 29: 63, July, 1947.

Davis, C. F., *The Voyage of the First Steamboat from Keokuk to Fort Dodge*, Annals (3), 7: 140-142, July, 1905.

Hussey, Tacitus, *History of Steamboating on the Des Moines River, from 1837 to 1862*, Annals (3), 4: 323-382, April, 1900.

Petersen, William J., *Iowa: The Rivers of Her Valleys*, 177-205. SHSI. 1941.

STEAMBOATING ON THE CEDAR AND IOWA RIVERS

Grahame, Russell C., *Voyages of the Black Hawk*, Palimpsest, 9: 157-169, May, 1928.

Lathrop, Henry W., *Early Steamboating on the Iowa River*, Historical Record, 13: 44-46, Jan., 1897.

Parish, John C., *The Ripple*, Palimpsest, 2: 113-122, April, 1921.

Petersen, William J., *Iowa: The Rivers of Her Valleys*, 119-156. SHSI. 1941

Shambaugh, Benj. F., *The Old Stone Capitol Remembers*, 182-208. SHSI. 1939.

FERRIES AND BRIDGES

Agnew, Dwight L., *Jefferson Davis and the Rock Island Bridge*, Iowa Journal, 47: 3-14, Jan., 1949.

Gallaher, Ruth A., *Guilty or Not Guilty*, Palimpsest, 19: 50-61, Feb., 1938.

Gallaher, Ruth A., *One More River to Cross*, Palimpsest, 8: 102-118, March, 1927.

Johnson, William S., *Crossing the Mississippi*, Palimpsest, 1: 169-182, Dec., 1920.

Lincoln and the Bridge Case, Palimpsest, 3: 142-154, May, 1922.

Mahan, Bruce E., *Bridging the Cedar*, Palimpsest, 4: 307-320, Sept., 1923.

Parish, John C., *The First Mississippi Bridge*, Palimpsest, 3: 133-141, May, 1922.

Petersen, William J., *The Story of Iowa*, 1: 523-538. Lewis Historical Co., New York. 1952.

Van der Zee, Jacob, *The Roads and Highways of Territorial Iowa*, Iowa Journal, 3: 181-191, April, 1905.

Whitley, Mrs. Francis E., *Across the Mississippi*, Palimpsest, 15: 10-16, Jan., 1934.

Wilson, Ben H., *The Plattsmouth Crossing*, Palimpsest, 30: 389-400, Dec., 1949.

Wilson, Ben H., *Steel Spans a River*, Palimpsest, 28: 207-217, July, 1947.

ROADS AND HIGHWAYS

Aldrich, Charles, *The Old Prairie Slough*, Annals (3), 5: 27-32, April, 1901.

Briggs, John E., *Along the Old Military Road*, Palimpsest, 2: 49-59, Feb.,

1921.

Brindley, John E., *History of Road Legislation in Iowa*. SHSI. 1912.

Gingerich, Melvin, *The Oskaloosa Road*, Palimpsest, 25: 353-357, Dec., 1944.

Glass, Remley J., *Early Transportation and the Plank Road*, Annals (3), 21: 502-534, Jan., 1939.

Grahame, Pauline P., *On the Highway*, Palimpsest, 8: 24-27, Jan., 1927.

Grahame, Pauline P., *On the Highway*, Palimpsest, 32: 24-27, Jan., 1951.

Hansen, Marcus L., *Phantoms on the Old Road*, Palimpsest, 2: 35-48, Feb., 1921.

Jackson, W. Turrentine, *The Army Engineers as Road Builders in Territorial Iowa*, Iowa Journal, 47: 15-33, Jan., 1949.

Mahan, Bruce E., *The Scotch Grove Trail*, Palimpsest, 4: 379-397, Nov., 1923.

Meyers, F. W., *The Great Ridge Road*, Palimpsest, 13: 410-415, Oct., 1932.

Parish, John C., *The Old Military Road*, Palimpsest, 2: 33-34, Feb., 1921.

Petersen, William J., *On River and Highway*, Palimpsest, 19: 73-88, March, 1938.

Petersen, William J., *The Story of Iowa*, 1: 539-550, 592-606. Lewis Historical Co., New York. 1952.

Petersen, William J., *Transportation by Land*, Palimpsest, 27: 301-316, Oct., 1946.

Plank Roads in Northeastern Iowa, Annals (3), 22: 77-81, July, 1939.

Van der Zee, Jacob, *The Roads and Highways of Territorial Iowa*, Iowa Journal, 3: 175-225, April, 1905.

Wilson, Ben H., *The Burlington Road*, Palimpsest, 16: 305-334, Oct., 1935.

Wilson, Ben H., *Plank Road Fever*, Palimpsest, 15: 289-318, Sept., 1934.

Wilson, Ben H., *Planked from Keokuk*, Palimpsest, 27: 369-380, Dec., 1946.

HIGHWAY ADMINISTRATION

Bodine, Marcy G., *The Administration of the Drivers' License Law in Iowa*, Iowa Journal, 40: 3-51, Jan., 1942.

Brindley, John E., *History of Road Legislation in Iowa*. SHSI. 1921.

Brindley, John E., *Road Legislation in Iowa*, Applied History, 1: 3-91. SHSI. 1912.

Kaloupek, Walter E., *The History and Administration of the Iowa Highway Safety Patrol*, Iowa Journal, 36: 339-386, Oct., 1938.

Pollock, Ivan L., *The Administration of Highways in the Country*, Applied History, 4: 416-471. SHSI. 1925.

Porter, Kirk H., *Managing a Campaign: An Account of the Good Roads Campaign in Johnson County, Iowa*, Iowa Journal, 24: 511-591, Oct., 1926.

Powers, Samuel C. E., *The Iowa State Highway Commission*, Iowa Journal, 29: 42-103, Jan., 1931.

Swisher, Jacob A., *Municipal Administration of Public Works*, Applied History, 6: 315-369. SHSI. 1930.

STAGECOACH DAYS

Cole, Harry E., *Stagecoach and Tavern Tales of the Old Northwest*. Arthur H. Clark, Cleveland. 1930.

Colton, Kenneth E., *Bringing the Stage Coach to Iowa: 1837-1842*, Annals (3), 22: 3-53, July, 1939.

Colton, Kenneth E., *Stagecoach Travel in Iowa*, Annals (3), 22: 175-200, Jan., 1940.

Grahame, Orville F., *Stagecoach Days*, Palimpsest, 5: 176-185, May, 1924.

Hansen, Marcus L., *Phantoms on the Old Road*, Palimpsest, 2: 35-48, Feb., 1921.

Larsen, Arthur J., *Roads and Trails in the Minnesota Triangle, 1849-1860*, Minnesota History, 11: 387-411, Dec., 1930.

Pelzer, Louis, *Pioneer Stage-Coach Travel*, Mississippi Valley Historical Review, 23: 3-26, June, 1936.

Petersen, William J., *The Story of Iowa*, 1: 539-550. Lewis Historical Co., New York. 1952.

See also the references on Roads and Highways.

POST OFFICES AND POST ROADS

Haefner, Marie, *Waiting for the Mail*, Palimpsest, 21: 209-217, July, 1940.

Hammer, Ilda M., *A History of the Des Moines Post Office*, Annals (3), 19: 146-155, Oct., 1933.

Ludwig, Mary C., *Beginnings at Morning Sun*, Palimpsest, 30: 142-148, May, 1949.

Ludwig, Mary C., *From Horseback to Jeep*, Palimpsest, 30: 149-160, May, 1949.

Ludwig, Mary C., *Service with a Smile—1949*, Palimpsest, 30: 161-168, May, 1949.

Petersen, William J., *Backgrounds of RFD*, Palimpsest, 30: 137-141, May, 1949.

Petersen, William J., *A Century of Mail Delivery*, Palimpsest, 27: 225-239, Aug., 1946.

Petersen, William J., *Some Beginnings in Iowa*, Iowa Journal, 28: 32-37, Jan., 1930.

Petersen, William J., *The Story of Iowa*, 1: 308-311, 539-550. Lewis Historical Co., New York. 1952.

Peterson, Harold D., *The Mail Was Late*, Palimpsest, 23: 47-56, Feb., 1942.

Proposals for Carrying the Mail in the State of Iowa, Annals (3), 20: 450-458, Oct., 1936.

Swisher, Jacob A., *Air Mail in the Twenties*, Palimpsest, 26: 12-20, Jan., 1945.

CONSTRUCTION OF RAILROADS

Agnew, Dwight L., *Iowa's First Railroad*, Iowa Journal, 48: 1-26, Jan., 1950.

Barkley, Alonzo J., *How Boonesboro Lost a Railroad Station*, Annals (3), 12: 540-543, Jan., 1921

Beard, Earl S., *Local Aid to Railroads in Iowa*, Iowa Journal, 50: 1-34, Jan., 1952.

Book of Iowa, The, State of Iowa, Des Moines. 1932.

Branch, E. Douglas, *Railroads Came to Council Bluffs*, Palimpsest, 10: 201-232, June, 1929.

Coffin, Lorenzo S., *Safety Appliances on the Railroads*, Annals (3), 5: 561-582, Jan., 1903.

Cole, Cyrenus, *A History of the People of Iowa*, 279-284, 399-406. Torch Press, Cedar Rapids. 1921.

Corliss, Carlton J., *Mainline of Mid-America: The Story of the Illinois Central*. Creative Age Press, New York. 1950.

Craig, James Thomas, *Great Western Builds Oelwein Shops*, Annals (3), 26: 90-123, Oct., 1944.

Craig, James Thomas, *Oelwein Secures the C. G. W. Shops, 1894*, Annals (3), 24: Part 1, 211-236, Jan., 1943.

The Davenport & Iowa City Rail Road, Iowa Journal, 49: 257-267, July, 1951.

Dodge, Grenville M., *Surveying the M. and M.*, Palimpsest, 18: 301-311, Sept., 1937.

Donovan, Frank P. Jr., *The Minneapolis & St. Louis Railway*, Palimpsest, 32: 249-280, July, 1951.

Donovan, Frank P., *Mileposts on the Prairie: The Story of the Minneapolis & St. Louis Railway*. Simmons-Boardman, New York. 1950.

Dusey, Frank W., *Two-story House Moved on Flat Cars*, Annals (3), 30: 135-141, Oct., 1949.

Galloway, John D., *The First Transcontinental Railroad: Central Pacific's Union Pacific*. Simmons-Boardman, New York. 1950.

Graves, Sarah E., *The Coming of the Railroad*, Palimpsest, 2: 240-243, Aug., 1921.

Hedge, Thomas, *Charles Elliott Perkins*, Annals (3), 8: 367-381, April, 1908.

Hoeltje, Hubert H., *The "First" Locomotive*, Palimpsest, 12: 64-69, Feb., 1931.

Hoeltje, Hubert H., *United by Rail*, Palimpsest, 10: 389-397, Nov., 1929.

Hussey, Tacitus, *How the Des Moines Valley Railroad Came to Des Moines*, Annals (3), 8: 125-134, July, 1907.

Johnson, E. A., *McMillan's Integrity and Loyalty*, Annals (3), 30: 539-544, Jan., 1951.

Johnson, Jack T., *Levi O. Leonard*, Palimpsest, 18: 349-380, Nov., 1937.

Johnson, Jack T., *Peter Anthony Dey*. SHSI. 1939.

Johnson, Jack T., *Plumbe's Railroad to the Moon*, Palimpsest, 19: 89-97, March, 1938.

King, John, *John Plumbe, Originator of the Pacific Railroad*, Annals (3), 6: 289-296, Jan., 1904.

Lathrop, Henry W., *The Pioneer Railroad of Iowa*, Historical Record, 8: 123-134, July, 1897.

Leonard, Levi O., and Jack T. Johnson, *Railroad to the Sea*. Midland Press, Iowa City. 1939.

McGlothlen, W. F., *Des Moines' Street Transit,* Annals (3), 31: 223-228, Jan., 1952.

Overton, Richard C., *Burlington West.* Harvard Press, Cambridge, Mass., 1941.

Peckham, Edward L., *A Journey Out West,* Palimpsest, 6: 233-249, July, 1925.

Perkins, J. R., *Trails, Rails and War.* Bobbs-Merrill, Indianapolis. 1929.

Petersen, William J., *Asa Whitney in Iowa,* Palimpsest, 18: 343-348, Oct., 1937.

Petersen, William J., *The Burlington Comes,* Palimpsest, 14: 381-395, Nov., 1933.

Petersen, William J., *The Freedom Train in Iowa,* Palimpsest, 29: 269-281, Sept., 1948.

Petersen, William J., *The Grand Excursion of 1854,* Palimpsest, 14: 301-314, Aug., 1933.

Petersen, William J., *The Illinois Central Comes,* Palimpsest, 14: 363-378, Oct., 1933.

Petersen, William J., *The Milwaukee Comes,* Palimpsest, 14: 413-428, Dec., 1933.

Petersen, William J., *The North Western Comes,* Palimpsest, 14: 317-333, Sept., 1933.

Petersen, William J., *The Rock Island Comes,* Palimpsest, 14: 285-300. Aug., 1933.

Petersen, William J., *The Story of Iowa,* 1: 551-591. Lewis Historical Co., New York. 1952.

Petersen, William J., *Transportation by Land,* Palimpsest, 27: 301-316, Oct., 1946.

Phillips, E. Bryant, *Early Street Railways in Council Bluffs,* Iowa Journal, 48: 121-132, April, 1950.

Preston, Ruth I., *The Lyons and Iowa Central Railroad,* Annals (3), 9: 284-301, Jan., 1910.

Quigley, Iola B., *Horse Railways,* Palimpsest, 12: 34-37, Jan., 1931.

Quigley, Iola B., *Some Studies in the Development of Railroads in Northeast Iowa,* Annals (3), 20: 219-231, Jan., 1936.

Rae, W. F., *Through English Eyes,* Palimpsest, 10: 412-418, Nov., 1929.

Riegel, Robert E., *The Omaha Pool,* Iowa Journal, 22: 569-582, Oct., 1924.

Sharp, Mildred J., *The M. and M. Railroad,* Palimpsest, 3: 1-15, Jan., 1922.

Thornton, Harrison John, *America's Freedom Train,* Palimpsest, 29: 257-268, Sept., 1948.

Throne, Mildred, *The Burlington & Missouri River Railroad in Iowa,* Palimpsest, 33: 1-32, Jan., 1952.

Throne, Mildred, *Streamliners in Iowa,* Palimpsest, 32: 217-248, June, 1951.

Titus, George M., *Building the "Kansas City Cut Off,"* Annals (3), 30: 63-68, July, 1949.

Usher, Isaac L., *Letters of a Railroad Builder,* Palimpsest, 3: 16-28, Jan., 1922.

Wick, Barthinius L., *John I. Blair and His Associates in Railway Building in Iowa,* Annals (3), 11: 489-496, Oct., 1914.

Williams, Ora, *Underground Railroad Signals*, Annals (3), 27: 297-303, April, 1946.

Williams, Ora, *When Railroads Were Sought*, Annals (3), 31: 161-176, Jan., 1952.

Wilson, Ben H., *Abandoned Railroads of Iowa*, Iowa Journal, 26: 3-64, Jan., 1928.

Wilson, Ben H., *The Narrow Gauge*, Palimpsest, 13: 133-177, April, 1932.

Wright, Luella M., *Cheers for the D. & S. C.*, Palimpsest, 18: 389-404, Dec., 1937.

REGULATION OF RAILROADS

Allen, Ethan P., *Gelpcke v. The City of Dubuque*, Iowa Journal, 28: 177-193, April, 1930.

Coffin, Lorenzo S., *Safety Appliances on the Railroads*, Annals (3), 5: 561-582, Jan., 1903.

Craig, James Thomas, *The Big Strike at Oelwein Shops*, Annals (3), 28: 116-138, Oct., 1946.

Dey, Peter A., *Railroad Legislation in Iowa*, Historical Record, 9: 540-566, Oct., 1893.

Grodinsky, Julius, *The Iowa Pool*. University of Chicago Press, Chicago. 1950.

Johnson, Jack T., *Peter Anthony Dey*, 173-189. SHSI. 1939.

Larrabee, William, *The Railroad Question*. Schulte Publishing Co., Chicago. 1893.

Pollock, Ivan L., *History of Economic Legislation in Iowa*, 35-66. SHSI. 1918.

Railroad Commissioners of Iowa, *Annual Report*. State of Iowa, Des Moines. Since 1878.

THE TELEGRAPH

Iowa Executive Council, *Annual Report of the Taxable Valuation of Telegraph and Telephone Property*. 29 vols. State of Iowa, Des Moines. 1901-1928. This information is now issued by the Iowa Tax Commission.

Petersen, William J., *The Story of Iowa*, 2: 607-613. Lewis Historical Co., New York. 1952.

Rice, Henry T., *Telegraphy First Used Here in 1862*, Annals (3), 30: 294-301, April, 1950.

Wilson, Ben H., *By Wire*, Palimpsest, 7: 233-260, Aug., 1926.

Wilson, Ben H., *Telegraph Pioneering*, Palimpsest, 6: 373-393, Nov., 1925.

Wright, Luella M., *A Telegraphic Scoop*, Palimpsest, 21: 181-183, June, 1940.

AVIATION

English, Emory H., *When Iowa Took to the Air*, Annals (3), 30: 81-104, Oct., 1949.

Petersen, William J., *Iowa City Municipal Airport*, Palimpsest, 11: 404-414, Sept., 1930.

Petersen, William J., *The Story of Iowa*, 2: 622-627. Lewis Historical Co., New York. 1952.

Ray, W. G., *Billy Robinson, Bird-Man*, Palimpsest, 11: 369-375, Sept., 1930.

Swisher, Jacob A., *From Ship to Shore*, Palimpsest, 23: 145-157, May, 1942.

Swisher, Jacob A., *Air Mail in the Twenties*, Palimpsest, 26: 12-20, Jan., 1945.

Wagner, Dorothy, *Destination—Unknown*, Palimpsest, 11: 376-397, Sept., 1930.

Waymack, W. W., *Good News*, Palimpsest, 11: 398-403, Sept., 1930.

RADIO

Heise, Marjorie Ross, *Two Friendly Farmer Stations*, Iowa Journal, 42: 405-419, Oct., 1944.

Petersen, William J., *The Story of Iowa*, 2: 618-620. Lewis Historical Co., New York. 1952.

Woolfries, A. G., *A Radio Pioneer, WOI-Ames, 1923-1940*, Annals (3), 23: 309-315, April, 1942.

THE TELEPHONE

Cone, Carl B., *Baseball and Telephony*, Palimpsest, 24: 248-254, Aug., 1943.

Cone, Carl B., *Hello Central*, Palimpsest, 24: 73-81, March, 1943.

Deering, Charles C., *The Telephone in Iowa*, Annals (3), 23: 287-308, April, 1942.

Petersen, William J., *The Story of Iowa*, 2: 613-618. Lewis Historical Co., New York. 1952.

Business and Industry

MANUFACTURING

Barnhart, Cornelia Mallett, *The Old Pottery Shop*, Palimpsest, 28: 239-246, Aug., 1947.

Belthuis, Lyda, *The Lumber Industry in Eastern Iowa*, Iowa Journal, 46: 115-155, April, 1948.

Book of Iowa, The, State of Iowa, Des Moines. 1932.

Briggs, John E., *Iowa Old and New*, 349-388. University Publishing Co., Lincoln, Nebr. 1939.

Cheever, Lawrence O., *The House of Morrell*. Torch Press, Cedar Rapids. 1948.

Christensen, Thomas P., *An Industrial History of Scott County, Iowa*, Annals (3), 22: 87-127, Oct., 1939, 259-311, 345-391, Jan., April, 1940.

Funk, A. B., *Fred L. Maytag*. Torch Press, Cedar Rapids. 1936.

Gingerich, Melvin, *Custom Built Coffins*, Palimpsest, 24: 384-388, Dec., 1943.

The Fruits of 100 Years 1827-1927. John Morrell & Co., Ottumwa. 1927.

Iowa: A Guide to the Hawkeye State, 91-99. Viking Press, New York. 1938.

Liebold, M. E., *Bookbinding in Iowa,* Midland Schools, 44: 60, Oct., 1929.

Logan, Guy E., *Iowa's Place in Manufacturing,* Midland Schools, 44: 8-9, Sept., 1929.

Petersen, William J., *Business and Industry,* Palimpsest, 19: 133-145, April, 1938.

Petersen, William J., *The Story of Iowa,* 2: 1066-1097. Lewis Historical Co., New York. 1952.

Petersen, William J., *The W. A. Sheaffer Pen Co.,* Palimpsest, 33: 257-288, Sept., 1952.

Swisher, Jacob A., *The Evolution of Wash Day,* Iowa Journal, 38: 3-49, Jan., 1940.

Swisher, Jacob A., *Mining in Iowa,* Iowa Journal, 43: 305-356, Oct., 1945.

Taylor, Loren, *The Colesburg Pottery,* Palimpsest, 29: 65-75, March, 1948.

Thornton, Harrison J., *The History of the Quaker Oats Company.* University of Chicago Press, Chicago. 1933.

Welch, F. A., *Cement and Gypsum Products of Iowa,* Midland Schools, 44: 245-247, March, 1930.

Welch, F. A., *Dairying as an Iowa Industry,* Midland Schools, 44: 115-117, Nov., 1929.

Welch, F. A., *A Few Outstanding Iowa Industries,* Midland Schools, 44: 349-351, May, 1930.

Welch, F. A., *The Industry of Iowa Ceramics,* Midland Schools, 44: 179-181, Jan., 1930.

Welch, F. A., *Iowa Canneries and Cereal Products,* Midland Schools, 44: 211-213, Feb., 1930.

Welch, F. A., *Iowa Manufacture of Farm Implements,* Midland Schools, 44: 305-307, April, 1930.

Welch, F. A., *Iowa's Meat Packing Industry,* Midland Schools, 44: 149-151, Dec., 1929.

Wilson, Ben H., *Abram Tuston Hay,* Palimpsest, 28: 193-206, July, 1947.

Wilson, Ben H., *The Ericsson,* Palimpsest, 14: 177-210, May, 1933.

Zorbaugh, Grace S. M., *Farm Background of Country Migrants to Iowa Industries,* Iowa Journal, 34: 312-318, July, 1936.

COAL MINING IN IOWA

History of Coal Mining in Iowa [State Mine Inspectors Report], Annals (3), 29: 61-63, July, 1947.

Hoffmann, Phil, *The Lost Creek Disaster,* Palimpsest, 26: 21-27, Jan., 1945.

Hoffmann, Phil, *The Powder House Explosion,* Palimpsest, 26: 247-256, Aug., 1945.

Kreiner, Carl B., *The Ottumwa Coal Palace,* Palimpsest, 3: 336-342, Oct., 1922.

Swisher, Jacob A., *The Rise and Fall of Buxton,* Palimpsest, 26: 179-192, June, 1945.

The Vanishing Iowa Coal Mine, Annals (3), 30: 142-143, Oct., 1949.

See also the various reports on coal mining by the Iowa Geological Survey.

Mills

Babbitt, Charles H., *The Old Pottawattamie Mill,* Palimpsest, 6: 319-334, Sept., 1925.

Duffield, George C., *Frontier Mills,* Annals (3), 6: 425-436, July, 1904.

Fishburn, Jesse J., *Ben Hershey—Lumber Baron,* Palimpsest, 28: 289-299, Oct., 1947.

Hartman, George B., *The Iowa Sawmill Industry,* Iowa Journal, 40: 52-93, Jan., 1942.

Hoeye, Frank, *Pioneer Water Power Mills of Dallas County,* Annals (3), 16: 43-48, July, 1927.

Hussey, Tacitus, *The Story of the Bonaparte Dam,* Annals (3), 7: 608-618, Jan., 1907.

New Steam Mill at Bloomington, Annals (3), 14: 381, July, 1924.

Swisher, Jacob A., *Iowa: Land of Many Mills.* SHSI. 1940.

Swisher, Jacob A., *The Old Rustic Mill,* Palimpsest, 17: 297-309, Sept., 1936.

Thornton, Harrison John, *History of the Quaker Oats Company.* University of Chicago Press, Chicago. 1933.

Weare, John, *Pioneer Perils,* Annals (3), 6: 437-443, July, 1904.

Regulation of Public Utilities

Downey, E. H., *The Regulation of Urban Utilities in Iowa,* Applied History, 1: 93-258. SHSI. 1912.

Haynes, Fred E., *Third Party Movements Since the Civil War,* 67-88. SHSI. 1916.

Trachsel, Herman H., *Municipal Administration of Public Utilities,* Applied History, 6: 373-443. SHSI. 1930.

Money and Banking

Book of Iowa, The, 216-221. State of Iowa, Des Moines. 1932.

Burrows, J. M. D., *Wildcat Currency,* Palimpsest, 14: 267-282, July, 1933.

English, Emory H., *Iowa Bank Law a Bulwark of Safety,* Annals (3), 30: 39-55, July, 1949.

Gallaher, Ruth A., *The First Bank in Iowa,* Palimpsest, 18: 103-112, March, 1937.

Gallaher, Ruth A., *Money in Pioneer Iowa 1838-1865,* Iowa Journal, 32: 3-59, Jan., 1934.

Herriott, Frank I., *Chapters in Iowa's Financial History,* Annals (3), 5: 352-373, 425-446, April, July, 1902.

The History of the First National Bank in the United States. Rand McNally, Chicago. 1913.

Iowa's Banking History, Midland Monthly, 2: 513-529, Dec., 1894.

Johnson, E. A., *Thrills and Perils of Country Banking,* Annals (3), 30: 343-358, July, 1950.

Lathrop, Henry W., *Some Iowa Bank History,* Historical Record, 13: 54-65, April, 1897.

Merritt, Fred D., *The Early History of Banking in Iowa.* University Press, Iowa City. 1900.

Miller, A. C., *Handling the Panic of 1907,* Annals (3), 8: 536-542, Oct., 1908.

Pollock, Ivan L., *History of Economic Legislation in Iowa,* 168-214. SHSI. 1918.

Price, Hiram, *The State Bank of Iowa,* Annals (3), 1: 266-293, Jan., 1894.

Preston, Howard H., *History of Banking in Iowa.* SHSI. 1922.

Redman, J. H., *Restored Confidence in Iowa Banks,* Annals (3), 30: 56-61, July, 1949.

Remey, J. T., *William F. Coolbaugh,* Annals (3), 7: 401-412, July, 1906.

Sherman, Hoyt, *Early Banking in Iowa,* Annals (3), 5: 1-13, April, 1901.

Sherman, Hoyt, *The State Bank of Iowa,* Annals (3), 5: 93-116, July, 1901.

Snyder, Charles E., *Two Sons of New York in Iowa,* Annals (3), 25: 147-173, Jan., 1944.

Talle, Henry O., *A Century of Banking in Iowa,* Annals (3), 28: 195-204, Jan., 1947.

INSURANCE

Swisher, Jacob A., *Life Insurance,* Palimpsest, 14: 101-134, March, 1933.

Swisher, Jacob A., *Insurance Comes to Iowa,* Palimpsest, 21: 218-228, July, 1940.

SALESMANSHIP

Mills, Frank M., *Early Commercial Travelling in Iowa,* Annals (3), 11: 328-335, April, 1914.

Ollivier, Lois Marie, *Berries for Sale,* Palimpsest, 23: 177-184, June, 1942.

Tjernagel, P. G., *Erik Kjyten,* Palimpsest, 12: 160-166, April, 1931.

Tjernagel, P. G., and H. M. Tjernagel, *Who Was Nagelsen,* Palimpsest, 13: 261-273, July, 1932.

Agriculture

AGRICULTURE

Agriculture, Palimpsest, 11: 269-320, July, 1930.

Aldrich, Charles, *The Old Prairie Slough,* Annals (3), 5: 27-32, April, 1901.

Aldrich, Charles, *The Repeal of the Granger Law in Iowa,* Iowa Journal, 3: 256-270, April, 1905.

Bessey, Charles E., *Laying the Foundation,* Annals (3), 9: 26-44, April, 1909.

Book of Iowa, The. State of Iowa, Des Moines. 1932.

Briggs, John E., *Iowa Old and New,* 301-348. University Publishing Co., Lincoln, Nebr. 1939.

Burrows, J. M. D., *Ventures in Wheat,* Palimpsest, 4: 53-62, Feb., 1923.

Coffin, Lorenzo S., *Agricultural Relief in 1873*, Palimpsest, 22: 293-300, Oct., 1941.

Coffin, Lorenzo S., *Breaking Prairie*, Annals (3), 5: 447-452, July, 1902.

Cunningham, J. C., *Sons of the Soil*, Iowa Journal, 35: 263-322, July, 1937.

Davidson, J. Brownlee, *Advent of Machine Production*, Palimpsest, 31: 85-95, March, 1950.

Davidson, J. Brownlee, *History of Farm Machines*, Palimpsest, 31: 96-112, March, 1950.

Davidson, J. Brownlee, *Influence of Farm Machinery*, Palimpsest, 31: 113-116, March, 1950.

Davidson, J. Brownlee, *Primitive Farm Implements*, Palimpsest, 31: 79-84, March, 1950.

Erwin, A. T., *Immigrants from Russia*, Palimpsest, 11: 311-315, July, 1930.

Farming in 1866, Palimpsest, 31: 484-490, Dec., 1950.

Frederick, John T., *The Farm in Iowa Fiction*, Palimpsest, 32: 121-152, March, 1951.

Gallaher, Ruth A., *Indian Corn as a Substitute*, Palimpsest, 27: 189-192, June, 1946.

Gallaher, Ruth A., *Science Versus Chance*, Palimpsest, 28: 350-352, Nov., 1947.

Gardner, Flora Clark, *The Business of Bees*, Palimpsest, 26: 332-348, Nov., 1945.

Haefner, John Henry, *Iowa State Department of Agriculture—Its Evolution*, Iowa Journal, 41: 113-175, April, 1943.

Hall, Reeves, *The Rockwell Cooperative*, Palimpsest, 24: 116-129, April, 1943.

Harbert, Albert N., *Joseph Lancaster Budd*, Annals (3), 7: 30-33, April, 1905.

Hayter, Earl W., *An Iowa Farmers' Protective Association*, Iowa Journal, 37: 331-362, Oct., 1939.

Heavy Breaking Plow, The, Annals (3), 21: 143-149, Oct., 1937.

Heise, Marjorie Ross, *Two Friendly Farmer Stations*, Iowa Journal, 42: 405-419, Oct., 1944.

Higgins, F. Hal, *Iowa's First Steam Tractor*, Annals (3), 22: 464-468, Oct., 1940.

Hughes, H. D., *The Coming of the Legumes*, Palimpsest, 11: 292-302, July, 1930.

Iowa: A Guide to the Hawkeye State, 65-76. Viking Press, New York, 1938.

Iowa Secretary of Agriculture, *Iowa Year Book of Agriculture*. State of Iowa, Des Moines. Since 1900.

Iowa State Agricultural Society, *Annual Report*. State of Iowa, Des Moines. 1854-1899.

Jarchow, Merrill E., *Life on a Jones County Farm, 1873-1912*, Iowa Journal, 49: 311-338, Oct., 1951.

Jarchow, Merrill E., *Social Life of an Iowa Farm Family*, Iowa Journal, 50: 123-154, April, 1952.

Jordan, Philip D., *Invention and Progress*, Palimpsest, 23: 253-263, Aug., 1942.

Petersen, William J., *In the Fields,* Palimpsest, 19: 275-285, July, 1938.

Petersen, William J., *J. Brownlee Davidson,* Palimpsest, 31: 77-78, March, 1950.

Petersen, William J., *The Story of Iowa,* 2: 1052-1065. Lewis Historical Co., New York. 1952.

Poage, Jean, *Tom Visits the Market,* Annals (3), 31: 215-222, Jan., 1952.

Pollock, Ivan L., *History of Economic Legislation in Iowa,* 67-80. SHSI. 1918.

Ross, Earle D., *Charles Mason and Federal Aid to Agriculture,* Palimpsest, 28: 12-24, Jan., 1947.

Ross, Earle D., *The Evolution of the Agricultural Fair in the Northwest,* Iowa Journal, 24: 445-480, July, 1926.

Ross, Earle D., *Farm Tenancy in Iowa,* Annals (3), 31: 36-40, July, 1951.

Ross, Earle D., *Green Pastures and Tall Corn,* Palimpsest, 27: 161-169, June, 1946.

Ross, Earle D., *Iowa Agriculture.* SHSI. 1951.

Ross, Earle D., *Lorenzo S. Coffin—Farmer,* Palimpsest, 22: 289-292, Oct., 1941.

Ross, Earle D., *The New Agriculture,* Iowa Journal, 47: 119-139, April, 1949.

Ross, Earle D., *Top Roots of Iowa Agriculture,* Annals (3), 27: 304-310, April, 1946.

Schmidt, Louis B., *Farm Organizations in Iowa,* Palimpsest, 31: 117-162, April, 1950.

Schmidt, Louis B., *The Internal Grain Trade of the United States 1850-1860,* Iowa Journal, 18: 94-124, Jan., 1920.

Schmidt, Louis B., *The Internal Grain Trade of the United States 1860-1890,* Iowa Journal, 19: 196-245, 414-455, April, July, 1921; 20: 70-131, Jan., 1922.

Schmidt, Louis B., *Some Significant Aspects of the Agrarian Revolution in the United States,* Iowa Journal, 18: 371-395, July, 1920.

Schmidt, Louis B., *The Westward Movement of the Corn Growing Industry in the United States,* Iowa Journal, 21: 112-141, Jan., 1923.

Schmidt, Louis B., *The Westward Movement of the Wheat Growing Industry in the United States,* Iowa Journal, 18: 396-412, July, 1920.

Schmidt, Louis B., *An Unworked Field in Mississippi Valley History,* Iowa Journal, 21: 94-111, Jan., 1923.

Swisher, Jacob A., *Chinch Bugs Rampant,* Palimpsest, 16: 201-210, July, 1935.

Swisher, Jacob A., *The Corn Gospel Train,* Palimpsest, 28: 321-333, Nov., 1947.

Thornton, Harrison John, *Oats in History,* Iowa Journal, 30: 377-394, July, 1932.

Throne, Mildred, *"Book Farming" in Iowa, 1840-1870,* Iowa Journal, 49: 117-142, April, 1951.

Throne, Mildred, *The Grange in Iowa, 1868-1875,* Iowa Journal, 47: 289-324, Oct., 1949.

Tillinghast, B. F., *Iowa Corn for Russians,* Palimpsest, 26: 47-64, Feb., 1945.

Wallace, Henry A., *The Civilization of Corn*, Palimpsest, 11: 269-281, July, 1930.

Waters, Geneva, *Friend of the Farm Wife*, Palimpsest, 22: 79-88, March, 1941.

Weeks, E. W., *Furrows*, Palimpsest, 9: 285-390, Aug., 1928.

Wright, Luella M., *The Farmer Supports All*, Palimpsest, 18: 128-142, April, 1937.

Wunderlich, Herbert J., *Foreign Grain Trade of the United States 1835-1860*, Iowa Journal, 33: 27-76, Jan., 1935.

HORTICULTURE

Erwin, A. T., *Immigrants from Russia*, Palimpsest, 11: 311-315, July, 1930.

Erwin, A. T., *Suel Foster*, Palimpsest, 24: 105-115, April, 1943.

Garretson, O. A., *The Lewelling Family—Pioneers*, Iowa Journal, 27: 548-563, Oct., 1929.

Harbert, Albert N., *Joseph Lancaster Budd*, Annals (3), 7: 30-33, April, 1905.

Iowa State Horticultural Society, *Transactions of the Annual Meetings*, State of Iowa, Des Moines. 1867 to date.

Ludwig, Mary Culbertson, *A Man and His Garden*, Palimpsest, 29: 204-213, July, 1948.

Mott, David C., *Gustavus Benson Brackett*, Annals (3), 421-434, Oct., 1936.

Ollivier, Lois Marie, *Berries for Sale*, Palimpsest, 23: 177-184, June, 1942.

Ollivier, Lois Marie, *The Orchards*, Palimpsest, 24: 237-247, Aug., 1943.

Petersen, William J., *Strawberry Time*, Palimpsest, 26: 161-178, June, 1945.

Wilson, Ben H., *Tesson's Apple Orchard*, Palimpsest, 4: 121-131, April, 1923.

FARM PLAGUES

Briggs, John E., *The Grasshopper Plagues in Iowa*, Iowa Journal, 13: 349-392, July, 1915.

Carpenter, Cyrus C., *The Grasshopper Invasion*, Annals (3), 4: 437-447, July, 1900.

Donovan, Josephine B., *Grasshopper Times*, Palimpsest, 4: 193-202, June, 1923.

Lyon, Bessie L., *The Menace of the Blue-stem*, Palimpsest, 21: 247-258, Aug., 1940.

Pellett, Frank C., *Some Farm Pests of Pioneer Times*, Iowa Journal, 41: 176-205, April, 1943.

LIVESTOCK RAISING

Bailey, Belle, *To Market with Hogs*, Palimpsest, 12: 57-63, Feb., 1931.

Book of Iowa, The. 94-105. State of Iowa, Des Moines. 1932.

Campbell, Robert, *Driving Sheep From Kentucky to the Hudson's Bay Country*, Annals (3), 15: 243-253, April, 1926.

Duffield, George C., *Driving Cattle from Texas to Iowa, 1866*, Annals (3), 14: 243-262, April, 1924.

Hopkins, John A., Jr., *Economic History of the Production of Beef Cattle in Iowa*, Iowa Journal, 26: 65-143, 204-294, 415-460, Jan., April, July, 1928.

Hopkins, John A., Jr., *The Passing of the Herds*, Palimpsest, 11: 282-291, July, 1930.

Murphy, Donald R., *Hogs to Feed*, Palimpsest, 11: 303-310, July, 1930.

Murray, Janette Stevenson, *Shipping the Fat Cattle*, Palimpsest, 28: 85-94, March, 1947.

Petersen, William J., *The Dairy Cattle Congress*, Palimpsest, 15: 357-386, Nov., 1934.

Pollock, Ivan L., *History of Economic Legislation in Iowa*, 67-80. SHSI. 1918.

Pugsley, Marcellus, *A Plains Adventure of an Iowa Man*, Annals (3), 10: 136-147, July, 1911.

Quaife, Elvin L., and Arthur L. Anderson, *The Hog in Iowa*, Palimpsest, 33: 193-224, July, 1952.

Teraberry, Hazel B., *Grandma's Wooden Sow*, Palimpsest, 23: 175-176, May, 1942.

Wentworth, Edward N., *America's Sheep Trails*. Iowa State College Press, Ames. 1948.

AGRICULTURAL PUBLICATIONS

Ainsworth, Peter, *The Meredith Publications*, Palimpsest, 11: 256-265, June, 1930.

Edwards, Everett E., *A Bibliography of the History of Agriculture in the United States*. U. S. Department of Agriculture, Miscellaneous Publication No. 84. 1930.

Smith, C. R. F., *The Iowa Homestead*, Palimpsest, 11: 229-241, June, 1930.

Thompson, Arthur T., *Wallaces' Farmer*, Palimpsest, 11: 242-255, June, 1930.

White, Hiram F., *The Career of Samuel R. Thurston in Iowa and Oregon*, Iowa Journal, 14: 239-264, April, 1916.

THE NEW DEAL FARM PROGRAM IN IOWA

Petersen, William J., *Agriculture and the AAA*, Palimpsest, 17: 255-261, Aug., 1936.

Petersen, William J., *Agriculture and Industry*, Palimpsest, 18: 262-269, Aug., 1937.

Petersen, William J., *Economics and Alphabeticals*, Palimpsest, 17: 262-270, Aug., 1936.

Petersen, William J., *Uncle Sam Lends a Hand,* Palimpsest, 16: 245-253, Aug., 1935.
Roberts, Richard H., *The Administration of the 1934 Corn-Hog Program in Iowa,* Iowa Journal, 33: 307-375, Oct., 1935.
Roberts, Richard H., *Economic Effects of the Corn-Hog Program in Iowa,* Iowa Journal, 34: 144-171, April, 1936.
Wallace, Henry A., *America Must Choose.* World Affairs Pamphlets, No. 3. Foreign Policy Association, New York. 1934.
Wallace, Henry A., *The American Choice.* Reynal & Hitchcock, New York. 1940.
Wallace, Henry A., *New Frontiers.* Reynal & Hitchcock, New York. 1934.
Wallace, Henry A., *Statesmanship and Religion.* Round Table Press, New York. 1934.
Wallace, Henry A., *Whose Constitution?* Reynal & Hitchcock, New York. 1936.

Iowa History

WHY STUDY IOWA HISTORY

Gallaher, Ruth A., *This Iowa,* Iowa Journal, 39: 3-51, Jan., 1941.
Gallaher, Ruth A., *What is History?,* Palimpsest, 27: 254-256, Aug., 1946.
Mahan, Bruce E., *State and Local History in the High School,* Bulletin of Information No. 12. SHSI. 1924.
Pelzer, Louis, *The Scope of Iowa History,* Iowa Journal, 8: 467-477, Oct., 1910.
Petersen, William J., *The Use of Local History as a Tool in Studying American History.* Ninth Yearbook of the National Council for the Social Studies, 101-110. 1938.
Petersen, William J., *Iowa History and American History,* Iowa Journal, 47: 34-49, Jan., 1949.
Shambaugh, Benj. F., *The Constitutions of Iowa,* 9-12. SHSI. 1934.
Teakle, Thomas, *The Romance in Iowa History,* Iowa Journal, 14: 159-172, April, 1916.

GENERAL HISTORIES OF IOWA

Andreas, A. T., *Illustrated Historical Atlas of the State of Iowa.* Lakeside Press, Chicago. 1875.
Brigham, Johnson, *Iowa—Its History and Its Foremost Citizens.* 3 vols. S. J. Clarke, Chicago. 1915. (Also in 2 vol. edition).
Cole, Cyrenus, *A History of the People of Iowa.* Torch Press, Cedar Rapids. 1921.
Cole, Cyrenus, *Iowa Through the Years.* SHSI. 1940.
Gue, Benjamin F., *History of Iowa.* 4 vols. Century History Co., New York. 1903.

Harlan, Edgar R., *A Narrative History of the People of Iowa.* 5 vols. American Historical Society, Chicago. 1931.

Petersen, William J., *The Story of Iowa,* 1: 1-606; 2: 607-1112. Lewis Historical Publishing Co., New York. 1952. The first two volumes of this 4-volume set are exclusively history and were written by Dr. Petersen. Two additional volumes containing almost 1,500,000 words are devoted to the biography of Iowans, most of whom subscribed for the set. This material was collected, written, and edited by the Lewis Historical Publishing Company.

Richman, Irving B., *Ioway to Iowa.* SHSI. 1931.

Sabin, Henry, and Edwin L. Sabin, *The Making of Iowa.* A. Flanagan Co., Chicago. 1916.

Salter, William, *Iowa: The First Free State in the Louisiana Purchase.* McClurg, Chicago. 1905.

BRIEF SURVEYS OF IOWA HISTORY

Gallaher, Ruth A., *The First Hundred Years,* Iowa Journal, 31: 531-575, Oct., 1933.

Gallaher, Ruth A., *This Iowa,* Iowa Journal, 39: 3-51, Jan., 1941.

Gallaher, Ruth A., *Pictures are History,* Palimpsest, 27: 321-356, Nov., 1946.

Petersen, William J., *A Day by Day Calendar of Historical Events in Iowa (January-June),* Iowa Journal, 44: 115-173, April, 1946.

Petersen, William J., *A Day by Day Calendar of Historical Events in Iowa (July-December),* Iowa Journal, 44: 227-290, July, 1946.

Petersen, William J., *Looking Backward on Hawkeyeland.* SHSI. 1947.

Petersen, William J., *Documents of Iowa Freedom,* Palimpsest, 29: 282-288, Sept., 1948.

Petersen, William J., *History of Iowa,* Who's Who in Iowa, 11-26. Iowa Press Association, Des Moines. 1940.

Petersen, William J., *Iowa.* Dictionary of American History. Scribners, New York. 1940.

SPECIAL REFERENCES FOR YOUNG PEOPLE

Aitchison, Alison E., *Iowa State Geography.* Ginn, New York. 1921.

Aurner, Clarence R., *Iowa Stories.* 3 vols. Clio Press, Iowa City. 1917.

Briggs, John E., *Iowa Old and New.* University Publishing Co., Lincoln, Nebr. 1939.

Christensen, Thomas P., *The Story of Iowa: A Children's History.* Holst Printing Co., Cedar Falls. 1931.

Erbe, Carl H., *Text and Workbook in the History of Iowa.* Holst Printing Co., Cedar Falls. 1931.

Erbe, Carl H., and Jacob A. Swisher, *Iowa History as Told in Biography.* Holst Printing Co., Cedar Falls. 1932.

Gallaher, Ruth A., *Pictures are History,* Palimpsest, 27: 321-356, Nov., 1946.

Mahan, Bruce E., and Ruth A. Gallaher, *Stories of Iowa for Boys and Girls.* Macmillan, New York. 1929.

Moeller, Hubert L., and Hugh C. Moeller, *Our Iowa: Its Beginnings and Growth.* Newsom & Co., New York. 1938.

Nicklin, Myrtle A., *My Progress Book in Iowa History.* American Education Press, Columbus, Ohio. 1931.

Petersen, William J., *Looking Backward on Hawkeyeland.* SHSI. 1947.

Rule, Edith, and William J. Petersen, *True Tales of Iowa.* Yelland & Hanes, Mason City. 1932.

Wallace, W. L., *Story of Iowa.* Klipto Loose Leaf Co., Mason City. 1931.

HISTORIANS

Charles Aldrich, Annals (3), 8: 563-639, Jan., 1909.

Briggs, John E., *Benj. F. Shambaugh,* Palimpsest, 21: 133-139, May, 1940.

Brigham, Johnson, *A Book of Iowa Authors by Iowa Authors,* 177-186. Iowa State Teachers Association, Des Moines. 1930.

Gallaher, Ruth A., *Benj. F. Shambaugh,* Iowa Journal, 38: 227-233, July, 1940.

Hill, James L., *Dr. William Salter,* Annals (3), 9: 561-644, Jan., 1911.

Mott, David C., *Benjamin F. Gue,* Annals (3), 20: 603-631, April, 1937.

Mott, David C., *Thomas Gregg, Local Historian and Author,* Annals (3), 14: 263-271, April, 1924.

Benjamin Franklin Shambaugh: As Iowa Remembers Him, 1871-1940. SHSI. 1941.

THE STATE HISTORICAL SOCIETY OF IOWA

Board of Curators of the State Historical Society of Iowa, *Biennial Report.* State of Iowa, Des Moines. 1857-1932.

Bourne, Henry E., *The Work of American Historical Societies,* Iowa Journal, 271-285, April, 1905.

Boyd, Julian P., *State and Local Historical Societies in the United States,* American Historical Review, 40: 10-37, Oct., 1934.

Opinions of American Historians on the Work of the State Historical Society of Iowa, Bulletin of Information No. 9. SHSI. 1920.

Petersen, William J., *The State Historical Society of Iowa: 1947-1949,* Iowa Journal, 47: 345-354, Oct., 1949.

Petersen, William J., *The State Historical Society of Iowa: 1949-1951,* Iowa Journal, 49: 193-210, July, 1951.

Proceedings of the Conference of Local Historical Societies of Iowa Held at Iowa City on Wednesday, May 25, 1910, Iowa Journal, 8: 522-552, Oct., 1910.

Shambaugh, Benj. F., *A Brief History of the State Historical Society of Iowa.* SHSI. 1907. Also in Iowa Journal, 1: 139-152, April, 1903.

Shambaugh, Benj. F., *The State Historical Society in War Times,* Iowa and War, No. 18, Dec., 1918. SHSI.

Some Information: The State Historical Society of Iowa. SHSI. 1942; 1948; 1951.

Thwaites, Reuben G., *State and Local Historical Societies,* Iowa Journal, 4: 245-266, April, 1906.

Iowa Songs, Seals, Slogans, and Flag

Gallaher, Ruth A., *The Iowa Banner,* Palimpsest, 5: 395-397, Oct., 1924.

Gallaher, Ruth A., *An Iowa Flag,* Iowa and War, No. 14, Aug., 1918. SHSI.

Gallaher, Ruth A., *Songs of Iowa,* Palimpsest, 5: 387-394, Oct., 1924.

Mahan, Bruce E., *Mottoes and Slogans of Iowa,* Palimpsest, 5: 384-386, Oct., 1924.

Mott, Frank L., *Pronunciation of Iowa,* Palimpsest, 5: 373-377, Oct., 1924.

Mott, Frank L., *The Pronunciation of the Word Iowa,* Iowa Journal, 23: 353-362, July, 1925.

Petersen, William J., *Looking Backward on Hawkeyeland.* 22-26. SHSI. 1947.

Shambaugh, Benj. F., *The Naming of Iowa,* Palimpsest, 5: 370-372, Oct., 1924; 16: 81-86, March, 1935.

Stiles, Cassius C., *The Great Seals of Iowa,* Annals (3), 11: 561-581, Jan., 1915.

Van Ek, Jacob, *Great Seals of Iowa,* Palimpsest, 5: 378-383, Oct., 1924.

Williams, Ora, *Stars on the Flag,* Annals (3), 27: 311-315, April, 1946.

Iowa Place Names

Barnhart, Cornelia Mallett, *Osceola and Oskaloosa,* Palimpsest, 28: 300-309, Oct., 1947.

Casady, P. M., *The Naming of Iowa Counties,* Annals (3), 2: 195-202, July-Oct., 1895.

Counties and County Names, Iowa Official Register, 1909-1910, 587-716.

Eriksson, Erik M., *The Name of Odebolt,* Palimpsest, 10: 432-441, Dec., 1929.

Fitzpatrick, T. J., *The Place-Names of Des Moines County, Iowa,* Annals (3), 21: 56-73, 127-140, July, Oct., 1937, 535-552, 604-640, Jan., April, 1939.

Fitzpatrick, T. J., *The Place-Names of Lee County, Iowa,* Annals (3), 17: 13-58, July, 1929.

Fitzpatrick, T. J., *The Place-Names of Van Buren County, Iowa,* Annals (3), 18: 12-41, 87-116, July, Oct., 1931.

Howe, Samuel S., *A Memoir of Indian Names in Iowa,* Annals (2), 1: 3-28, Jan., 1882.

Hull, John A. T., *Iowa Historical and Comparative Census, 1836-1880,* 384-421. State of Iowa, Des Moines. 1883.

Iowa: A Guide to the Hawkeye State. Viking Press, New York. 1938.

Keyes, Charles Rollin, *Des Moines River, and Origin of the Name*, Annals (3), 3: 554-559, Oct., 1898.

Ludwig, Mary Culbertson, *Namer of Towns*, Palimpsest, 29: 161-173, June, 1948.

Mott, Frank L., *Pronunciation of Iowa*, Palimpsest, 5: 373-379, Oct., 1924.

Mott, Frank L., *Pronunciation of the Word Iowa*, Iowa Journal, 23: 353-362, July, 1925.

Petersen, William J., *Iowa: The Rivers of Her Valleys*. SHSI. 1941.

Read, Allen W., *Literary Place Names*, Palimpsest, 9: 450-457, Dec., 1928.

Shambaugh, Benj. F., *The Naming of Iowa*, Palimpsest, 5: 370-372, Oct., 1924; 16: 81-86, March, 1935.

Shambaugh, Benj. F., *The Origin of the Name Iowa*, Annals (3), 3: 641-644, Jan., 1899.

HISTORIC SITES IN IOWA

Iowa: A Guide to the Hawkeye State. Viking Press, New York. 1938.

Leggett, Richard C., *An Historic Indian Agency*, Annals (3), 25: 257-274, April, 1944.

Petersen, William J., *Great Journeys from Little Homes*, Palimpsest, 29: 255-256, Aug., 1948.

Petersen, William J., *Historical Setting of the Mound Region in Northeastern Iowa*, Iowa Journal, 31: 47-86, Jan., 1933.

Petersen, William J., *Some Beginnings in Iowa*, Iowa Journal, 28: 3-54, Jan., 1930.

Swisher, Jacob A., *Historic Iowa*, Palimpsest, 15: 257-266, Aug., 1934.

Swisher, Jacob A., *The Hoover Birthplace*, Palimpsest, 29: 241-254, Aug., 1948.

Swisher, Jacob A., *Plum Grove*, Palimpsest, 29: 19-32, Jan., 1948.

Swisher, Jacob A., *Some Historic Sites in Iowa*, Iowa Journal, 32: 195-259, July, 1934.

CENSUS OF IOWA

Census of Iowa for the Year 1925. State of Iowa, Des Moines. 1926. Territorial and State census figures were compiled in 1836, 1838, 1844, 1846, 1847, 1849, 1851, 1852, 1854, 1856, 1859, 1863, 1865, 1867, 1869, 1875, and every ten years thereafter until 1925.

Gallaher, Ruth A., *Vagaries of the Census*, Palimpsest, 29: 127-128, April, 1948.

Haefner, Marie, *The Census of 1838*, Palimpsest, 19: 185-192, May, 1938.

Howard, Winifred M., *The Census of 1840*, Palimpsest, 21: 165-180, June, 1940.

Hull, John A. T., *Census of Iowa for 1880, with other Historical and Statistical Data*. State of Iowa, Des Moines. 1883.

Shambaugh, Benj. F., *The First Census of the Original Counties of Dubuque and Demoine (Iowa)*. Historical Department, Des Moines. 1897.

Seventeenth Census of the United States: 1950. Government Printing Office, Washington. 1951. Specific data regarding Iowa begin with the Sixth Census of the United States in 1840.

STATISTICAL SURVEYS

Book of Iowa, The. State of Iowa, Des Moines. 1932.
Iowa Official Register. State of Iowa, Des Moines. 1873 to date.
Iowa State Planning Board, *A Preliminary Report of Progress.* State of Iowa, Des Moines. 1934.
Iowa State Planning Board, *The Second Report.* State of Iowa, Des Moines. 1935.

BIBLIOGRAPHIES

Brigham, Johnson, *A General Survey of the Literature of Iowa History,* Iowa Journal, 1: 77-104, Jan., 1903.
Budington, Margaret, *A Bibliography of Iowa State Publications for 1898 to 1903,* Iowa Journal, 1: 362-403, July, 1903; 2: 399-429, July, 1904; 3: 101-145, Jan., 1905.
Dondore, Dorothy, *The Prairie and the Making of Middle America: Four Centuries of Description.* Torch Press, Cedar Rapids. 1926.
Edwards, Everett E., *A Bibliography of the History of Agriculture in the United States.* U. S. Department of Agriculture, Miscellaneous Publications No. 84. 1930.
Fitzpatrick, T. J., *A Bibliography of Iowa State Publications for 1904 and 1905,* Iowa Journal, 5: 337-408, July, 1907.
Fitzpatrick, T. J., *Bibliography of the Iowa Territorial Documents,* Iowa Journal, 5: 234-269, April, 1907.
Mott, Frank L., *Literature of Pioneer Life in Iowa.* SHSI. 1923.
Petersen, William J., *Two Hundred Topics in Iowa History.* SHSI. 1932.
Petersen, William J., *A Reference Guide to Iowa History.* SHSI. 1942.

STATE AND LOCAL ARCHIVES

Collection and Preservation of the Materials of War History—A Patriotic Service for Public Libraries, Local Historical Societies, and Local Historians, Bulletin of Information No. 8. SHSI. 1918.
English, Emory H., Ed. *Pittman's Useful Life,* Annals (3),31: 309-310, April, 1952.
English, Emory H., *Ora Williams—An Appreciation,* Annals (3), 28: 249-252, April, 1947.
Harlan, Edgar R., *Ethics Involved in the Handling of Personal Papers,* Annals (3), 16: 610-621, April, 1929.
Herriott, Frank I., *The Preservation of Iowa's Public Documents,* Annals (3), 5: 293-306, Jan., 1902.

Indiana Historical Bulletin, *Value of a County Historical Unit,* Annals (3), 27: 161-162, Oct., 1945.

Iowa's New State Office Building, Annals (3), 30: 385-389, July, 1950.

Lyon, Bessie, *Importance of Keeping Records and Archives,* Annals (3), 25: 129-134, Oct., 1943.

Martin, Ethyl E., *Organization, Purpose, and Activities of Local Historical Societies in Iowa,* Bulletin of Information No. 16. SHSI. 1941.

Shambaugh, Benj. F., *A Report on the Public Archives,* Annals (3), 7: 561-591, Jan., 1907.

Spaulding, Ellen D., *A System of Handling and Depositing Personal Archives,* Annals (3), 17: 67-73, July, 1929.

Stiles, Cassius C., *Iowa Public Archives,* Annals (3), 16: 241-308, 331-394, 448-466, April, July, Oct., 1928.

Stiles, Cassius C., *Public Archives Division,* Annals (3), 16: 107-130, Oct., 1927.

Stiles, Cassius C., *Public Archives of Iowa,* Annals (3), 10: 166-193, 273-319, Oct., 1911, Jan.-April, 1912.

Stiles, Ray C., *The Historical, Memorial and Art Department of Iowa,* Annals (3), 21: 6-16, July, 1937.

Suggestions to Public Libraries and Local Historical Societies Relative to Collecting and Preserving Materials of Local History, Bulletin of Information No. 3. SHSI. 1904.

Virtue, Ethel B., *Principles of Classification of Archives,* Annals (3), 12: 1-10, April, 1915.

War and the Record of War, Annals (3), 24: Part 1, 200-210, Jan., 1943.

Williams, Ora, *The Iowa Historical Department,* Annals (3), 23: 267-286, April, 1942.

Williams, Ora, *That Our Memory May be Green,* Annals (3), 24: 93-104, Oct., 1942.

Williams, Ora, *War Record Work in Iowa,* Annals (3), 26: 61-63, July, 1944.

Wissler, Clark, *State and Local Archaeological Surveys,* Bulletin of Information No. 11. SHSI. 1923.

SOURCES OF MATERIAL ON THE HISTORY OF COUNTIES

Allen, Arthur F., *Northwestern Iowa,* 2: 571-898. 2 vols. S. J. Clarke, Chicago. 1927.

Andreas, A. T., *Illustrated Historical Atlas of the State of Iowa.* Lakeside Press, Chicago. 1875.

Cook, Luella E., *Histories of Iowa Counties,* Iowa Journal, 36: 115-151, April, 1938.

Gue, Benjamin F., *History of Iowa,* 3: 293-438. 4 vols. Century History Co., New York. 1903.

Who's Who in Iowa. Iowa Press Association, Des Moines. 1940.

See also the various county histories, plat books, and atlases.

History of Northeastern Iowa

Keyes, Charles Reuben, *Shall Iowa Have National Monuments,* Iowa Journal, 31: 31-46, Jan., 1933.

Lees, James H., *The Geology and Topography of Northeastern Iowa,* Iowa Journal, 31: 3-30, Jan., 1933.

Petersen, William J., *Historical Setting of the Mound Region in Northeastern Iowa,* Iowa Journal, 31: 47-86, Jan., 1933.

Shimek, Bohumil, *The Switzerland of Iowa,* Palimpsest, 16: 289-298, Sept., 1935.

The Significance of Iowa in Frontier History

Boynton, Percy H., *The Rediscovery of the Frontier.* University of Chicago Press, Chicago. 1931.

Branch, E. Douglas, *Westward.* Appleton, New York. 1930.

Clark, Dan E., *The West in American History.* Crowell, New York. 1937.

Colegrove, Kenneth W., *The Attitude of Congress Toward the Pioneers of the West from 1789 to 1820,* Iowa Journal, 8: 3-129, Jan., 1910; 9: 196-302, April, 1911.

Dondore, Dorothy A., *The Prairie and the Making of Middle America,* 153-209. Torch Press, Cedar Rapids. 1926.

Gallaher, Ruth A., *This Iowa,* Iowa Journal, 39: 3-51, Jan., 1941.

Goodwin, Cardinal, *The Trans-Mississippi West.* Appleton, New York. 1922.

Hafen, LeRoy R., and C. C. Rister, *Western America.* Prentice-Hall, New York. 1941.

Hutton, Graham, *Midwest at Noon.* U. of Chicago Press, Chicago. 1946.

Jordan, Philip D., *Preserving Our National Heritage,* Annals (3), 25: 99-104, Oct., 1943.

Larson, Laurence M., *The Changing West of Other Essays.* Norwegian-American Historical Association, Northfield, Minn. 1937.

Paxson, Frederic L., *History of the American Frontier 1763-1893.* Houghton Mifflin, New York. 1924.

Pelzer, Louis, *History Made by Plain Men,* Iowa Journal, 11: 307-322, July, 1913.

Petersen, William J., *Iowa History and American History,* Iowa Journal, 47: 34-49, Jan., 1949.

Riegel, Robert E., *America Moves West.* Henry Holt, New York. 1930.

Schlesinger, Arthur M., *New Viewpoints in American History.* Macmillan, New York. 1922.

Shambaugh, Benj. F., *The History of the West and the Pioneers,* Proceedings of the State Historical Society of Wisconsin for 1910, 133-145. State Historical Society of Wisconsin, Madison. 1911.

Thwaites, Reuben G., *The Romance of Mississippi Valley History,* Proceedings of the Fiftieth Anniversay of the Constitution of Iowa, 115-142. SHSI. 1907.

Turner, Frederick J., *Essays in American History.* Henry Holt, New York. 1910.

Turner, Frederick J., *The Frontier in American History*. Henry Holt, New York. 1921.

Turner, Frederick J., *The Significance of the Mississippi Valley in American History*, Proceedings of the Mississippi Valley Historical Association, 1909-1910, 159-184.

Van der Zee, Jacob, *Amendments to the Constitution of the United States Proposed in the State Legislature of Iowa, 1846-1909*, Iowa Journal, 7: 379-401, July, 1909.

Weld, Laenas G., *Decisive Episodes in Western History*. SHSI. 1914.

Williams, Ora, *The Constitution*, Annals (3), 25: 185-191, Jan., 1944.

TOPICS FOR IOWA HISTORY WEEK

Iowa, Palimpsest, 5: 355-399, Oct., 1924. Also issued as a special number, 7: 1-56, May, 1926.

The Pioneers, Palimpsest, 8: 1-56, Jan., 1927.

Indians of Iowa, Palimpsest, 9: 33-85, Feb., 1928.

The Past at Play, Palimpsest, 10: 33-90, Feb., 1929.

Iowa and the Nation, Palimpsest, 11: 1-542, Jan.-Dec., 1930.

Ioway to Iowa, Palimpsest, 12: 73-134, March, 1931.

Black Hawk and the Treaty of 1832, Palimpsest, 13: 41-92, Feb., 1932.

The Settlers Came: 1833, Palimpsest, 14: 41-100, Feb., 1933.

The Establishment of Civil Government in Iowa, Palimpsest, 15: 33-80, Feb., 1934.

A Century Ago: 1835, Palimpsest, 16: 65-104, March, 1935.

Wisconsin Territory: 1836, Palimpsest, 17: 69-116, March, 1936.

Iowa in 1837, Palimpsest, 18: 65-112, March, 1937.

Iowa in 1838, Palimpsest, 19: 1-524, Jan.-Dec., 1938.

THE CENTENNIAL OF THE TERRITORY AND STATE OF IOWA

The Centennial of Iowa Territory, Annals (3), 21: 210-223, Jan., 1938.

Colton, Kenneth E., *Iowa's Struggle for a Territorial Government*, Annals (3), 21: 363- 396, July, 1938.

Directory of Iowa Territorial Officials, Iowa Journal, 35: 256-262, July, 1937.

Dolliver, James I., *Iowa Contributes to Nation's Progress*, Annals (3), 28: 212-233, Jan., 1947.

Gallaher, Ruth A., *A Decade of Iowa Centennials: 1938-1947*, Iowa Journal, 35: 227-255, July, 1937.

Gallaher, Ruth A., *The Evolution of Stamps*, Palimpsest, 28: 95-96, March, 1947.

Iowa Centennial Anniversary, Annals (3), 27: 62-70, July, 1945.

Iowa in 1838, Palimpsest, 19: 1-524, Jan.-Dec., 1938.

Iowa Measures the Centuries, Annals (3), 29: 57-60, July, 1947.

Iowa Statehood Centennial, (a report of progress), Annals (3), 24: Part 1, 237-241, Jan., 1943.

Klingaman, O. E., *Background to the Establishment of the Territory of Iowa,*
Annals (3), 21: 335-362, July, 1938.

Mason City Globe-Gazette, *Looking to Iowa's Centennial,* Annals (3), 24:
315-317, April, 1943.

Petersen, William J., *The Postage Stamp Centennial,* Palimpsest, 28: 78-84,
March, 1947.

Petersen, William J., *The State Centennial Stamp,* Palimpsest, 28: 65-77,
March, 1947.

Petersen, William J., *The Territorial Centennial of Iowa,* Iowa Journal,
37: 3-51, Jan., 1939.

Swisher, Jacob A., *The Iowa City Centennial,* Iowa Journal, 37: 363-378,
Oct., 1939.

Williams, Ora, *The Quality of Iowa Citizenship,* Annals (3), 28: 188-194,
Jan., 1947.

THE CONTEMPORARY IOWA SCENE

Millsap, Kenneth F., *Iowa in 1950,* Palimpsest, 32: 345-376, Sept., 1951.
Petersen, William J., *Iowa in 1934,* Palimpsest, 16: 233-270, Aug., 1935.
Petersen, William J., *Iowa in 1935,* Palimpsest, 17: 249-296, Aug., 1936.
Petersen, William J., *Iowa in 1936,* Palimpsest, 18: 245-284, Aug., 1937.
See also the yearbooks of the standard encyclopedias.

PAGEANTS

Hurley, George O., *Pageantry for Iowa Communities,* Bulletin of Information No. 10. SHSI. 1923.

Mahan, Bruce E., *The Pioneers—A Pageant of Early Iowa,* Bulletin of
Information No. 13. SHSI. 1927.

Mahan, Bruce E., *The Story of the Indian—A Pageant of Early Iowa,*
Bulletin of Information No. 14. SHSI. 1928.

Petersen, William J., *The Territorial Centennial of Iowa,* Iowa Journal,
37: 3-51, Jan., 1939.

Biographies of Iowans

BIOGRAPHICAL SKETCHES — COLLECTIONS

Aurner, Clarence R., *Some Early Educational Leaders in Iowa,* Iowa Journal,
22: 532-568, Oct., 1924.

Brigham, Johnson, *Iowa: Its History and Its Foremost Citizens.* 3 vols.
Arthur H. Clark, Cleveland. 1915.

Clark, Dan E., *History of Senatorial Elections in Iowa.* SHSI. 1912.

Dictionary of American Biography. 21 vols. Scribners, New York. 1928-
1936.

Gue, Benjamin F., *History of Iowa,* IV. 4 vols. Century History Co., New
York. 1903.

Harlan, Edgar R., *A Narrative History of the People of Iowa*, III, IV, V,
5 vols. American Historical Society, Chicago. 1931.

Lake, Frank C., and Lloyd N. Prince, *Who's Who in Iowa*. Lake and Prince,
Sioux City. 1920.

Lewis Historical Publishing Co. Inc. *The Story of Iowa*. Vols. 3 and 4 's
devoted to "Family and Personal History."

Shambaugh, Benj. F., *Messages and Proclamations of the Governors of Iowa*.
7 vols. SHSI. 1903-1905.

Stiles, Edward H., *Prominent Men of Early Iowa*, Annals (3), 10: 194-201,
Oct., 1911, 250-264, 435-449, Jan.-April, July, 1912, 629-633, Jan.,
1913.

Stiles, Edward H., *Recollections and Sketches of Notable Lawyers and Public
Men of Early Iowa*. Homestead, Des Moines. 1916.

Who's Who in Iowa. Iowa Press Association, Des Moines. 1940.

For additional biographical material see also the table of contents and index.
The county histories contains many brief biographical sketches.

PROMINENT IOWANS

ADAMS, AUSTIN

Adams, Mrs. Mary N., *Austin Adams*, Historical Record, 8: 49-70,
April, 1891.

Swisher, Jacob A., *An Adams in Iowa*, Palimpsest, 29: 39-48, Feb., 1948.

ALLISON, WILLIAM BOYD

Boyd, William R., *William B. Allison*, Annals (3), 23: 118-125, Oct.,
1941.

Brigham, Johnson, *James Harlan*, 260-274. SHSI. 1913.

Clark, Dan E., *History of Senatorial Elections in Iowa*, 152-167. SHSI.
1912.

Cooper, Vernom, *A Diligent Public Servant*, Palimpsest, 6: 265-283,
Aug., 1925.

Eriksson, Erik M., *Presidential Hopes*, Palimpsest, 6: 284-294, Aug.,
1925.

Lodge, Henry C., *William B. Allison*, Annals (3), 11: 321-327, April,
1914.

Robeson, George F., *Young Men for Old*, Palimpsest, 6: 295-302, Aug.,
1925.

Sage, Leland L., *The Early Life of William Boyd Allison*, Iowa Journal,
48: 299-334, Oct., 1950.

White, Edward A., *A Woman Promotes the Presidential Candidacy of
Senator Allison, 1888*, Iowa Journal, 48: 221-246, July, 1950.

ANSON, ADRIAN CONSTANTINE

Swisher, Jacob A., *Adrian C. Anson*, Palimpsest, 3: 374-378, Nov., 1922.

ATKINSON, WILLIAM I.

Flowers, Montaville, *William I. Atkinson—An Appreciation*, Annals
(3), 16: 81-97, Oct., 1927.

CARVER, GEORGE WASHINGTON
  Reed, Charles D., *George Washington Carver, Mystic Scientist*, Annals
    (3), 24: Part 1, 248-253, Jan., 1943.
CHAMBERS, JOHN
  Clarke, William Penn, *Governor John Chambers*, Annals (3), 1: 425-
    445, July, 1894.
  Johnson, Jack T., *John Chambers*, Palimpsest, 22: 129-160, May, 1941.
  Letters of Governor John Chambers on Indian Affairs, 1845, Iowa
    Journal, 19: 246-286, April, 1921.
  Letters of Gov. John Chambers to I. C. Spender, Washington, Annals
    (3), 28: 234-236, Jan., 1947.
  Parish, John C., *John Chambers*. SHSI. 1909.
  Parish, John C., *The Autobiography of John Chambers*, Iowa Journal,
    6: 247-286, April, 1908. Also published separately. SHSI.
CHAPMAN, WILLIAM WILLIAMS
  Colton, Kenneth E., W. W. *Chapman, Delegate to Congress from Iowa
    Territory*, Annals (3), 21: 283-295, April, 1938.
  Johnson, Jack T., *Pioneer and Politician*, Palimpsest, 19: 350-359, Sept.,
    1938.
  Letters of W. W. Chapman, Annals (3), 22: 328-339, April, 1940.
  Parvin, Theodore S., W. W. *Chapman, First Delegate in Congress from
    the Territory of Iowa*, Historical Record, 2: 241-258, April, 1886.
CLARK, SAMUEL MERCER
  Swisher, Jacob A., *Samuel Mercer Clark*, Palimpsest, 29: 111-120, April,
    1948.
CLARK, WAREHAM G.
  Gardner, Flora Clark, *Wareham G. Clark*, Palimpsest, 25: 298-310,
    Oct., 1944.
CLARKE, JAMES
  Johnson, Jack T., *James Clarke*, Palimpsest, 20: 385-399, Dec., 1939.
  Salter, William, *James Clarke*, Historical Record, 4: 1-12, Jan., 1888.
CLARKE, WILLIAM PENN
  Eriksson, Erik M., *A Career of Energy*, Palimpsest, 7: 65-75, March,
    1926.
  Eriksson, Erik M., *William Penn Clarke*, Iowa Journal, 25: 3-61, Jan.,
    1927.
  Lloyd, Frederick, *In the Name of Free Soil*, Palimpsest, 7: 76-82, March,
    1926.
  Swisher, Jacob A., *Constitution Making in 1857*, Palimpsest, 7: 83-93,
    March, 1926.
COATES, A. U.
  An Autobiographer's Life in Iowa, Annals (3), 30: 175-197, Jan., 1950.
CODY, WILLIAM FREDERICK
  Fryxell, F. M., *The Codys in Le Claire*, Annals (3), 17: 3-11, July, 1929.
  Wagner, Dorothy, *Buffalo Bill, Showman*, Palimpsest, 11: 522-540,
    Dec., 1930.
COLE, CYRENUS
  Cole, Cyrenus, *I Remember, I Remember*. SHSI. 1936.

CONWAY, WILLIAM B.

 Johnson, Jack T., *The Man Who Would be Governor*, Palimpsest, 19: 251-263, July, 1938. See also the Lucas-Conway Controversy.

COPPOC, BARCLAY

 See references on Barclay Coppoc—Follower of John Brown.

COUSINS, ROBERT GORDON

 Maxson, Virginia, *Robert G. Cousins*, Palimpsest, 14: 253-266, July, 1933.

 Swisher, Jacob A., *Robert Gordon Cousins*. SHSI. 1938.

COX, THOMAS

 Reid, Harvey, *Thomas Cox*. SHSI. 1909.

 Reid, Harvey, *Colonel Thomas Cox*, Annals (3), 7: 241-269, Jan., 1906.

CUMMINS, ALBERT BAIRD

 Cummins as an Orator, Annals (3), 29: Part 1, 152-154, Oct., 1947.

 Harrington, Elbert W., *Albert Baird Cummins as a Public Speaker*, Iowa Journal, 43: 209-253, July, 1945.

 Harrington, Elbert W., *A Survey of the Political Ideas of Albert Baird Cummins*, Iowa Journal, 39: 339-386, Oct., 1941.

CURTIS, SAMUEL RYAN

 Colton, Kenneth E., *With Fremont in Missouri, in 1861. The Letters of Samuel Ryan Curtis*, Annals (3), 24: 105-167, Oct., 1942.

 Colton, Kenneth E., *Frontier War Problems, The Letters of Samuel Ryan Curtis*, Annals (3), 24: 298-314, April, 1943.

 Colton, Kenneth E., *The Irrepressible Conflict of 1861, The Letters of Samuel Ryan Curtis*, Annals (3), 24: 14-58, July, 1942.

 Gallaher, Ruth A., *Samuel Ryan Curtis*, Iowa Journal, 25: 331-358, July, 1927.

 Gallaher, Ruth A., *Samuel Ryan Curtis*, Palimpsest, 11: 129-140, April, 1930.

DAVENPORT, GEORGE

 Wilkie, Franc B., *Davenport Past and Present*, 145-165. Luse, Lane & Co., Davenport. 1858.

 See also references on Davenport.

DEAN, HENRY CLAY

 Cheney, J. W., *Glimpses of Henry Clay Dean, A Unique Individual*, Annals (3), 10: 320-330, Jan.-April, 1912.

 Rippey, J. R., *Henry Clay Dean*, Annals (3), 8: 299-304, Jan., 1908.

 Robeson, George F., *Henry Clay Dean*, Palimpsest, 5: 321-333, Sept., 1924.

 Twain, Mark, *The Power of Words*, Palimpsest, 23: 224-228, July, 1942.

DEY, PETER ANTHONY

 Johnson, Jack T., *Peter Anthony Dey*. SHSI. 1939.

DILLON, JOHN FORREST

 CLARKE, GOV. GEORGE W., *John Forrest Dillon, Lawyer and Man*, Annals (3), 28: 167-187, Jan., 1947.

 Stiles, Edward H., *Judge John F. Dillon*, Annals (3), 9: 1-18, 104-133, April, July, 1909.

 Swisher, Jacob A., *John F. Dillon*, Palimpsest, 10: 317-327, Sept., 1929.

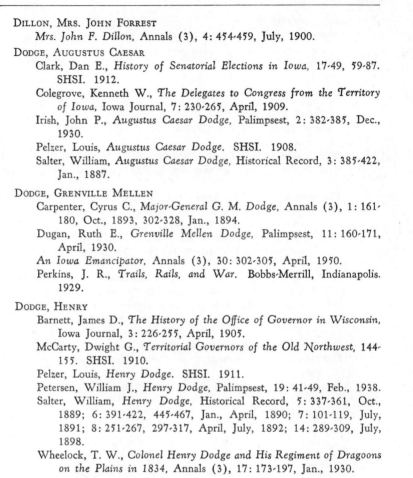

DILLON, MRS. JOHN FORREST
    Mrs. John F. Dillon, Annals (3), 4: 454-459, July, 1900.

DODGE, AUGUSTUS CAESAR
    Clark, Dan E., History of Senatorial Elections in Iowa, 17-49, 59-87.
        SHSI. 1912.
    Colegrove, Kenneth W., The Delegates to Congress from the Territory
        of Iowa, Iowa Journal, 7: 230-265, April, 1909.
    Irish, John P., Augustus Caesar Dodge, Palimpsest, 2: 382-385, Dec.,
        1930.
    Pelzer, Louis, Augustus Caesar Dodge. SHSI. 1908.
    Salter, William, Augustus Caesar Dodge, Historical Record, 3: 385-422,
        Jan., 1887.

DODGE, GRENVILLE MELLEN
    Carpenter, Cyrus C., Major-General G. M. Dodge, Annals (3), 1: 161-
        180, Oct., 1893, 302-328, Jan., 1894.
    Dugan, Ruth E., Grenville Mellen Dodge, Palimpsest, 11: 160-171,
        April, 1930.
    An Iowa Emancipator, Annals (3), 30: 302-305, April, 1950.
    Perkins, J. R., Trails, Rails, and War. Bobbs-Merrill, Indianapolis.
        1929.

DODGE, HENRY
    Barnett, James D., The History of the Office of Governor in Wisconsin,
        Iowa Journal, 3: 226-255, April, 1905.
    McCarty, Dwight G., Territorial Governors of the Old Northwest, 144-
        155. SHSI. 1910.
    Pelzer, Louis, Henry Dodge. SHSI. 1911.
    Petersen, William J., Henry Dodge, Palimpsest, 19: 41-49, Feb., 1938.
    Salter, William, Henry Dodge, Historical Record, 5: 337-361, Oct.,
        1889; 6: 391-422, 445-467, Jan., April, 1890; 7: 101-119, July,
        1891; 8: 251-267, 297-317, April, July, 1892; 14: 289-309, July,
        1898.
    Wheelock, T. W., Colonel Henry Dodge and His Regiment of Dragoons
        on the Plains in 1834, Annals (3), 17: 173-197, Jan., 1930.

DOLLIVER, JONATHAN PRENTISS
    Boyd, William R., Possessed Rare Oratorical Ability, Annals (3), 29:
        335-347, July, 1948.
    English, Emory H., Dollivers Justification, Annals (3), 29: 352-365,
        July, 1948.
    Eriksson, Erik M., A Tribune of the People, Palimpsest, 5: 37-46, Feb.,
        1924.
    Hostettler, Gordon F., Jonathan Prentiss Dolliver: The Formative Years,
        Iowa Journal, 49: 23-50, Jan., 1951.
    Mott, Frank L., Master of Oratory, Palimpsest, 5: 60-77, Feb., 1924.
    Parker, Addison, Dolliver's New Alignment, Annals (3), 29: 350-352,
        July, 1948.
    Titus, Geo. M., Dolliver as a Campaigner, Annals (3), 29: 347-350,
        July, 1948.

Van Ek, Jacob, *Two District Conventions*, Palimpsest, 5: 47-59, Feb., 1924.

DRUMMOND, THOMAS

Cummins, Albert B., *Sacrifices for State and Nation*, Annals (3), 30: 339-342, July, 1950.

English, Emory H., *Thomas Drummond*, Annals (3), 30: 315-327, July, 1950.

Harbert, A. N., *Military Service Conspicuous*, Annals (3), 30: 328-332, July, 1950.

Sells, Cato, *Memorial Tablet Presented to State*, Annals (3), 30: 337-338, July, 1950.

Tobin, T. F., *Drummond's Life Fruitful*, Annals (3), 30: 333-337, July, 1950.

DUBUQUE, JULIEN

See references on Julien Dubuque and the Mines of Spain.

DUNCOMBE, JOHN F.

Dey, Peter A., *John F. Duncombe*, Historical Record, 18: 587-595, Oct., 1902.

DYER, JOHN JAMES

Parvin, Theodore S., *John James Dyer*, Historical Record, 13: 1-10, Jan., 1897.

EASTMAN, ENOCH WORTHEN

Parvin, Theodore S., *Enoch Worthen Eastman*, Historical Record, 1: 49-57, April, 1885.

EDMUNDSON, JAMES DEPEW

Weaver, James B., *James Depew Edmundson*, Palimpsest, 14: 1-40, Jan., 1933.

FLEMING, WILLIAM HENRY

The Autobiography of a Private Secretary, Annals (3), 15: 3-46, July, 1925.

FOSTER, JUDITH ELLEN

Mott, David C., *Judith Ellen Foster*, Annals (3), 19: 127-138, Oct., 1933.

FOSTER, SUEL

Mott, David C., *Suel Foster*, Annals (3), 20: 497-509, Jan., 1937.

GEAR, JOHN HENRY

Dey, Peter A., *John Henry Gear*, Historical Record, 18: 497-509, July, 1902.

Fleming, William H., *Gov. John Henry Gear*, Annals (3), 5: 583-600, Jan., 1903.

GRANT, JAMES

Honorable James Grant, Annals (1), 11: 561-588, Oct., 1873.

GRIMES, JAMES WILSON

Carpenter, Cyrus C., *James W. Grimes, Governor and Senator*, Annals (3), 1: 505-525, Oct., 1894.

Clark, Dan E., *History of Senatorial Elections in Iowa*, 104-119, 129-131. SHSI. 1912.

Grimes, James W., *High Aims of Government*, Annals (3), 30: 209-
210, Jan., 1950.

Haefner, Marie, *A Man of Character*, Palimpsest, 22: 184-192, June,
1941.

Herriott, Frank I., *James W. Grimes Versus the Southrons*, Annals (3),
15: 323-357, 403-432, July, Oct., 1926.

Letters of James W. Grimes, Annals (3), 22: 469-504, Oct., 1940.

Lewellen, Fred B., *Political Ideas of James W. Grimes*, Iowa Journal,
42: 339-404, Oct., 1944.

Nealley, Margaret E., *Letters of Mrs. James W. Grimes*, Iowa Journal.
1: 329-333, July, 1903.

Pelzer, Louis, *The Origin and Organization of the Republican Party in
Iowa*, Iowa Journal, 4: 487-525, Oct., 1906.

Salter, William, *James W. Grimes*, Historical Record, 8: 337-360, Oct.,
1892.

Salter, William, *The Life of James W. Grimes*. Appleton, New York.
1876.

Senator Grimes Backed Ericsson, Annals (3), 30: 368-375, July, 1950.

GRINNELL, JOSIAH BUSHNELL

Parker, Leonard F., *Josiah Bushnell Grinnell*, Annals (3), 2: 249-259,
Jan., 1896.

Payne, Charles E., *Josiah Bushnell Grinnell*. SHSI. 1938.

HADDEN, DAVID E.

Reed, Charles D., *A Half Century of Service*, Annals (3), 25: 229-
230, Jan., 1944.

Wilson, Ben H., *David E. Hadden*, Palimpsest, 25: 257-288, Sept., 1944.

HADDOCK, GEORGE CHANNING

Petersen, William J., *George C. Haddock*, Palimpsest, 14: 233-248,
June, 1933.

HALL, JONATHAN C.

Stiles, Edward H., *Judge Jonathan C. Hall*, Annals (3), 8: 18-31,
April, 1907.

HARLAN, JAMES

Brigham, Johnson, *James Harlan*. SHSI. 1913.

Brigham, Johnson, *Toombs of Georgia Champions Harlan of Iowa*,
Annals (3), 10: 34-41, April, 1911.

Clark, Dan E., *History of Senatorial Elections in Iowa*, 120-128, 132-
142. SHSI. 1912.

Clark, Samuel M., *Hon. James Harlan*, Midland Monthly, 1: 227-243,
March, 1894.

Dyall, Martha T., *The Harlan Home*, Palimpsest, 12: 347-353, Sept.,
1931.

Harlan, Mrs. Ann E., Annals (3), 2: 489-508, Oct., 1896.

Swisher, Jacob A., *Harlan's Defense of Grant*, Palimpsest, 15: 17-29,
Jan., 1934.

HARRINGTON, KATE (Rebecca Harrington Smith Pollard)

Haefner, Marie, *An American Lady*, Palimpsest, 12: 169-178, May,
1931.

HATTON, FRANK
  Davis, S. R., *Ex-Postmaster-General Frank Hatton,* Midland Monthly,
    2: 209-212, Sept., 1894.
HAY, ABRAM TUSTON
  Wilson, Ben H., *Abram Tuston Hay,* Palimpsest, 28: 193-206, July,
    1947.
HAYNES, GLENN C.
  Haynes, Fred E., *Warden Haynes,* Palimpsest, 23: 305-316, Oct., 1942.
  Haynes, Fred E., *The Warden's Theories,* Palimpsest, 23: 330-336, Oct.,
    1942.
  Swisher, Jacob A., *A Good Soldier,* Palimpsest, 23: 317-329, Oct., 1942.
HEMPSTEAD, STEPHEN
  Lloyd, Frederick, *Stephen Hempstead,* Historical Record, 1: 3-12, Jan.,
    1885.
HEPBURN, WILLIAM PETERS
  Briggs, John E., *William Peters Hepburn.* SHSI. 1919.
HERRON, GEORGE D.
  McCowan, Hervy S., *A Misunderstood Man: Professor George D.
    Herron,* Midland Monthly, 2: 204-208, Sept., 1894.
HERSHEY, BENJAMIN
  Fishburn, Jesse J., *Ben Hershey—Lumber Baron,* Palimpsest, 28: 289-
    299, Oct., 1947.
HIGLEY, JENNETTE ROBERTSON
  Bartholomew, Amanda L., *Jennette Robertson Higley,* Historical Record,
    13: 145-162, Oct., 1897.
HOOVER, HERBERT CLARK
  Hoover, Herbert C., *Boyhood in Iowa,* Palimpsest 9: 269-276, July,
    1928.
  Hoover, Herbert, *The Memoirs of Herbert Hoover.* 3 vols. *Years of
    Adventure: 1874-1920; The Cabinet and the Presidency: 1920-
    1933; The Great Depression, 1929-1941;* Macmillan, New York.
    1951, 1951, 1952.
  Hoover, Herbert, *Boyhood in Iowa,* Palimpsest, 29: 225-233, Aug., 1948.
  Hoover, Herbert, *Boyhood in Iowa,* Palimpsest, 32: 409-416, Nov., 1951.
  Hoover, Herbert, *Iowa Through Eyes of a Ten-Year-Old,* Annals (3),
    27: 231-235, Jan., 1946.
  Hoover, Herbert, *The Meaning of America,* Palimpsest, 32: 433-438,
    Nov., 1951.
  Petersen, William J., *Great Journeys from Little Homes,* Palimpsest,
    32: 439-440, Nov., 1951.
  Swisher, Jacob A., *Bert Hoover,* Palimpsest, 9: 263-268, July, 1928.
  Swisher, Jacob A., *Bert Hoover,* Palimpsest, 29: 234-240, Aug., 1948.
  Swisher, Jacob A., *The Hoover Birthplace,* Palimpsest, 29: 241-254,
    Aug., 1948.
  Throne, Mildred, *Herbert Hoover,* Palimpsest, 32: 417-432, Nov., 1951.
HOWE, ORLANDO CUTTER
  Herriott, Frank I., *Judge Orlando C. Howe,* Annals (3), 19: 163-186,
    267-311, 323-351, 406-443, Jan., April, July, Oct., 1934.

KIRKWOOD, SAMUEL JORDAN

Clark, Dan E., *Samuel Jordan Kirkwood*. SHSI. 1917.

Lathrop, Henry W., *The Life and Times of Samuel J. Kirkwood*. Published by the author, Iowa City. 1893.

Lathrop, Henry W., *Samuel J. Kirkwood—Iowa as Affected by One Man's Influence*, Midland Monthly, 1: 163-167, Feb., 1894.

Reizenstein, Jacob E., *Kirkwood Elected Road Supervisor*, Annals (3), 26: 305-306, April, 1945.

Samuel Jordan Kirkwood, Historical Record, 10: 145-158, Oct., 1894.

Shambaugh, Bertha M. H., *The Scrap-Books of a Quiet Little Lady with Silvery Hair*, Palimpsest, 4: 401-427, Dec., 1923.

Swisher, Jacob A., *A Convention Stampeded*, Palimpsest, 9: 349-356, Oct., 1928.

LANGWORTHY, EDWARD, LUCIUS H., AND SOLON M.

Parish, John C., *The Langworthys of Early Dubuque and Their Contributions to Local History*, Iowa Journal, 8: 315-355, July, 1910.

LARRABEE, WILLIAM

Gallaher, Ruth A., *From Connecticut to Iowa*, Palimpsest, 22: 65-78, March, 1941.

Larrabee, William, *The Railroad Question*. Schulte Publishing Co., Chicago. 1893.

Parker, Daniel M., *That Good Old Man*, Palimpsest, 7: 113-115, April, 1926.

LEA, ALBERT MILLER

Gallaher, Ruth A., *Albert Miller Lea*, Palimpsest, 16: 65-80, March, 1935.

See also references on Albert Miller Lea and His Place in Iowa History.

LECLAIRE, ANTOINE

Snyder, Charles E., *Antoine LeClaire, The First Proprietor of Davenport*, Annals (3), 23: 79-117, Oct., 1941.

LEES, JAMES HENRY

James H. Lees, Annals (3), 20: 309-311, April, 1936.

LORAS, MATHIAS

Hoffmann, M. M., *The First Bishop of Iowa*, Palimpsest, 11: 321-333, Aug., 1930.

Lenehan, B. C., *Rt. Rev. Mathias Loras, D. D., First Bishop of Dubuque*, Annals (3), 3: 577-600, Jan., 1899.

LOVE, JAMES MADISON

Judge James Madison Love, Historical Record, 8: 241-250, April, 1892.

LOWE, ENOS

Parvin, Theodore S., *Dr. Enos Lowe*, Historical Record, 8: 289-296, July, 1892.

LOWE, RALPH PHILLIPS

Lowe, Edson A., *Ralph P. Lowe*, Historical Record, 7: 145-158, Oct., 1891.

LUCAS, ROBERT

Johnson, Jack T., *The Years Parvin Remembered*, Palimpsest, 19: 323-332, Aug., 1938.

Clarkson, John T., *A Life of Achievement,* Annals (3), 29: 583-588, April, 1949.

Successful Farming Staff, *Tribute to a Successful Life,* Annals (3), 29: 569-582, April, 1949.

MERRILL, SAMUEL

Fleming, William H., *Governor Samuel Merrill,* Annals (3), 5: 335-351, April, 1902.

MILLER, SAMUEL FREEMAN

Fairman, Charles, *Mr. Justice Miller and the Supreme Court, 1862-1892.* Harvard University Press, Cambridge, Mass. 1939.

Gregory, Charles N., *Samuel Freeman Miller.* SHSI. 1907.

Strong, Henry, *Justice Samuel Freeman Miller,* Annals (3), 1: 241-257, Jan., 1894.

MINOTT, JAMES SHERMAN

Keyes, Charles Reuben, *James Sherman Minott,* Palimpsest, 24: 1-7, Jan., 1943.

MOREHOUSE, DANIEL WALTER

Wilson, Ben H., *Daniel Walter Morehouse,* Palimpsest, 23: 337-369, Nov., 1942.

NOBLE, REUBEN

Studebaker, T. H., *Reuben Noble,* Annals (3), 3: 193-199, Oct., 1897.

NORTH, ADA

Mrs. Ada North, Librarian, Annals (3), 2: 540-549, Oct., 1896; 6: 624-626, Jan., 1905.

NUTTING, CHARLES CLEVELAND

Taylor, Wilson L., *Charles Cleveland Nutting,* Palimpsest, 24: 269-300, Sept., 1943.

PARKER, LEONARD FLETCHER

Swisher, Jacob A., *Leonard Fletcher Parker.* SHSI. 1927.

PARVIN, THEODORE SUTTON

Aldrich, Charles, *Theodore S. Parvin,* Annals (3), 5: 199-208, Oct., 1901.

Springer, John, *Theodore Sutton Parvin,* Historical Record, 17: 335-344, July, 1901.

PERKINS, GEORGE DOUGLAS

George D. Perkins, Palimpsest, 5: 273-317, Aug., 1924.

PRICE, HIRAM

Gue, Benjamin F., *The Public Services of Hiram Price,* Annals (3), 1: 585-602, Jan., 1895.

RAGUE, JOHN FRANCIS

Hoffmann, M. M., *John Francis Rague—Pioneer Architect of Iowa.* Annals (3), 19: 444-448, Oct., 1934.

Shambaugh, Benj. F., *The Old Stone Capitol Remembers,* 91-110. SHSI. 1939.

REASER, WILLBUR A.

Williams, Ora, *Willbur A. Reaser, Portrait Artist,* Annals (3), 24: Part 1, 245-247, Jan., 1943.

REMEY, GEORGE COLLIER
> Rear Admiral George Collier Remey, 1841-1928, Annals (3), 19: 403-405, Oct., 1934.

REYNOLDS, "DIAMOND JO"
> Petersen, William J., Joseph Reynolds, Palimpsest, 24: 205-214, July, 1943.

RICHMAN, JACOB SCOTT
> Brannan, William F., J. Scott Richman, Annals (3), 7: 361-366, April, 1906.

ROBERTS, GEORGE E.
> Boyd, William R., Broadcast Over Station WSUI, Annals (3), 29: 413-424, Oct., 1948.
> English, Emory H., Capable Public Service, Annals (3), 29: 425-433, Oct., 1948.
> Roberts, George E., The Economics of a Boom, Annals (3), 29: 434-453, Oct., 1948.

RORER, DAVID
> Briggs, John E., An Eloquent Plea, Palimpsest, 26: 270-274, Sept., 1945.
> Briggs, John E., A Rare Man, Palimpsest, 26: 257-269, Sept., 1945.
> Stiles, Edward H., David Rorer, Annals (3), 8: 116-124, July, 1907.
> Swisher, Jacob A., Eminence at the Bar, Palimpsest, 26: 275-288, Sept., 1945.

SALTER, WILLIAM
> Jordan, Philip D., Forty Days with the Christian Commission: A Diary by William Salter, Iowa Journal, 33: 123-154, April, 1935.
> Jordan, Philip D., William Salter's Letters to Mary Ann Mackintire 1845-1846, Annals (3), 24: Part 2, 103-185, Jan., 1943.
> Jordan, Philip D., William Salter's "My Ministry in Iowa 1843-1846," Annals (3), 24: Part 2, 1-102, Jan., 1943.
> Salter, William, Journal of a Missionary in Jackson County, Iowa Territory 1843-46, Annals (3), 7: 592-607, Jan., 1907.
> William Salter, Annals (3), 10: 63-66, April, 1911.

SARGENT, GEORGE BARNARD
> Ross, Earle D., George Barnard Sargent — Western Promoter, Iowa Journal, 45: 115-132, April, 1947.
> Sargent, George B., Lecture on the West, Iowa Journal, 45: 137-174, April, 1947.
> Speech by George B. Sargent Before the Boston Board of Trade, Iowa Journal, 45: 133-136, April, 1947.

SCHAEFFER, CHARLES ASHMEAD
> Swisher, Jacob A., Charles Ashmead Schaeffer, Palimpsest, 28: 49-62, Feb., 1947.

SCHEE, GEORGE WORTH
> Peck, J. L. E., George Worth Schee, Annals (3), 16: 421-431, Oct., 1928.

SCOTT, WILLSON ALEXANDER
> Huntington, Ida M., Willson Alexander Scott, Annals (3), 13: 243-262, April, 1922.

Swisher, Jacob A., *Willson Alexander Scott*, Palimpsest, 28: 225-238, Aug., 1947.

SELLS, ELIJAH

Davis, John M., *Elijah Sells*, Annals (3), 2: 518-530, Oct., 1896.

SHAMBAUGH, BENJAMIN FRANKLIN

Benjamin Franklin Shambaugh: As Iowa Remembers Him. SHSI. 1941.

Briggs, John E., *Benj. F. Shambaugh*, Palimpsest, 21: 133-139, May, 1940.

Gallaher, Ruth A., *Benj. F. Shambaugh*, Iowa Journal, 38: 227-233, July, 1940.

SHAW, LESLIE MORTIER

Ross, Earle D., *A Yankee-Hawkeye*, Palimpsest, 28: 353-366, Dec., 1947.

SHEAFFER, WALTER A.

Petersen, William J., *The W. A. Sheaffer Pen Co.*, Palimpsest, 33: 257-288, Sept., 1952.

SHELLEY, KATE

Fiske, Horace S., *An Epic of Iowa*, Midland Monthly, 9: 493, 494, June, 1898.

Swisher, Jacob A., *Kate Shelley*, Palimpsest, 6: 45-55, Feb., 1925.

SHERMAN, BUREN ROBINSON

Lloyd, Frederick, *Governor Buren R. Sherman*, Historical Record, 5: 241-249, April, 1889.

STODDARD, DRUSCILLA ALLEN

Clarkson, Anna H., *A Beautiful Life—A Biographical Sketch*, Annals (3), 11: 188-199, July-Oct., 1913.

STREET, JOSEPH

See references on Indian Agents.

SUDLOW, PHOEBE W.

Barnhart, Cornelia Mallett, *Phoebe W. Sudlow*, Palimpsest, 28: 25-32, Jan., 1947.

TEETERS, WILBER JOHN

Swisher, Jacob A., *Wilber John Teeters*, Palimpsest, 30: 72-78, March, 1949.

THOMPSON, JAMES L.

Snyder, Charles E., *Forgotten Men—James L. Thompson*, Iowa Journal, 43: 357-369, Oct., 1945.

WEAVER, JAMES BAIRD

Haynes, Fred E., *James Baird Weaver.* SHSI. 1919.

WHICHER, STEPHEN

Whicher, George M., *Stephen Whicher*, Annals (3), 4: 494-521, Oct., 1900.

WILLIAMS, JESSE

Johnson, Jack T., *Jesse Williams*, Palimpsest, 21: 184-196, June, 1940.

WILLIAMS, JOSEPH

Babbitt, Charles H., *Peter in the Pumpkin*, Palimpsest, 5: 172-175, May, 1924.

Johnson, Jack T., *A Judge Well Met*, Palimpsest, 19: 370-378, Sept., 1938.

INDEX

185